Being Yourself

Essays on UG Krishnamurti
and Other Topics

JSRL Narayana Moorty

Copyright © 2014 JSRL Narayana Moorty
All rights reserved.
ISBN: 13:978-1495422621
ISBN: 10:1495422623

*This book is dedicated
to my teacher and friend
UG Krishnamurti*

CONTENTS

Introduction vi
Part 1: UG 9
1. How I Met UG 10
2. Later Visits to Mill Valley (and Sausalito) 16
3. Notable Travels and Visits 26
4. My Last Visit with UG 54
Part 2: Essays on UG 67
5. Science And Spirituality: Any Points of Contact? 68
6. Thought, the Natural State and the Body 85
7. Being with UG -- His Teaching Process 95
8. Further Remarks About UG 117
PHOTOS 119
Part 3: Being 139
9. Thought, Thinking and the Self 140
    Features Of The Self 146
10. Reflecting on Reflection 153
11. On the Division between Spiritual and Worldly Goals 154
12. Desire, Pleasure and Tension 165
13. The Self is a Set of Habits 158
14. In and Out of Mental States 159
15. Ending the Downward Spiral 162
16. The Self, Meaning and Significance of Life 164
Part 4: Other Philosophical Essays 170
17. Whither Morality? 171
18. Is There Such a Thing as Selflessness? 179

19. The Paradox of Being Yourself 183
20. Why I am a Vegetarian, On Taking Life, and On Abortion 185
    Why I am a Vegetarian……..………………………………..185
    On Taking Life…………………………...………………...186
    On Abortion……………………………...…………………188
21. Looking Within 191
22. Reflections on Meditation 194
23. The Bugbear of Spiritual Progress 201
Conclusion 203
NOTES...210

Introduction

I have always thought a photograph reveals the photographer more than it does the subject. In that sense the following writing is rather autobiographical.

My association with UG, which started in 1981, has been long. He visited me and my family at least once every year since then, till the beginning of 2006, after which time he stopped visiting the US. This book not only tells about my acquaintance and association with UG, but also about how he affected me personally in my thought and in my life in general. It's hard to pinpoint and say definitely this is where UG's influence stops and my own thinking and life start.

The other influences in my life have been Gora, the atheist follower of Gandhi, Chalam, the famous Telugu writer and J. Krishnamurti. Yet, there has been a certain ongoing inquiry in my mind ever since I was conscious, namely, "Who am I?" You can say it is that which gave me a core identity and drove my thinking. It is what made me interested in all these people in the first place. After all is said and done, if there is anything called the "I" remaining, it is that which makes me question everything and everyone I have been exposed to, including UG. In my investigations in this book, I combine my skepticism with the critical and analytical skills I have acquired in my study of philosophy.

UG never minded my critical remarks in my essays on him. Once, after reading my Introduction to the book *No Way Out*, he asked if I was rethinking my (critical) comments on him. I answered, "No, I am not taking any of it back." Then I was relieved to hear him say, "That's the only way to write." He did not want people to merely repeat what he said: "What hasn't helped you can't help others." The essays in this book, although they tell of my acquaintance and relationship with UG, do not merely rehash what UG says, nor are they merely an interpretation of UG's teachings. Even when I am open to someone's ideas, I always question and test them and add my own investigations to them. It is in that spirit that I hope the reader will look at the following essays.

Almost all the chapters included here are essays I have posted on my blog site http://moortysblogpage.blogspot.com for about two years. For the sake of completion, I have added my paper "Science and Spirituality." There is a little history behind this essay which was initially read in 1995 at the Krishnamurti Centenary Conference in Oxford, Ohio. When the organizer of the conference, my friend Professor Rama Rao Pappu, asked me to write about J. Krishnamurti, I told him that since I had already published an article about J. Krishnamurti[1], I would rather write about UG. After some hesitation, he agreed to my proposal.

When I was visiting UG in Corte Madera, California, in the beginning of 1995, I mentioned to him that it was possible to put up one of his books on the Internet. Mario Viggiano and Julie Thayer, friends of UG, were also present on the occasion. Mario immediately jumped on the idea and said, "Let's do it!" Thus the UG website was set up at Julie's http://www.well.com/user/jct and UG's *Mind is a Myth* with a picture of his taken by Julie in New Zealand was put up. UG, who had by then read my article "Science and Spirituality," insisted that it also be put up. Later, I had seen him handing a copy of this article to a visitor or two.

Part 1 of this book consists of articles about how I met UG and an account of some of my meetings with him. I have deliberately avoided giving biographical details about UG as they have been frequently mentioned in books like *The Mystique of Enlightenment, Mind is Myth, UG Krishnamurti, A Life*, by Mahesh Bhatt, and *The Other Side of Belief* by Mukunda Rao. *Part 2* of the book comprises a set of articles about UG's teachings as well as his teaching process. *Part 3* contains my ruminations about thinking, the self and mental states. *Part 4* deals with my views about assorted issues such as meditation, morality and selflessness. I can't say the articles in Parts 3 and 4 are all inspired by UG's teachings, but they are related to them in some fashion or other. Although all the essays in the book except my memoirs might require careful reading, they should be fairly accessible to the general reader.

My philosophical essays may not impress the professional philosopher and may not seem to advance any current discussion of specific philosophical problems. To be sure, they are neither scholarly nor technical, but purely informal. I have not even provided extensive documentation in them. My interest here is to tackle some problems from a rather commonsense point of view, mostly starting from my own experience. Of course, what I have learned from both Western and Eastern philosophy, as well as what I have learned from UG, does come into play in my explorations. I hope my suggestions to solve those problems might trigger the reader's own inquiries.

Needless to say, I have to use my thinking and logical skills to present my understanding of the issues presented here. I don't know if it is possible to arrive at a totally consistent theory about them or fit them into a coherent and meaningful picture. Indeed, the reader may find that in several places my conclusions are hesitant and tentative. I may seem to be expressing doubts about my own previous conclusions or debating with myself. That's why I would like to call this book a "work in progress."

My aim here is to approach some issues without presupposing any religious or spiritual beliefs, taking a commonsense point of view and remaining always within the limits of the known. The book should also demonstrate how I have translated, as best as I can, what I have understood or learned from UG into my own life. Standing on such a ground of experience I have tried to chip away, as it were, bit by bit, at some of the concepts in understanding oneself (despite UG's rejection of the very idea of understanding oneself). Of course, you can never know the unknown. But what has been considered mystical or mysterious before could, at least to a minor degree, be unraveled. In my opinion, that was indeed what UG was trying to achieve as well, as the title of the book *Mystique of Enlightenment* indicates.

You may find it difficult to draw a clear line separating between what UG said from my own analysis and investigation. That's in the nature of things. I never separated myself from UG. Just like in life, I consider my work as an extension of his teachings.

My central concern when I discuss moral issues is always to find out how I can relate to these subjects and what difference they would make in my life or my reader's life.

You will find some repetition of ideas in a few chapters. Unfortunately, the nature of the subject-matter is such that different topics require inclusion of the same ideas to discuss the various facets of a problem and make the discussion complete. Repetition is also used sometimes to reinforce an idea.

Thanks to Wendy Moorty for her meticulous editorial help for both the text and the photographs, and for her design of the cover.

Several photographs from the collections of Lisa Taranto, Julie Thayer, and Wendy Moorty have been used in this book. My thanks to all four for letting me include them here. Also thanks to Jean-Pierre Kolle for letting me use his picture of me on the back cover.

Narayana Moorty
Seaside, California
April, 2014

Part 1: UG

1. How I Met UG

First Introduction: The first time I heard about UG was from Terry Newland (then Terry Agnew). I knew Terry in Berkeley around 1969 when I was living in Berkeley. I once saw an announcement in the UC Berkeley campus newspaper that there was going to be a J. Krishnamurti discussion group meeting in the Student Union Building on campus. I went there mainly out of curiosity (and perhaps also out of a need to belong to a Krishnamurti group). Terry was conducting what seemed like an organizational meeting. After the meeting we became friends.

It must have been some months later in the same year, Terry had taken a fancy to me and invited me to Sonoma State University for a talk in a philosophy professor's class. He also asked me to talk to a student group. Then I visited an elementary school where Terry was teaching at the time. He asked me to speak to the kids there and then showed me his yoga class. Before that time he had a falling out with the Krishnamurti people, particularly in Switzerland: Terry was duly kicked out of the Krishnamurti circles. Earlier, he had been specially invited to go to Switzerland to meet and spend time with Krishnamurti. At the same time, he was also listening to UG.

Later, Terry invited me and three of my friends to spend the night in his place in Sebastopol on our way to Carson City where we were also going to visit another friend who was teaching in the Indian Reservation School. Early in the morning, I got to watch Terry do yoga. He looked like the image of health – sounds of breath coming out of his nostrils like steam from pipes and perfectly precise and graceful *asanas*, all done seemingly effortlessly with a robust and statuesque body.

That morning Terry gave us a breakfast of Musilex cereal. He also showed me a picture of UG and described him as an enlightened man. As I mentioned above, Terry had heard him speak in Switzerland. He told me later how UG had taken him out for a coffee and talked to him about himself.

UG had invited him, Terry said, to spend three months in India (in Bangalore) with him and write his biography. Terry described how UG's physical features had changed because of the transformation he had undergone: ashes falling out of his forehead, arms turning backward, glands swelling, eyes not blinking, and so on.[2]

Terry was obviously quite touched by the attention UG showered on him. Apparently, UG would get up early in the morning before Terry and

1. How I Met UG

fix hot water for his bath!(3) The biography he was supposed to write, for which purpose he took a typewriter with him, never came to pass.

I heard several such accounts about UG from Terry and simply stored them away in my memory without thinking much about them.

Second Introduction: The next occasion I heard about UG was when I was in Hawaii with Terry around 1971. My then-partner Linda and I had just gotten married and gone on a trip to Hawaii in response to an invitation from Terry to spend a month with him and learn Yoga. Soon after we arrived at his cabin in Molokai, there was an accident: while Terry was lighting a stove to make dinner for us, the lighter fluid caught fire, the fire quickly spread through the whole cabin, and the cabin was burnt down to ashes. We escaped with a few belongings, but lost our air tickets in the fire. We spent the night in Terry's friends' house and the next day moved to another friend's rather large house miles away. There Linda and I stayed for a week and learned some yoga from Terry anyway. We came to the main island of Oahu after that, got replacement airline tickets and headed back to the mainland.

A day or two after the cabin had burned down, I went with Linda and Terry to one of his lady friends' place. It was a lone house amid fields and pineapple plantations. There Terry played a tape of UG speaking. Again, I had no reaction. I remember UG's voice in the tape being somewhat screechy.

Third Introduction: I went to India with Linda and our daughter Shyamala in the summer of 1975. We spent a few days in Chennai and then went to Tiruvannamalai, visiting my old friend Chalam, the famous Telugu writer. Just as I entered Chalam's front yard (across the street from the Ramanashram) and was approaching the house, I heard an audio cassette of UG being played. I distinctly remember him saying in the tape something about the space between two thoughts. At that time, I was suffering from a bout of flu. I went upstairs in a few minutes, as the talk didn't make much impression on me. Some kind of Vedanta, I thought. I also noticed for the first time a picture of UG on a wall in Chalam's house. Sowris, Chalam's daughter, who was a mystic, told me that UG was her distant cousin. I later learned from Chandrasekhar that a few years before this visit, he had told Chalam and his family about UG and showed them a picture of him.(4) Sowris had recognized him as the person to whom she could have been married when she was young, except that UG wasn't interested. Chalam and his family subsequently met UG through Chandrasekhar.

Sowris, Chalam and Sowris's "gang" used to visit UG in Bangalore. Apparently, after the initial visits, UG, in his usual fashion, started tightening screws on Sowris, bluntly telling her that if she wanted to see him, she should come without her entourage. He also forbade her to sing in his presence (singing was one of her 'hang-ups'!). Later, when Chalam was confined to a wheelchair, UG apparently said, "Why should that old man come here all the way? I will go and visit him myself," and did make a trip to Tiruvannamalai.

My First Meeting with UG: Then, some years later, sometime in 1981, I got a letter from Nartaki, the woman who lived with Chalam's family for much of her life.[5] She wrote that UG was coming to the U.S., and suggested that I should go and visit him. She gave me a phone number to call. I, of course, promptly ignored her suggestion.

At about the same time (I think it was around September, 1981), Terry also called from Mill Valley saying that UG was in town and was asking about me ("Where is this Dr. Narayana Moorty?"). Apparently, Nartaki had given UG my phone number and address both of which he had promptly lost. He could, however, remember my name. Nartaki later told me that she had said to him, "You go and see everyone everywhere; why don't you go see this man when you go the U.S.?" Terry asked me if I would like to come and visit UG in Mill Valley. I replied that I was too old to go see "teachers" (I was already burned out with J. Krishnamurti), and that if he was passing through here in Seaside, he would be welcome. So, I didn't go then.

It must have been about a month or so later,: one morning ,[6] I got a phone call from Ramesh Ganerwala, an engineer who worked for the California Energy Commission. He was driving UG and Valentine from San Louis Obispo after visiting James Brodsky (later Jane) or some other person. He said that he was with UG and Valentine nearby in Carmel and that UG wanted to know if they could come and visit. I said they would be most welcome and that they could have lunch at my place as well.

I had a large quantity of *upma* made for my in-laws who had just visited me that morning. After breakfast, they had all gone out with my present wife, Wendy. I was home alone. The time was about noon. Ramesh drove UG and Valentine in his small old beat-up BMW. I watched through the living-room window as UG got out of the car and walked on the pavement toward my house. With his arms hanging loose, he had the gait of a zombie. His face was devoid of expression and he looked like a man on the death row. (Recently, in spite of my denials, UG interpreted this as my saying that I saw "death" walking in!)

Valentine and Ramesh, as well as UG, all came in. I greeted them, led them into the kitchen and seated them at the kitchen table. UG sat next to the wall in the kitchen and I sat across the table from him. I served lunch to everyone. UG was praising my *upma* to Ramesh saying that it was the "authentic stuff". UG started talking mostly about himself. During the conversation he and I exchanged notes about our backgrounds -- he coming from Gudivada and I from Vijayawada, both towns in Andhra

Pradesh, just twenty miles apart, and about the people we had known in common. He went to Chennai (then Madras) University for his Honors studies and had as his professor T.M.P. Mahadevan who was also my M. Litt. thesis supervisor. Apparently he dropped out of his Philosophy Honors class in Chennai University, not having taken the final examinations. We both knew my Sanskrit lecturer in S.R.R. & C.V.R. College, Vijayawada, and a few others. Also, my old atheist friend in Vijayawada, Gora, was his botany lecturer in college in Masulipatam.

During the conversation, UG joked about Satya Sai Baba, saying how earlier he used to materialize Swiss watches, but now was only materializing Hindustan watches after Indira Gandhi had imposed import restrictions on Swiss watches.

They stayed for about two hours. As they were leaving, I tried to put my arm around UG's shoulder as a gesture of affection, but he quickly moved away. I realized that he was not open to such physical contact. I was also aware how in Indian culture, touch is a sensitive issue. In the living room, as he was leaving, I shook his hand to say goodbye, addressing him as "Mr. Krishnamurti." He said that I could just as well call him "number 69," like a jail convict, and that people just called him "UG."

It was a pleasant experience meeting UG. I had the strange feeling, as we were standing at the kitchen door and holding each other's hands, that he was so similar to me in many ways and that I was meeting myself. The feeling was one of closeness. I was already bonded with UG!

As he left, he invited me to visit him in Mill Valley. I thought that it was merely a formal invitation. I said, "Yes, thank you," and didn't take the invitation seriously.

First Visit to UG: I think UG visited me a second time, when Elena, a Russian young woman, was also present.[7] It must have been about a month or so after his first visit. I can't remember much about this visit except that this time he invited both Elena and me to visit him in Mill Valley. Again, I didn't respond except saying "OK, thank you." But the night before Thanksgiving that year, I got a phone call from Ramesh saying that UG would like to see me, could I come? Earlier, I had built all kinds of excuses in my mind not to go to see UG, such as that the invitation was just a formality and he wasn't probably very serious about it; that I didn't like driving long distances; that my old AMC Rambler car wouldn't make it that far; and that I didn't like traveling, to mention a few. But all those excuses had evaporated now, as the invitation this time was so specific and personal that I couldn't as well turn it down. Also, Kodvatiganti Subba Rao, an engineer from Berkeley who worked for the FEMA, was visiting us for Thanksgiving. He was leaving on the

Thanksgiving Day and was willing to give me and Elena a ride to Mill Valley. So, we all three drove up to Mill Valley.

We arrived at UG's house in Mill Valley around 5 o'clock in the afternoon. Subba Rao and UG quickly got into an argument on the subject of the Bhagavad Gita. The argument got nowhere and Subba Rao left after about an hour.

Julie Wellings, whom I had met once long ago in 1975 in Tiruvannamalai, when she was living in Chalam's household and learning Telugu from Sowris being her companion, was also visiting UG. She brought her own beer that night and drank it, to my surprise. (I thought one didn't drink or smoke in front of "holy men.") The next day a few pictures were taken. I have included one of here.

UG gave me a room upstairs with a big soft bed and some sheets. Not much else. I couldn't sleep well. I was there a couple of nights. The next day in the kitchen, UG asked me if I could "look into" the cooking which Kim (a friend of UG from New York) was doing. I put a few spices like cumin (or anything suitable I could find on the shelf) in the food.

On the second day I was there, Ramesh visited. UG went on talking hours on end about his past life, his wife and family, and so on. Then a young man walked in. He sat at the table and they talked about Zen. UG challenged the man, holding a cup in his hand, "Tell me what this is." "Do you really see this? What do you really see here?" And he kept on pounding him with such questions. Soon, he enlisted my help. I remember saying, "There is something funny about Zen. How can anyone certify that someone had *satori* or enlightenment and to what degree?" UG appeared to agree with me.

It was during this visit that Terry brought mimeographed copies of conversations with UG (later to become part of *The Mystique of Enlightenment*) and distributed them to people around. He collected five dollars per copy for the cost of mimeographing. I got myself a copy.

This was when Elena met Krim, a young American of Russian origin, who had known UG in Switzerland for a number of years. I remember going out for a short walk with them. Apparently, UG cautioned to Krim as we were leaving, "Make it short — *kurtze promenade*!" That was the beginning of a disastrous relationship between Krim and Elena which ended several years later. UG repeatedly mentioned how he had warned him. I wonder if he foresaw the outcome of that relationship.[8]

That afternoon, an elderly man and a young couple, all Americans, came to visit UG. I was told that they were friends of Alan Watts. UG received them cordially and soon got involved in a discussion with them. At one stage, I interjected, saying something trying to help the discussion, and UG immediately interrupted me saying, "I want to stop him right there." I got the message and kept quiet.

When I arrived, I had noticed that Valentine was coughing. Trying to help, I gave her a dose of homeopathic pills of Tuberculinum 200. Later, I heard from UG that in India she had had an attack of TB. I regretted giving her the pills, as I worried that my pills might have brought about or worsened the attack. But apparently, all was well after that, as I saw her later in Mill Valley, hale and healthy.

I was ready to leave after two days of staying with UG. Kim was driving Ramesh's BMW car for UG in those days. On the third day, sometime in the afternoon, Kim was ready to drive me to the bus depot in San Francisco. (I was going to take a local bus to go there, but UG would have none of that.) I remember giving a hug to Ramesh and Terry and whoever before I left. UG decided to drive with us to the bus depot. I felt honored. At the bus depot, he got out of the car and bid me farewell. I felt so special that he came to see me off there. I bought myself a ticket, got on the bus and returned to Monterey.

2. Later Visits to Mill Valley (and Sausalito)

It was Wendy's and my wedding anniversary in January 1982. Just before then, I had my first dental treatment (at the age of 48). And that day we visited my colleague, Bob O'Brien. I finally got our wedding gift from him – a salad bowl which he had so deftly crafted. It took him so long (we were married in January 1981) because he made it himself. It's extremely well made with teak wood. We still have it.

Then we drove up to Mill Valley. We were pretty late in arriving, probably around 3:00 PM. And UG said he hadn't eaten his lunch yet. It looked like he was waiting for us. (Although, later, when I mentioned the fact, he dismissed it saying he had probably already eaten once before [but when?]). I apologized. Wendy and I were shown our room. Wendy was given her first sewing chore ("sweatshop", as UG used to call it) of mending some pants for Valentine. Valentine talked to me in the balcony for a minute. She said UG liked being with me. We both stood in the balcony overlooking the canyon. Wendy took a picture of us from the side.

On the second day, I made cauliflower *pakodis* for everyone. Terry kept the place immaculately clean, the glass table in the living room and all. I sat there in the morning and UG was sitting across the table. I remarked that I sometimes felt as if there was no separation between him and me, as if we were one continuous person. He replied that he felt that way all the time.

The next morning, there was a large group of people, probably around 20, who gathered in the living room. Douglas Rosestone was there with his wife. Also present were Bob Carr with his video camera and his friend Paul Arms. Before or after the meeting, there was a bit of exchange between UG and me. I was telling him how Douglas had called me in Seaside from a local hotel (he was visiting the area), how he tried to hook me into inviting him for dinner and how I wouldn't be conned into it. UG remarked in reply, "conned?" His remark felt like a lashing to me.

At the meeting, I was sitting by the fireplace and UG came and sat next to me. I learned then and later that that was how he felt people's bodies. I remarked during the discussion how a master desire runs all our thoughts and other desires. He seemed to agree with me (although he wouldn't comment).

2. Later Visits to Mill Valley (and Sausalito)

I think it was also during that visit that I was telling UG how he was shooting everyone down, and he replied that yes, he was shooting at us all the time, but "you duck!"

When Wendy and I were visiting him in Sausalito, one afternoon, we all went for a ride. Valentine, Wendy and whoever went into the fields for a walk, and I stayed in the car with UG, because he didn't want to go. I asked him why he visited people everywhere and especially me. His answer was, "I always did that in my life." It was not much of an answer to my mind.[9] A few minutes later, he said he was "sinking", meaning that his senses would become numb and he was ready to pass out. I understood that after his calamity he would literally "die" every day for about 45 minutes; that is, his body would become cold, his breathing and heartbeat would stop, and then suddenly for no apparent reason he would come back alive.

At one point, I was talking about Chalam and Sowris, describing how I had parted ways respectfully with Sowris, telling her that I couldn't believe that God was incarnate in her and speaking through her. Then I told UG how I was first an atheist and to this day, I couldn't believe in anything religious (or otherwise). He was emphatic in agreeing with me saying that no belief was necessary. Of course, Sowris had replied to my remark by asking me to keep an open mind. And I think to this day I have an open mind, although I always find myself at crossroads. In that same conversation, UG pooh-poohed Sowris and her so-called amorous delusions concerning him, and recalled how his grandmother used to refer to Chalam in a rhyming fashion as *"Chalam gari malam* (the filth of Chalam)."

After the walk, either because I volunteered to drive or UG asked me to, I drove my Horizon UG and others back to his place. I was extremely nervous and slow; but I made it OK. And UG, of course, was encouraging.

It must be on this visit that the following conversation took place: I said to UG: "Your talk is like sweet poison. No wonder people are attracted to it." I said "poison" because people would turn whatever UG says into some kind of teaching, drawing a direction (or as UG says, a "directive") from it, and try to apply it to themselves. UG asked, "Why 'sweet'?" I answered, "sweet," because what you say represents the end of a search."

His next visit to Seaside happened sometime later. UG called me once from Mill Valley or Sausalito and said he wanted to visit me because he needed my "spiritual advice" on something. Of course, that was just a joking way for him to preamble his visit.

When he visited, he recounted to me some of the questions people showered on him wherever he went, such as "Why do you go to all these places? Why do you talk to people?". I told him that he didn't owe an explanation to anyone on these matters, that he could do just as he pleased and that if people didn't like to come and listen to him that was their problem. He repeated my answer to people everywhere (he himself told me later), quoting me, of course.

Months later, I received a copy of the newly printed book, *Mystique of Enlightenment*, mailed from Mountain View. Obviously UG had it sent to me. When he visited after I received his book, he asked me if I had read it and what I had thought of it. I said I did read the book and that I thought he had made some issues very clear. He seemed satisfied with my reply.

It might be on the same visit that I mentioned how I felt great around him and was going to say more in that vein. He replied, "Let's not talk about it. Let's eat some *upma* together and forget about it."

I used to invite people whenever UG visited and have a discussion gathering. I would prepare *upma* and *raita* or something else and offer lunch to everyone. *What Am I Saying?* is a video produced at one of those meetings (1985). Bob Carr invited friends of his who were videographers and arranged for the discussion. A lot of people were there: Jean-Michel Terdjman, Vito and Shalom Victor, Mr. Said, Sunim, Shivashankaran, Linda, Roberto Lupetti, the Italian painter, and also perhaps my colleague Robert O'Brien and Mr. Chu. The discussion recorded on that tape is a typical example of how frustrating it is to argue or debate about anything with UG. How could it be otherwise, when he wouldn't respect any rules of logic like non-contradiction and couldn't really explain how he came to know some things? The discussion was dead-ended.

That was probably why I never really argued with him again.

UG always said that it is not possible to "figure him out" or make sense of what he says (maybe because he constantly shifted from one position or statement to another), and that you can't get a "directive" out of what he says.

In the early visits, particularly when I saw him in Mill Valley, I noticed some physical changes in myself. At least the first night of the visit, my body would be so wired up and tense that I would have hard time falling asleep for hours. It was getting activated for some reason. There was this agitation from the bottom of my belly, as if some energy was being stirred up. Observing other people experiencing similar changes, it became clear to me that my body as well others' was responding to UG's presence.

A third visit to UG occurred when Valentine was still traveling with him. I drove all the way to Sausalito in my Horizon. UG gave me a small bedroom in the basement. To my surprise, he was feeding a cat with food from a can. When the cat tried to jump into his lap he would gently push

2. Later Visits to Mill Valley (and Sausalito)

it away. (He was still a Brahmin in that and in many other respects.) He sat with me in the living room for lengths of time listening to tapes of Indian music I had brought to play. (I didn't know then that he was listening just to keep me company.) I even watched a Telugu movie with him, *Sagarasangamam* or *Saptapadi*, I am not sure which (with lots of dances and songs). As I was leaving, he asked me to return it in the video store in Berkeley. I asked him if he would like me to rent another movie for him, and he told me no, he had only rented it for me.

After a few visits, UG was complaining about his loose teeth, about having to place Valentine somewhere, as she was getting too old to travel with him, and so on. Not much later, on one of his trips to India he did take her to Bangalore and leave her there with the family of Chandrasekhar. This was slightly before I went to visit him in Bangalore in 1986, after I had spent six days with him in Gstaad, Switzerland, with my daughter, Shyamala.

UG later moved to the "Crow's Nest", Terry Newland's place in Mill Valley. In this arrangement, Terry would move out to sleep in Dr. Paul Lynn's house or his own trailer which he parked elsewhere, while UG stayed in his studio apartment located on the main street in Mill Valley. Of course, UG paid Terry's rent while he stayed there. On at least one of my visits, I slept in the back attic room of that apartment when I stayed there. UG slept in a closet-like room there. Once, in the afternoon, when I had returned from my walk and he was sleeping there, I had gone into the living room and asked someone there jokingly whether the Master was sleeping. UG must have heard this and later quoted me as referring to him as my "Master". I didn't bother to correct it. Well, after all, he could be the Master (or my Master), although I never quite thought of him in those terms.

The next morning or so, very early in the morning (around 5 AM) I woke up and was standing in the doorway talking to UG. I told UG: "UG, because of seeing you, anything can go in my life, including myself." (I guess that was a declaration of faith.) He answered, "If you go, Sir, I go." I am not sure what that meant. You never dared to ask UG for clarification (not that sometimes he wouldn't give one). You just didn't have the guts. Perhaps, it meant he would go out of my system along with myself.

Maybe that same morning, I remember sitting with him in the living room and reading aloud the entire book *No Way* by Ram Tzu; we both relished the book.

Several incidents happened during my visits to the Crow's Nest. I will recount them here as I remember:

Terry Newland always had to have a cause -- if it wasn't Henry George, it was UG. (I used to say that Terry was the champion of lost causes.) If it wasn't UG, it was selling plastic tongue cleaners that he somehow had acquired a fancy for. Terry would also chastise people for their insincerity or half-heartedness or for the games they play. He never really got along with anyone. He worked for brief periods at Bob and Paul's restaurant (Marvin's Gardens in Larkspur), but didn't quite get along with them. For one thing, he had terrible health problems: for instance, due to urinary problem, he had to pee so often that it was hard for him to keep a job. He applied for federal disability and he wanted me to write a letter for him supporting his case. I wrote a good letter. He had a very nice girlfriend who really cared for him. But he would put too many demands on his girlfriends or become too critical of them. He would eventually spurn them off.

But Terry really cared for people. Once, as we were standing outside of Crow's Nest on the far side of the road, a couple of kids were crossing the street when a car was coming by. He was really shook up and yelled at the kids not to cross while the car was coming. His face was plain red.

One night when I stayed over in Mill Valley, I slept in Paul Lynn's house in the basement. I think it was on that occasion that Terry gave me part of the manuscript of *The Sage and the Housewife* by Shanta Kelker, asked me to read and make corrections and comments. I read it and returned it to him with my comments. I told UG that both Terry and I both thought that the manuscript was quite interesting and that Shanta should be encouraged to write more. UG, of course, did just that. Later, the question came up as to who should edit it, because it would be redundant for both Terry and me to do it. Either he or I, but not both of us, should do it, I said. That was how it came about that the manuscript was sent to me in stages in small notebooks for editing. I did the editing in Seaside, and the book was eventually published by Frank Naronha in Delhi under the title, *The Sage and the Housewife*[10]. It was a bit after I had gotten introduced to using computers by my friend and colleague Vito Victor and was developing my computer word-processing skills that I edited the book.

UG was impressed by my editing skills, telling people that I was the best editor he had ever known. He also had Terry send me the manuscript of *Mind is a Myth* (the title was given later by UG after much thought; I remember discussing it with him in a bookstore in Berkeley) and asking me to edit it. It was well written, so I didn't have to do much editing (Terry did such a good job himself); but I made the glossary more systematic.

About that time, Chandrasekhar and his wife Suguna were visiting from India. They and I were put up in Terry's girlfriend's apartment. I remember food being brought from a restaurant. The next morning, I drove Chandrasekhar and Suguna to Monterey where they spent a couple

2. Later Visits to Mill Valley (and Sausalito)

of days in my place. Suguna promptly had a migraine headache and hardly ate anything. We went to K-Mart where she shopped for dresses for her daughters. It was at that time that Chandrasekhar wanted me to edit a transcribed conversation between UG and some scientists, a piece in which UG said something to the effect that just as cells have to cooperate with other cells for self-preservation, human beings have to do the same. Chandrasekhar and UG both liked my editing.

On one of those visits to the Crow's Nest, I took UG, Krim and Terry (and perhaps also Douglas) on a ride into the mountains next to Mill Valley in my temperamental Horizon. Promptly the car stalled on one of those roads. I told everyone that the car wouldn't start again for another half hour. UG said, "You guys go for a walk, I will rest here." We all went for a little walk and UG pushed the seat back and lay down there and fell asleep! He was absolutely worriless in spite of the fact we were stuck.

I think it was on the same visit that Sajid Hussein, (later changed to Sajid Martin) was going to visit UG in Mill Valley. UG had asked him when they spoke on the phone earlier to come around 1:00 PM. We arrived there after the drive a minute or so after 1:00 PM. And Sajid had left a note saying he was there and was about to leave. UG said, "I told you I would be back at 1:00 PM." So precise!

On one of the visits, Sajid and Jean-Michel also came with me to visit UG in Mill Valley. We all drove together. UG wanted me to sleep in his place while the other two were going to stay at a Howard Johnsons nearby. I told UG that as they came with me, I couldn't as well take the privileged position and let them go to a hotel. So I went with them and stayed in the hotel. Jean-Michel and I shared a room.

On one of those early visits, we all went to Pasand's, an Indian restaurant in San Rafael for lunch. As we were about to cross the road to get to the restaurant, I noticed that UG, as usual, threw up stuff into a garbage bin. I also saw how parts of his face were trembling. I understood that the tremblings were energy outbursts.

I paid for the food with my credit card, but being so nervous I forgot the card in the restaurant when we left. After we got back to the Crow's Nest, I remembered it and called the restaurant; luckily the card was still there. Then some pictures that had been taken by someone were shown. And UG gave me one of mine, which was pretty ugly. I was reluctant to take it, but UG insisted. As I got into the car, the thermos I was carrying tilted and much of the coffee in it was spilled. I thought this was probably a punishment for my reluctance to accept the ugly picture.

A couple of times I slept in Bob and Paul's house. I remember on one occasion having a beer with them and talking about the paper I had written on J. Krishnamurti: "Fragmentation, Meditation and Transformation." Paul was pretty incisive in his critique, I thought.

On another visit, one of my friends, K.S. Sastry, a professor of Metallurgy at UC Berkeley, came to visit UG, on my persuasion. He talked a little, but neither he nor UG seemed impressed with each other. It might be on the same visit that Jeffrey Mishlove came for an initial conversation with UG as a preamble to a TV interview with him. I wasn't too impressed with him. But the TV interviews, at least one of them, turned out to be a success. Mishlove was pretty passive in those interviews (there were three of them). The interviews are still sold commercially. I think one of those interviews of UG is bundled with another with John Searle, the famous philosopher from UC Berkeley, whom I assisted as a TA in my final year there.

Terry was also trying to make efforts to "sell" UG to the media. This was during a time when UG was announcing that he was interested in getting on the media. "Just so, someone somewhere will get the message that there is nothing to get," he said. Terry was sending copies of *Mystique* to various people, including Larry King.

On one occasion, in the Crow's Nest, Terry tried to pick an argument with me in front of UG, attacking my "wishy-washiness" or something (just because I wouldn't say much in front of UG). I tried to defend myself and in the process UG was putting his arm out wanting to stop our argument, and in the counterattack I gently pushed UG's arm away, saying, "Wait, UG." Of course, UG withdrew his arm.

Douglas, Krim, Paul and Bob were all around once. There was some discussion going on (this time about sex and pleasure, I think). And we so marveled at the quality of the discussion that we regretted not having a tape recorder to record the conversation. But we all admitted that the quality of the discussion would have suffered drastically if a tape-recorder was put in the middle (making us all self-conscious). Those electrifying conversations could never be repeated. We couldn't even remember much of them.

I remember there were about ten people one night; UG offered to make a quick dinner for them all. In about ten minutes he had produced a delicious potato-buds-and-cheese dish for the ten people! We were all duly impressed.

Terry had a hard time getting along with people. One night, Larry Morris and I went to his place (which he must have rented while UG stayed at the Crow's Nest) to spend the night. Terry recently had returned from an unsuccessful trip to Mexico. He had gone there, with the help of money from UG, to try to find a different way of living. He wasn't doing very well. (He had sold his motorcycle to make the trip.) He had his usual troubles of meeting girls and making friends. He would alienate

2. Later Visits to Mill Valley (and Sausalito)

people quickly because he was so demanding. He still had trouble making a living and keeping jobs because of his poor health condition. He had some problem with his urinary tract (he had intestinal cancer). On top of it, he had had an unsuccessful septum surgery which he went through to correct a deviated septum (to help his breathing in Yoga – what a stupid idea!). He had infection upon infection which were not cured by antibiotics. He was in a miserable shape. And he had memories of a troubled childhood. His father had been hunted by the McArthur House Committee for Un-American Activities for being a Communist. Apparently, he had been beaten by his father even when he was a teenager. That night, for the first time, I saw Terry crying. He was in pain. His whole life was in total darkness, except for a little light at the end of the tunnel -- UG. I felt so sorry for Terry.

Soon after, Terry died in pretty miserable circumstances. This happened in September, 1990 (a few months before Valentine died in India).

UG had dropped by in Seaside on his way to Mill Valley from Los Angeles, I think. He might have spent a day here. But that afternoon UG and others all went to Costco and from there they left. As he was getting into the car, UG looked pretty strange. He must have already a premonition of Terry's death.

When UG arrived in Mill Valley, apparently, he couldn't find Terry. The next morning, the hospital called for Terry, looking for him for his missed appointment. Then UG sent Julie Thayer and someone else to look for Terry. Terry was found by Julie dead in Dr. Paul Lynn's house, where he had been house-sitting while the Lynns were away.

Here is Julie's account of it:

> We stopped at your (Moorty's) house on the way down to L.A. in September of 1990 (Valentine died later, in January of 1991) – UG, Douglas and Olivia, and I. When we returned to Mill Valley a few days later, Terry was missing... I found him dead in Paul Lynn's house. He had suffered a massive heart attack and was lying on his stomach in the living room, near the telephone.

The body was soon brought to the mortuary next door to the Crow's Nest, the last place Terry ever wanted to enter. UG never bothered to look at the dead body or go to the funeral. But when Terry's parents arrived for the burial, UG offered to buy Terry's sofa and other furniture from the parents to help them pay for the funeral, the same furniture which he had helped Terry buy in the first place.

Some or all of the stuff he later gave away to Krim and whomever, because that was the end of the Crow's Nest and of Mill Valley for UG. The landlady was willing to rent it to UG, but he wasn't interested.

On one visit, Scottie from Ojai came with a friend of his, Ted, who was an editor of some sort. We all three went to the town center café for coffee on a Sunday morning. Ted started pouring out his gripes about UG, how UG said the same thing over and over again and how boring he was. I tried to defend UG a bit saying that you don't go to UG if you are looking to be entertained. I don't think I ever saw Ted again. But, of course, I saw Scottie many times, including once in his house in Ojai, California, with UG.

In some ways I was responsible for Julie meeting UG. It happened sometime (maybe about a year or two) before. I used to place some UG books for sale in the Pilgrim's Way bookstore in Carmel and also leave a card with my phone number and a note in each of the books saying that if the reader was interested in meeting UG, he or she should contact me. Julie was visiting Carmel. Her friend Tom Head was a part owner of K-Mart and lived in Carmel Valley. Julie was then a disciple of Andrew Cohen, along with some other women, one of whom, Luna Tarlo, was Andrew's mother. Julie had seen *The Mystique of Enlightenment* once on Andrew's shelf and had looked into it. In Carmel at the Pilgrim's Way she bought a copy of it and called me up after she saw the card.

She and Tom came over to my house and talked about UG, expressing an interest in meeting him. Apparently Julie was involved in some Zen group doing community service or whatnot. Julie and Luna, her friend, met UG at my house. Then they and their other lady friends all went to see him again in Mill Valley two days later, as they were moving into a house not far from the Crow's Nest. UG in his usual forceful fashion apparently told them, "Obviously the book has not done its job, or you wouldn't be here." Immediately after that meeting with UG, they all left Andrew's community.

Later on, Julie came to see me with the other three women (one of them was Polish, called Elisabeth, another was Luna and I can't recall the third one.) I made buttermilk pancakes for them all that morning.

One evening, when I was at the Crow's Nest, there was a row between UG and Julie. It had something to do with the videos Julie was shooting. UG was asking her to catalog them and edit them; and Julie was resisting the idea saying that she had neither the equipment nor the skills to do it. I tried to clarify to her exactly what UG was saying, and UG agreed with my interpretation. She could have just done that much and no more and let things take their own course. But Julie could be stubborn too.

I think at that time Julie was staying at UG's place for a month or so sleeping in the bedroom. UG himself was sleeping in a little room in the attic which he had asked Scottie to build for him so that Julie could have the bedroom.

2. Later Visits to Mill Valley (and Sausalito)

Another time, Julie came over to Seaside to see me for a couple of days. Apparently, she had another row with UG .[11] I also noticed the disciplining type of schoolteacher-pupil relationship developing between them, UG correcting every move of hers.

Then UG asked her to "go see Moorty, spend a couple of days with him and talk things over." She and I went to Point Lobos for a walk. It was useless to talk to her or point out things to her; she would never quit her attachments, attitudes and beliefs. It was by then obvious to me that she was simply in love with UG. After all these years, she still is. I believe she is still grieving the loss of UG, like several others I know.

* * *

Those were just the beginnings of the strong connection between UG and me. UG visited us here in Seaside at least once almost every year since the first few meetings, and I in turn, on his invitation, visited him many times on various occasions and in many places including Corte Madera, San Rafael, Los Angeles, Hemet, and Palm Springs in California and Lake Havasu in Arizona. I also spent times with him in Bangalore, Chennai, Yercaud and Mysore in India on various occasions, and on one visit, once, in 1990, my wife and children and I spent a week with him in Bangalore. I (sometimes with my family) spent, again on his invitation, several summers with him in Gstaad, Switzerland.

On all those trips, I had memorable conversations, car rides and restaurant meals with UG as well as delectable meals cooked by him. I made numerous acquaintances around UG's gatherings and some close friendships as well, although I had lost some close friends too because of my friendship with UG.

It's hard for me to recall every detail now, but in the following chapter I will include the trips or events that have made an indelible mark.

3. Notable Travels and Visits

For many people, knowing UG involved travelling to places all over the world, for as UG would boast, ever since he was in his teens, he never stayed in one place more than six months. Even at an advanced age, he managed to keep moving. He rented the same Chalet Sunbeam in Gstaad Switzerland in the summer for many years and people would visit him there from all over. He would make brief trips to other countries in Europe from that base. While I knew him, he visited California almost every year, first staying in the Mill Valley area, then in Palm Springs. He also made regular brief visits to New York, passing through, as it were. He often went to India, staying for some time with Chandrasekhar and Suguna in Bangalore before and during the time they cared for Valentine, and after. He of course made trips to Bombay, a few times to Delhi, but rarely to Hyderabad where his two daughters and their families lived. (They visited him, instead, wherever he stayed.) He also made many trips to Australia, New Zealand and even China and Japan, although his forays into China and Japan were always solo. He traveled simply and insisted on carrying his own small suitcase or carry-on bag, his total sum of luggage and a point of pride. In his last years, he had forgone travel to Australia and China, but made short trips by car to Germany and more extended ones to Italy, his final destination.

I visited UG in several of these places, at his invitation, and was always treated with great hospitality. Here are some highlights.

First Trip, Gstaad and Bangalore, 1986

Late in 1985, UG suggested I should visit him in Gstaad. I told him that I wanted to bring my 12 year-old daughter, Shyamala, with me, and that I would also like to go to India too, since it would be so much closer — less miles and less cost. But, I said I wouldn't go to India unless he was there, because half the fun of going to India would be to visit him there. So he promised to be there at the same time.

It was arranged that Shyamala and I would go for about two weeks, spending six days in Gstaad, and then also go to see friends in Marseille, Paris and Heidelberg, Germany, after which I would send Shyamala back to the US. I would then go on to India, spend some time visiting family members, as well as some time with UG in Bangalore. My wife, Wendy, and one year-old son, Kiran, would remain at home in Seaside.

Gstaad, 1986

UG stayed in touch with us constantly by sending train schedules, picture postcards and whatnot. The first leg of the travel was difficult, with Shyamala getting airsick on the plane and in the Frankfurt airport, and I having to clean up after her. In the airport I had difficulty finding a money exchange bureau and getting us on the train to Berne. Making a phone call to UG on the train involved some fumbling and help from a German man, as I didn't know that I wasn't supposed to dial the initial "0" in the number. Once the call was successfully made, I informed UG of our arrival time, and also of Shyamala's sickness, and to my great relief, when I returned to my seat, Shyamala suddenly was feeling better.

We both were starved. We had to change the trains in Basel, carrying our stuff across the train tracks, which was another hassle. Finally, around 7:30 PM or so in the evening we arrived in Berne and were met at the train station by UG and Paul Sempé who drove us to Gstaad in an hour and a half. It was dark, so we couldn't see much. Once arrived, we had some soup and bread, which revived us. Kim was cooking for UG and Valentine (and others too). We were given two small rooms upstairs to sleep, and we were ready to rest.

The next day, I had a better picture of the Chalet Sunbeam and its surroundings in Gstaad. It was a two-storied chalet, with the landlord, Herr Grossman and his wife, living upstairs. Also from a side staircase you could go to an upstairs apartment and a room for guests. There was a bath with a shower downstairs. The Chalet stands on a small hill and you could see the town's main street and tennis courts, and the surrounding magnificent mountains all around covered with green grass mown in the summer time by owners of the properties (and fertilized with cow urine which causes the whole town to smell strongly for a couple of days). In winters, Gstaad turns into a ski resort and in summers, a venue for world-class tennis tournaments. The place is abuzz with tourists in summers. The weather is pleasant with occasional showers. Gstaad is a delight to tourists.

I met many people visiting UG that were new to me, but whom I would see many times again on future visits. These included Paul Sempé, Marissa, Salvatore, Henk Shoneville, Robert Geissman, and Herr Grossman, the rather peculiar resident-owner of the chalet. Paul was once a pacifist and used to listen to J. Krishnamurti regularly. Salvatore and Marissa were also once followers of Krishnamurti. Henk, who ran an Advaita ashram in Amsterdam, once took me out for a beer and complained about how badly UG would treat him in spite of the fact that he made all the arrangements for UG's visits in Amsterdam. Paul Sempé would discuss Descartes with me. Being a Frenchman, Paul was quite enamored by Descartes. Once, UG was listening in to our conversation, but I was too self-conscious to speak freely. Of course, UG was critical of Descartes.

Shyamala was entertained by Marissa and Kim. Marissa's teenage son, Lorenzo, being there was very helpful. They all took good care of Shyamala. Kim took Shyamala on hikes on the mountains and they all played Dungeons and Dragons. Marissa even did our laundry.

In the morning of the second day or so of our arrival, UG took us down to Mount Egli and took our picture at the bottom of the hill with our camera. That was touching. He left us there, asking us to take the lift to go up on the mountain. We did, and Shyamala and I walked on the Alps. Shyamala shouted, "I am not going home. This is my home!" I was pleased with her response. When we got back down to the town, it was 2:30 or so in the afternoon, too late to expect lunch at UG's. So we decided to have lunch at a restaurant downtown. We went into an Italian restaurant and ordered some minestrone soup. I had to make sure, in my broken French, that there was no meat in it. (I used the word "*viande*".) Shyamala thought the soup was delicious.

Generally, the food we had with UG in "Sunbeam" was good — the usual UG menu of soups with cream, bread, cheese and yogurt.

We went on car trips to various places. Paul Sempé drove us to Zurich one day, where we ate lunch in an Indian restaurant. In Zurich we met this young German psychiatrist and his wife whom I had occasion to meet again much later. Paul also drove us to see Berne and Lucerne. The night before that drive, the weather was predicted to be dismal. The television showed a picture of the whole of Switzerland overcast with a forecast of rain. But the next day, it was sunny! In Berne, UG walked around the shops with us, and bought us some freshly-squeezed orange juice and chocolate for Shyamala. Only when we had returned to Gstaad did it begin to get cloudy. Observing this, I asked UG, "Should we say it was UG's miracle or simply that the weather man was mistaken?" UG replied quietly, "Let's say that the weather man was mistaken."

During our stay, Shyamala and I took pictures all over the place. Once Shyamala's camera fell on the street. I later had to supplement my pictures with Chandrasekhar's either because mine were lost or there was not enough film left.

I think it was on this trip that I asked UG if he would be interested in reading the article I wrote about J. Krishnamurti ("Fragmentation, Meditation and Transformation"). It was published later (in 1988) in the *Journal of the Indian Council of Philosophical Research*. UG said that he would always be interested in reading what I had to write. So, I gave it to him. He read it overnight and the next morning he nicely slipped it under a couple of other books or papers so that it would not be easily noticed. I

3. Notable Travels and Visits

asked him what he thought of the paper. He said I made clear some of the difficulties which the reader might have in understanding Krishnamurti, and the conversation ended there.

I commented to UG at one point about how all the people who gathered around UG for his sessions (I had in mind Robert Geismann and Bernard, the mailman from England) were so mature. And UG's reply was astonishing: "The Old Man (meaning J. Krishnamurti) prepared them all, Sir!" That told me the regard in which he held J. Krishnamurti, contrary to all appearances.

Sometimes, UG would flare up at one person or another. Once, I saw him flare up at Kim and another time, at Paul Sempé. I remember Kim saying, "You want me to leave now?" Then UG would say, "if you want to…" and then soften. There was no apparent reason to flare up at Paul either. UG's rationale was always, "This gun shoots wherever and whenever it sees the movement of thought."

One day, maybe on another trip, I saw UG yelling at Herr Grossman, calling him a bastard or whatever, because Grossman had just raised his rent. And of course, UG didn't relish the idea. Grossman was quite money-conscious and, in spite of his riches (apparently he owned some businesses in town as well as Chalet Sunbeam), lived very modestly.

Grossman engaged me in conversation once when I was climbing down the stairs in the night. For at least 40 minutes or an hour he bored me with his talk about the Rosicrucian teachings.

People would often gather informally outside UG's apartment on the small lawn next to the chalet, with the backdrop of the town below and mountains behind. They sat in plastic chairs or on the ground. One afternoon, I was standing there and UG asked me to please sit down. I told him I didn't mind standing. He replied that it hurt him if I kept standing. Without making a fuss, I sat down.

Another car trip we made was with Salvatore, the Italian architect. We went to Geneva to receive Chandrasekhar at the airport (he was returning from the US after a training course in automobile engineering in Detroit). It rained and hailed heavily in Geneva, and on our return we found a dent on Salvatore's car top from the hail.

Our stay in Gstaad was filled with trips, conversations and new acquaintances. It was memorable.

On the day of our departure, we were driven by Paul Sempé early in the morning around 3 AM to a border train station and dropped off there to go to France via Milan. (UG went with us to the travel agent to book the train tickets -- we bought tickets also for a fast train from Marseilles to Paris.) After bidding goodbye to UG and Paul, Shyamala and I put the luggage in the cloak room and went out to a restaurant across the street for breakfast. We got on the train, and it went through a very long tunnel

(I think it was about 15 kilometers long) on the borders between Switzerland and Italy. When we got through the tunnel it just stopped raining, everything was wet and fresh after a recent shower. The mountain sides were green. The train stopped at a station. All the surroundings were fresh and sparkling, the wet pavement reflecting the sun. It was one of the most beautiful sights you could see. We continued our journey to Marseille where we were met by my old friend Paul Albert.

After a couple of days with Paul and his family, five days in Paris and four days in Heidelberg, I returned with Shyamala to Frankfurt. I sent her back to the U.S. and took a plane to Bombay, India.

Bangalore, 1986

After visiting my relatives in Bombay, I went to Hyderabad to visit my brother. From there I tried to contact Chandrasekhar in Bangalore by phone to find out about UG's arrival and stay. I couldn't locate him, so I left a message. Chandrasekhar never answered my message.

I then went on a trip south, first to see my friend Kumaraswami Raja in Annamalai. Raja was a professor of linguistics in Annamalai University. He used to be a close friend of mine in Visakhapatnam where we both worked in the University. He was very much into J. Krishnamurti, having read many of his books. Many years ago he had helped me go to the U.S. by encouraging me to send him my papers and submitting them to the philosophy department at UC Berkeley. I spent a couple of days with him in Annamalai, met his new wife Saraswati (he had had a previous short-lived and broken marriage in the US) and his son Mohan. I played all my Amsterdam tapes of UG for him on his tape recorder. (Henk had given me these tapes in Gstaad. He had made them himself from interviews he had had with UG. He was actually selling them to others, but he gave me a complimentary set.) The tapes must have made an impression on Raja. He said, "This must be another Krishnamurti looming on the horizon." After a couple of days of visiting, Raja dropped me off at the Annamalai bus station about 10 in the night to travel to Bangalore. He promised he would come to Bangalore a day or two after I arrived there, and I asked him to put himself up in a hotel and come to 40 K.R. Road, Chandrasekhar's house, where UG was living.

The next morning, after a sleepless night and with a back that felt broken, I arrived in Bangalore. I hired an auto rickshaw and went to 40 K.R. Road. Just as I was getting out of the vehicle, I saw UG walking away on the street in an Indian dress (*lalchi* and *pajamas*). I hailed him. He turned around and recognized me, and took me into the house. He and Chandrasekhar showed me the room where I was going to sleep. It was adjacent to the street, but quite decent. They arranged for a smoke device

3. Notable Travels and Visits

to keep the mosquitoes away. Usha, UG's daughter, was there and also Valentine, living in the downstairs room at that time. There were a couple of servants and a constant traffic of people. I chastised Chandrasekhar for not answering my phone messages, but UG calmed me down, saying that since I was there anyhow, it didn't matter. There was also a mention of *Sudha*, my translation of Chalam's Telugu poetry and Chandrasekhar was critical of it and seemed not to like it.

I stayed in Bangalore for six days. I was planning to stay there for less, but UG charted out my itinerary, insisting that I should stay in Bangalore for six days. (I had stayed for six days in Gstaad, so I must stay there for six days -- so went the reasoning.)

There were all kinds of visitors there: Shanta Kelker and her children Mittu and Prashant were frequent visitors. And there was Gopikrishna and Niranjan, the bicycle shop owner, Radhakrishna, the tea merchant, Ramachandra and his partner, Rechal Das, financiers to the movies, Chandrasekhar, the architect and his wife Sudha, Gopi Krishna and his wife, Brahmachari, the would-have-been Sankaracharya of the Kudali Math, Satyanarayana, the statistician/astrologer, and so on and on. We all sat on the floor or on a cot, while UG sat in a chair. There were few chairs. Lots of gossip and joking around made for a party-like atmosphere.

Kalyani was one of the visitors. She would sing and dance, and beg for money. She was well-to-do, being the sister of a civil service officer. Later, she died of breast cancer. She was apparently pretty psychic and a bit crazy. All kinds of stories about her are told in *Stopped in Our Tracks*, *Series I*, by Chandrasekhar.

Mahesh Bhatt was also there, staying at the Woodlands hotel. A couple of days after I arrived, we went to see him there. And Mahesh ordered some beer. Brahmachari, the swamiji, was there. Then Raja was ushered in, as he had arrived at 40 K.R. Road and someone brought him over. Apparently, he was given the room which Usha was occupying, so he didn't have to stay in a hotel. UG asked Usha to sleep in the living room instead. Raja, myself, Mahesh and Nagaraj, all drank beer in UG's presence -- generally unheard of. Brahmachari, who would not normally approve such things, nevertheless joined the merriment minus the drinking.

Another night, UG asked me to join him to go to Mahesh's room where a drinking session for me and Mahesh had been arranged. We took an elevator to go to Mahesh's room. Mahesh wasn't in his room. But UG had a key, and on entering the room we could hear a big band playing next-door downstairs. The noise was so loud that I thought UG would do something to quell it. He went into the bathroom and closed the curtain there and came back into the main room. As he was sitting down in the armchair he swung his right arm broadly. A minute later the band noise stopped and never returned. Mahesh and I did have a couple of drinks in the room, and then the three of us went downstairs for dinner.

Nagaraj (the personal assistant to the Postmaster General) was always around, on "French leave" from his work so he could be with UG, taking shorthand notes of conversations with UG. He was addicted to smoking. He wanted to quit smoking but couldn't. UG would advise him not to quit. If he quit, UG warned, it would be a great shock to his system. Sometime later, Nagaraj even called me at home in Seaside (while UG was visiting) and asked me for tips to quit smoking. I told him to "just quit." Anyway, apparently he did, and he died soon after. UG, I heard, went to visit his family to console them.

There were two servant maids in the house taking care of Valentine. I noticed how their faces would expand with broad smiles whenever UG walked into a room. They were happy to see him. Of course, he always rewarded them generously for their work. Why wouldn't they be happy? Besides, UG's aura was such.

One night, Chandrasekhar and I brought *vadais* and hot chutney from a nearby restaurant. We all ate them to spare the women at home the trouble of cooking.

During my stay, I was offering to spend some money on this or that, but UG would always stop me, saying, "Wait, your turn will come." We went into a *sari* shop looking for a *sari* for Wendy, my wife. UG let me pay for a piece of fabric for him and he helped me to pick a nice sari for Wendy, a blue one.

That was the last time I saw my friend Raja. While there, he once participated in a conversation with UG. As usual, the topic was enlightenment. UG in his usual fashion downplayed the idea of "waiting for something to happen." I wrote to Raja later (from the US) a couple of times, but never had a response from him. I learned a couple of years later from his son Mohan that one evening around 5 p.m. he went out for a walk to the downtown area and never returned. His family and friends advertised in the papers and other venues searching for him, but to no avail. No one knew what happened to him.

I mentioned this later to UG and mused aloud that he might have been murdered. UG replied, "Murdered, no!" I didn't know how to take that answer.

As my time in Bangalore was coming to a close, I remarked to UG that it seemed about 90% of the people who came to see him there were really there for the supernatural effect and not for his teaching. He replied, "Why 90%? All of them!"

After the six days had passed, I bade goodbye to everyone. Suguna made some *upma* for me (as it was too early for dinner). As a parting gift,

UG gave me some incense sticks to give to my family. I was going out to get an auto-rickshaw and Chandrasekhar wanted to accompany me to the bus station. I said I could go alone. UG supported me by saying that a man who can go all around the world doesn't need company to go the bus station.

Bangalore, 1990

On one of his visits to Seaside, UG invited Wendy to come to Switzerland, with our two children, 4 year-old Kiran and by then a 16 year-old Shyamala. I told him that if we went all the way to Switzerland, it would be only a bit longer to go to India, but it would cost too much to go to both places. UG said that it would be more interesting for Wendy to go to India. I pointed out that I wouldn't care to go to India if he weren't there, so as before, he said he would make a point of being there when we got there. So, the trip was arranged.

The four of us traveled from Seaside first to Chennai and then took another plane to Bangalore. Julie and Chandrasekhar received us at the airport around midnight.

At 40 K.R. Road, our family was given a big room upstairs and was treated like royalty. The food was great. And I remember going for a walk with UG in the Lalbagh gardens. And also, UG took us all to the M.T.R Restaurant where everything was made with *ghee*.

We stayed in Bangalore for 10 days. On the third day, it was June 25, my birthday. For that day, I arranged that Julie would take my family in a taxi to Mysore and show them around while I spent time with UG in Bangalore. But at 6 AM, just as I went downstairs in my pajamas to get some coffee, I learned that Julie had backed out of going -- she couldn't tear herself away from UG! UG suggested that I should take them to Mysore -- after all, they were my family. I agreed and got ready in 15 minutes. I did have a great birthday celebration, with a lovely beer and cashew nuts in the luxury hotel located in the Brindavan Gardens near Mysore.

One morning, UG arranged for me to go and get a Nadi reading (I think it was called Agasthya Nadi). I had anticipated this possibility even while I was back in the US, as there was talk about it then. So I had my horoscope that had been done by my late father sent to me from Hyderabad and I took it with me to the reading, along with information about Wendy's birthplace and date and time of birth. We had both our readings done. Brahmachari and Chandrasekhar were with us, as well as Wendy, and I think also Shyamala and Kiran. The session took place for no more than an hour. At the end I gave the Nadi reader a hundred rupees. The Nadi reader had long matted hair and read the palm leaves inscribed in archaic Tamil which he translated into contemporary Kannada. (Chandrasekhar recorded and translated it and typed it up that night.) There were some predictions that I would become famous and rich in some sort of international business, that I would live till I was 93, that Wendy was my second wife, and that my mother was going to die in the next year or two, due to her past karma. The reading was right about Wendy, and perhaps my mother (my mother did die about a year later), but not about the "international business." Neither I nor UG believed that I would be good in any kind of business. I just don't have such talents or interest. At the end of the session, I was prompted by the *nadi* reader to ask three questions. One of the questions I asked was whether I would get enlightened (or, when I would get enlightened.) The answer came that I would be enlightened when I was 93 (just before I die?!). When this was reported to UG, he chide me for my question. I said I just asked out of curiosity, although, I told him, I believed that in some sense I felt that I was already enlightened. That put an end to the conversation.

One afternoon, there was a big gathering at 40 K.R. Road. The upstairs living room was packed with people. A little girl from a Telugu family was brought to perform classical dance for UG, her teacher accompanying her with her singing. It was painful to watch. The dance was so long that the girl was literally in pain. Julie shot a video of this and other events. At some point in the late afternoon, everyone moved to the rooftop terrace. Even Valentine was carried up the stairs in her wicker chair. There Shyamala charmed everyone with her dance as well as her dramatization of Dr. Seuss's poem, "What Was I Scared Of?" While everyone was chatting, Shyamala and the other girls, Mittu, Aruna and Archana, taught each other some dance movements. Mittu and Prashant were Shanta's children. Aruna and Archana were Chandrasekhar's daughters. Bharati, UG's elder daughter, was also present. The women had a grand time decking Shyamala with *saris*.

Another day, I invited everyone for lunch at the Woodlands Hotel. We all ate pizza and other foods. Indian food was served, but in another part of the restaurant where you ate in Indian style.

The night before we left, we saw UG off at the airport. He left to go somewhere. The same night, after 10 o'clock, Chandrasekhar took me to see his friend Satyanarayana, the statistician, who was also an astrologer, for a reading. Satyanarayana was kind enough to give a detailed reading. I did take some notes. When I looked over the notes later, the reading didn't seem all that striking to me,

Apparently, Satyanarayana was a psychic too. He could cite phrases from a page of a book, along with the page number, of UG's *Mind is a Myth* before it ever came to be published! He told us that his father was a monk before he died. I noticed a picture of him in monk's robes in one of the rooms.

On our final day, we were all invited for lunch by Ramachandra and Rechal Das. They were partners and billionaires. There were snacks and beer and all that. But we didn't see their families. There was some philosophical talk, part of it turning around who would succeed UG. I felt that they got interested in me because somehow they suspected that I might be the one to succeed UG. Not a chance! (In fact, I commented once on UG in everyone's presence: "UG is an 'odd ball'. I don't want to be an odd ball!") After the lunch, Ramachandra dropped us off at the airport.

From there we flew to Hyderabad where we visited my brother and his family for a couple of weeks. In Hyderabad, my family was treated for lunch or dinner parties by UG's daughters Bharati and Usha, and UG's friend Dr. Kameswari. UG's grandson Kamesh drove us around showing his place of work, the Defense Research Laboratories.

We then briefly visited several other places, Bombay, Guntur, Delhi, Agra, Banaras and Chennai, partly on a lecture tour, arranged by my former teacher and friend Professor K. Satchidananda Murty, before returning to Seaside.

Carmel, 1991

This period of four weeks of being with UG did not involve traveling on my part. This was the only time that UG stayed in the area where I live for more than two or three days. The occasion was to provide Mahesh Bhatt a place to write UG's biography (*UG Krishnamurti, A Life*, published later in 1992 by Penguin Books, India), with some assistance from me and UG.

UG sent some money from Europe, asking me to find a place for him and Mahesh to stay while they visited the US with the plan of Mahesh writing UG's biography. Wendy and I found a vacation rental home in Carmel for them and rented it for a month. They arrived and set up house there. I brought in my 286 PC computer and a dot-matrix printer. The idea was for me to help Mahesh write the biography in the afternoons when I wouldn't be busy teaching in the college. For a whole week there was no movement, as Mahesh didn't make even the first stab at writing. I was beginning to doubt if the biography would ever come to pass. But soon after, he picked up speed and would dictate material to me and I would type it up on the computer while simultaneously editing it where it needed.

There were few visitors – UG made sure of that. There was this odd and odoriferous couple whose story I recounted below in Chapter 7.

Larry Morris came for a couple of weeks to help with the writing. UG himself had newspaper and magazine clippings as well as some old letters with him, and he would dictate some of those to me. At times, he and Larry (and I too) would work together on a paragraph or two. Also, Douglas Rosestone visited, giving an account of the night of UG's "calamity," which was video-graphed and reported in the biography. A few others, mostly from the San Francisco Bay area and Santa Cruz, managed to drop in for short visits.

Mahesh was intense in his work. When he was not working, he was talking to his daughter on his birthday or to some others in Bombay about his films. He never cared much about what he ate or drank, and lived practically on what UG had provided him. At nights, when he was alone, he would write his stuff and dictate the material the next day when I was on the computer.

The last night of the writing of the biography, at about 10 p.m., the computer keyboard promptly broke down. Not knowing what else to do, I called the shop person who had sold me the computer. Fortunately, not only did he answer, but he said that he could replace the one I had with another one right then! I told Mahesh I would go down to this man's shop to fetch the replacement keyboard, and Mahesh said he would go with me. After we returned at about 11 PM, I told Mahesh that it was my job now to put all the material of the book together and he could retire for the night. But Mahesh insisted that he would sit with me: he said that in his movie-making work he was used to things breaking down in the middle of the night and to sitting with people working with him late into the night. I started working.

Around 2 AM, UG suddenly walked in from his bedroom and declared, "I still sense a block here. These two chapters (whatever they were) should not be separate. They should be merged together." I told him that then the resulting chapter would be too long and that some material would have to be cut. The material that could be cut was mostly about Mahesh's relationship with Parveen Babi. Mahesh said that he couldn't do it because the material was too close to him. So, I said I would do it. In about 10 minutes time I merged the chapters and cut down the size. This was another of the many instances where being with UG meant things could change instantly, at any time; one could not hesitate or ponder, but had to act quickly.

The book was ready to be printed by 6 AM. I sat down with UG to design the cover page and was wondering if UG had a picture of himself to put on the cover page. UG went into his bedroom and returned with a very nice picture, although it was not the one on the published book. It seemed to fit the cover perfectly. As the book had to be finished immediately (they were scheduled to leave the next day), I called my work and excused myself for the day, and set about printing the biography using double-strike printing on a dot-matrix printer. The two hundred pages took about five and-a-half hours. By 11:30 AM the manuscript was ready to be taken to Kinkos to be copied and bound. I was exhausted; so I rested for a couple of hours in the middle of the day.

The next morning, Mahesh and UG left the house in Carmel, dropping by our house for breakfast on their way to Corte Madera. I told UG that the work had been hard, but I loved every minute of it. I also said that my work was my "*guru dakshina*" (gift to the guru) to him. UG replied that if there was anybody like a guru, he wouldn't call himself that.

By all counts, the writing of the biography was a memorable event. To commemorate the event Wendy took a bunch of photographs on different occasions, a couple of which are included in the Photos section below..

Yercaud, Mysore, Bangalore and Chennai, 1994

While I was visiting UG in San Rafael some months earlier, UG invited me to go to India that winter of 1994 and he even provided me with a round-trip ticket. I was to spend a month in India, about three weeks with him and a week with all my extended family in Hyderabad.

My brother had died the year before (in November 1993) from a heart attack. I hadn't gone to his funeral, so I thought it would be a good gesture on my part to visit my sister-in-law, his widow, after a year of his death, to offer my condolences.

After one night in Chennai, I first spent about two weeks in Yercaud with UG, a night at Brahmachari's ashram in Mysore, a few days in Bangalore at Chandrasekhar's, then a week with my family in Hyderabad, and then went back to Chennai to spend another week with UG before I left the country.

I flew from Los Angeles on Malaysian Airlines directly to Chennai. UG, besides sending me the ticket, also arranged for Chandrasekhar to meet me at the airport and take me to Mr. Malladi Krishnamurti's house to spend the night. I was quite touched by the cordiality with which the Malladi's received me. They had supper ready for me. I slept, took a bath in the morning and had some coffee. I learned that Mr. Krishnamurti was the roommate of my childhood friend Parthasaradhi when they had both studied at the Indian Statistical Institute in Calcutta. (I later told Parthasaradhi, who, like me, has lived in the U.S. for many years, about him and I was able to connect the two.)

Well rested, the next morning, Chandrasekhar and I took a train to Salem. We traveled in an air-conditioned compartment where seats were already reserved for us. We ate some *idlis* sold by vendors on the train for breakfast and talked to our hearts' content.

When we arrived in Salem after about 4-6 hours of travel, UG and Major Dakshinamurti were waiting at the station to receive us. We went into a nearby restaurant for lunch. UG chided the major for the measly tip he gave to the waiter.

Later, we arrived at the Radha Estate, in Yercaud. Yercaud is a resort village located on a hill near Salem. Driving there involved quite an uphill curving road with sharp hairpin turns which the Major negotiated well. The house had a West Wing and an East Wing; UG, the Major and I occupied the East Wing. In my room, as I opened my suitcase to pull out some small gifts (like almond rocca), I heard UG talking about them as "junk". Of course, I was hurt a little. Yet he appropriated the whole box of the almond rocca, only part of which I had intended to give to Chandrasekhar and Suguna and the rest to my family, and never even mentioned a thing about it. UG gave me some rupees in exchange for dollars (with his usual "commission" – as this was his usual practice and how he made some money, the exchange rates varying, depending on the customer!).

Nartaki also came to see me (I had written to her before), and, of course, UG. She was put up in the West Wing along with Godfried and Bodil.

My room was comfortable enough, and there was a bathroom where I could get hot water and wash my underwear and hang them up to dry. I remember one morning I came out after my bath, not quite fully dressed, and UG was sitting cross-legged in the living room on a sofa, clad in white clothes. I was standing in front of him, hands closed, watching him in reverence. Earlier, when I was taking my bath, I had been having all kinds of negative thoughts going in my head, but now when I stood there, my mind was swept clean of all those negative thoughts, and I could feel a nice clean energy running through me. UG looked like a freshly blossomed flower.

One evening, after dinner, UG was asking all the foreigners (it must have included me) to go to the West Wing. I teasingly said something to the effect, "We all belong over there!" UG took it as if I was feeling hurt. The next afternoon, he himself made some coffee with cream and brought over to me. I knew he was making up for his remark the previous night. The coffee was absolutely delicious.

I saw him also abetting a drunkard by giving him money each time he came by or UG passed him on the street.

One evening, UG again started his tirade against Chandrasekhar for his gathering so many personal letters of people to UG, as well as photographs of him, and videos and audios of UG talking with people.

UG's claim was that others might access those letters and glean personal information the authors or involved parties wouldn't want seen. Also, he maintained that the photographs and videos were the general property of people (of everyone) and Chandrasekhar had no business keeping them for himself. Another claim I heard was that people who keep these videos and other materials might eventually use them to make money. That night things came to a head with a movement to destroy the photographs. UG started throwing pictures (he only did that to a few) into the fire. I said I would help him and threw one of them into the fire myself. Everyone was aghast at what I did. Later, on several occasions, I would brag about how I had committed UG's picture to flames.

Early in my visit there was a talk about taking me to a Nadi astrologer somewhere in Salem. Godfried, the elderly German painter, and Bodil, his Swedish wife, had already consulted that Nadi. The Nadi reader had told them about their previous lives, including their past names, and everyone had been impressed. Arrangements were made for us all to go in a hired van. I was mildly interested. On the morning of the reading, I was taking a bath, getting ready to go, and UG shouted from the living room addressing me, "You're not really interested in going, are you?" "No, not really," I said. Then he cancelled the trip, on that pretext! That's UG's style. He can throw surprises at you at any turn!

One cold night, the fireplace was lit. UG's room was right next door. There was a billow of smoke coming out of the fireplace, and quite a bit of it was being drawn through a small window into UG's room. UG, however, continued to sleep in his room with his door closed and did not come out for hours. Later, he bragged about this and would say, "Fresh air is only a psychological necessity!" "Right" I would say to myself sarcastically. In fact, I remember in Palm Springs and in the Crow's Nest in Mill Valley, people practically choking from the heat and rushing out of the room gasping for a breath of fresh air. Suffocation is not a psychological necessity!

It was during that trip that Brahmachari showed a sudden interest in me which he never had before, perhaps because he had read my paper on non-duality ("The Viability Non-Duality") by that time. He started showing some respect for what I had to say.

One afternoon, we two and Chandrasekhar went out for a walk into the village and sat on top of a couple of boulders. The view of the valley from there was magnificent. Brahmachari told me stories from his past about UG and we exchanged notes about our experiences with UG.

One afternoon, Chandrasekhar asked me if I would look into his translation of Mahesh Bhatt's biography of UG into Telugu. I said I would and asked him whose idea it was to ask me, his or UG's. It was UG's, he said. UG remembered that I had some experience in translating when I worked for the Telugu Encyclopedia many years ago, and probably thought that it would do some good to the translation if I looked into it.

There was this lawyer of the Supreme Court of India, Sushil Kumar, visiting from Delhi. He wore a Rajnishi style *sannyasi* ochre robe. Obviously he was a *sannyasin* before. One morning there was a big meeting in the living room with several people around. Sushil Kumar was quite brilliant. A big repartee session went on between him, Brahmachari and UG. Mahesh was also present. I think someone even filmed it. It was simply hilarious. People roared with laughter.

The next day, Sushil Kumar and UG were standing in the porch, involved in some discussion. I was present. At some point UG for some reason turned the discussion over to me. I answered to the best of my ability.

On the New Year's Eve, Dakshinamurti, Chandrasekhar, Suguna and I watched the TV while UG was resting in his room. The celebration was quite interesting. Among other entertainment items, there was a woman from Malaysia singing in Tamil -- she was quite good. It was quite amazing to me how many channels (including Western channels like CNN and BBC) you could get on the TV in India. Of course, you had to have the appropriate cable to receive them.

After the New Year's, it was time for us to leave Yercaud. Brahmachari had left before us. We planned to visit him in Mysore at his ashram (which is really a house where he taught Vedanta or whatnot to a few *brahmacharis* (bachelors). They cooked food and ate there. There were several rooms there; the house was his family house and probably his share of the family property. His brothers, according to UG, were king makers. They were noted for their corruption and graft. Brahmachari had connections with liquor dealers and could get you illicit liquor!

I rewarded the servants well for their work before we left the house in Yercaud for Mysore. The Major drove UG, Nartaki and me. We dropped Nartaki off at the bus stop to take a bus to Tiruvannamalai where she worked in the Ramanashram. It was in the morning around 8 AM. We then drove for quite some time through a National Forest, up in the hills. The forest was like a jungle, but had wide enough dirt roads to go on and lots of trees, but it wasn't a dense forest. We must have driven through the forest for about an hour. We played several tapes of Balamuralikrishna, the famous South Indian classical singer, in the car.

We arrived at Brahmachari's ashram at about lunch time. Brahmachari made me wear a *dhoti*, and we sat on the floor for lunch. The food was cooked by Brahmachari. It was quite tasty. There were cots with mosquito nets in the neighboring rooms. After lunch, an astrologer came by and a hilarious conversation followed. UG and Brahmachari were talking to each other through the astrologer, joking, of course. I interrupted them saying, "Why are you guys talking to each other through him, instead of directly?" That added more spice to the hilarity. We slept there that night and the next morning we left for Bangalore, which was about a six-hour drive. Brahmachari saw us off after blessing me and receiving UG's blessings.

I stayed in Bangalore at Chandrasekhar's place, Purnakutee on 40, K.R.Road. There I saw Gottfried and Bodil again as well as Frank Naronha. That was the first time I met Naronha. He was a high level civil servant in the Central Government and had edited a couple of UG's books, *No Way Out* and *Thought is Your Enemy*. He was trying to touch UG's feet to show respect and UG was preventing him by trying to touch Naronha's feet in turn. So you could see both of them ending up pushing each other's arms away from themselves as though they were wrestling. It was funny. When he was making some appeals to UG (about his job), I said to Naronha: "You don't have to ask him, whatever is good for you, UG will do it." UG looked at me and echoed questioningly, repeating, "Without asking?"

Chandrasekhar brought out his translation of Mahesh's book, and I started making corrections with my limited abilities. UG and I discussed the correct translation for "Calamity" and we finally settled on "*vipattu*". I spent several days making the corrections. In the process, Chandrasekhar also brought out journals he had kept of his encounters with UG. I glanced through them and told him that they deserve to be published in English, as many Westerners wouldn't know about most of the things that had happened around UG in India in the early years after his calamity.

One evening, Brahmachari brought a poem of his (he called it a *dandakam* on UG) which he wrote in Kannada and wanted me to translate it into English. He, Chandrasekhar and I sat together for about two hours and did the translation and got it typed up. It is now in Chandrasekhar's book, *Stopped in Our Tracks, Series I* with the title "Who is this UG?"

My next stop was Hyderabad, where I visited my sister-in-law and other relatives and friends for a week, out of UG's orbit, and then went on to Chennai where UG was waiting in the airport, along with Chandrasekhar and the Major. We again were put up at the Malladi's, where I had a grand time.

Chandrasekhar played a tape of Jnanachakravarti's astrology readings and some music. We were invited the next morning for breakfast at Madurai Mani's place. The *idlis* were great and to top it off Mr. Mani sang. The Manis are a domiciled Telugu family. Obviously, the man is well known. His music was good, except it wasn't my favorite.

After three nights, Chandrasekhar, Suguna, the Major, UG and I went out scouting for a place to spend the next three nights. After looking at a resort place one day and not being satisfied with it, we returned to Chennai. The next day, we decided to go to Pondicherry. We went to the Aurobindo Ashram Hotel there and found that there were no vacancies. So we headed out of Pondicherry. About 15 kilometers away, UG spotted a hotel from a distance and declared that that was "it." We went there, and found it was the Government-run Ashoka hotel. It was pretty clean and was standing on an immaculate beach with a fantastic view from the back where you could sit on chairs and watch the ocean, the beach and the lone boat parked in the sand on the beach. The Major and I occupied one room, Chandrasekhar and Suguna another and UG a third. The food wasn't great, but we tipped well anyway. Once, UG asked how much I tipped and I mentioned that it was 10% of the amount of the bill. He made no comment. Chandrasekhar was going to pay for the hotel, but I insisted on paying for it.

On the second day, I arranged for a ride back to Pondicherry to meet with my French friend, Paul Albert, at the hotel where he was staying. Albert was living in Pondicherry at that time trying to do some field work in linguistics in a local tribe. The Major drove and Chandrasekhar and Suguna went with us. UG opted to stay back at the hotel. I caught Albert in the restaurant at the hotel. Looking at the picture on one of UG books I gave him, Albert remarked that UG looked like a movie star. I introduced Chandrasekhar, Suguna and the Major to him. They were to come back in the late afternoon and pick me up after I had spent the day with Albert. I drank some beer with him and then we went into the local tavern with food stalls lined up alongside, a place where local wine was served. There were hordes of flies on the foodstuff. Paul said that if it weren't for the flies, he would have loved to eat the food. We went up to his room, which was clean. He made a tape copy of a couple of 45 rpm albums of Sita and Anusuya's folk songs and gave it to me as a gift. (Alas, I lost the tape and I don't know how.) Then we went for a short walk along the street.

In the late afternoon, my three friends came to pick me up. Paul said *namaskaram* to Suguna and we all left.

One night while we were there, it was a beautiful full-moon night and all four of us went to the beach. Suguna was complaining about some personal things in her life, particularly about how she didn't want to see or hear about Kaka, Chandrasekhar's former wife, whom he divorced on UG's prompting.

We returned to Chennai. I called Satchidananda Murty, my former philosophy professor at Andhra University, on the phone. I had called him once earlier from Yercaud. He had already met UG before in

3. Notable Travels and Visits

Albuquerque, so when I was on the phone with him in Yercaud, he asked if UG would come to his village and receive his hospitality. UG politely declined. I made an appointment to see Murty in Chennai at the hotel where he was staying. He was there on some official business.

I asked Malladi if he could spare a couple of copies of the organizers he had gotten made for his company, which he graciously gave me. I took one of those and a copy of one of UG's books as gifts to Murty. That morning, UG had his hair cut at the Taj Mahal Hotel. UG, Major, Chandrasekhar, Suguna and I had some coffee there after the haircut and then drove by the hotel where Murty was staying. I was dropped off at the hotel. I asked UG if he wanted to come in to see Murty. UG promptly declined. I went and knocked at Murty's door. He opened it but looked pretty annoyed as I was there a few minutes earlier than the appointed time (I was supposed to see him at 12 noon, and it was about 11:50 AM). He let me in anyway. Others, all professors, also came. I spent the afternoon in their company discussing issues of promoting Indian studies abroad. After lunch and a meeting with the professors in Murty's room, I took an auto rickshaw back to the Malladi's.

At the Malladi's, the food was delicious. UG, the Major and I were all put up in the rooms upstairs. Mahesh was visiting UG at the time. And also a woman from Sri Lanka called Sylvia.

Parvati Kumar, a wealthy retired chartered accountant, once came with his wife and about fifty foreigners. They were on their way to somewhere in the South to visit one of the "Masters'" places. Malladi's house had a collection of the pictures of the Masters. I once heard the whole family chanting in Sanskrit at the shrine downstairs. The sound of chanting sent shivers up my spine. Parvati Kumar prostrated before UG, and, of course, UG, withdrew his feet, saying that they were dirty. Kumar is into occult Vedic thinking and has published in poor English plenty of literature concerning it. UG is considered a Master in the lineage of Masters by Kumar's group to which the Malladi's also belonged.

That night, the whole group Kumar had brought was asked for dinner. UG and the rest of us were invited too. UG was made to sit on an elevated seat. He introduced Mahesh Bhatt as "Public Enemy No. 1," and Chandrasekhar as "Public Enemy number 2," and I added that I was the Public Enemy Number 3. Anyway, we ate dinner. UG gave a small speech, and not saying very much, got up and mingled nicely with the people around. Soon after, we all left to go upstairs, leaving the group to their own devices.

The last night I was there, I was leaving in the middle of the night to fly back to the U.S. from Chennai. UG was supposed to leave the next night. I asked him where he was going. He said he had four plane tickets in his pocket -- one to go to Australia, a second to the U.S., a third to

China and Japan and the last one to Europe. He said he would first go to Singapore and then decide in which direction he would go from there. I am sure he made his decision by tossing a coin. That's some traveler!

UG was debating whether he should go with me to the airport to see me off. I discouraged him saying why should he trouble himself driving in the car at such a late hour in the night. Notwithstanding, around 10 PM, he decided to go. At the airport I got everything taken care of and was about to go in the gate and board the plane. As usual, I shook UG's hand and saluted him. He tapped me on my shoulder and made some kind of a blessing gesture with his arm as he was leaving. It had to be a blessing!

That was the end of my trip to India in 1994.

Hemet, California, and Gstaad Switzerland -- 1995

At the end of 1994, UG and gang visited us in Seaside for a couple of days, staying through the New Year's day. As usual, he stayed in the modest Magic Carpet Lodge (a Best Western motel) down the street where I live. During that time, UG insisted that I go travel with them in Southern California right after the New Year's day. There was no specific destination. Rather, he wanted to make good of his threats to find a new "base" in California: he said he was "finished" with the Bay area.

I had to stay home for a few days to take care of Kiran's injured leg; but soon after the New Year's day, I flew to LA and was received by UG at the airport. My daughter Shyamala was also there to meet me at the airport and spend a little time with me. We all got into a van driven by Julie. While Julie was driving out of the parking lot she ran into competition with another woman for space on the driveway and neither of them would budge. UG kept yelling at Julie, "Don't let that bitch in!" egging her on. Finally, after both women took considerable risks, Julie prevailed. This scene certainly freaked Shyamala out.

We drove to a nearby hotel where the Malladi's were waiting for us with *idlis* and other goodies. We had our lunch with them. Shyamala was introduced to Malladi Krishnamurti and his wife Prasanna. Larry was with us on the trip too. Shyamala left us to return home.

We spent the night in a hotel, UG, Larry and I, occupying the same suite. In the morning, we all set out on our trip with nothing but a cup of coffee or tea and some peanuts from the plane. And, looking for places to stay, we drove toward San Diego, via a valley where we didn't find anything suitable. We had lunch in an Indian restaurant in San Diego. Then we were driving again when UG asked us to stop and picked up one of those papers where hotels, apartments and other accommodations

3. Notable Travels and Visits

were listed. He found a Best Western motel for a price of $19 a night in a place called Hemet. He couldn't have been happier!

We immediately drove and found ourselves in a small non-descript town some distance southeast of Los Angeles. The rent at the motel was actually somewhat higher, probably around $29 and the apartment suites were even higher. Julie rented an apartment, Mario and Lisa one and the Guhas another. (Some of these must have travelled with us and others come in later.) Larry rented one for himself. I was to crash in UG's suite, sleeping on the living room sofa-bed which could be folded back into a sofa in the daytime for people to sit on. The arrangement was that I would pay rent for the suite for one month (that was the scheduled duration of our stay) and in his turn UG would feed me.

Sometime during our stay, I coined a nickname for Hemet: "Hemet, damn it!" UG liked it.

In India, Mahesh was going to write a press release on pornography and government censorship and he sought UG's help on the phone. To help with the matter, UG dictated his pronouncement on the subject to me. I didn't have a computer with me, so I wrote it down by hand. It was entitled, "The Role of Godmen in the Next Millennium." I edited it and then fair-copied it in all capitals, and Julie faxed it to Mahesh in Bombay. It was an indictment of censorship, showing how it never works. A key sentence in the piece reads:

> If we admit that our interest in spirituality is not essentially different from our interest in varieties of food, varieties of girls, and every other form of pleasure, then everything falls into its natural rhythm of life.

While we were in Hemet we made several trips to various places. One time we went to a billionaire's place (I can't recall his name.) The man had once been a professor of mathematics or economics at the University of Chicago. Once, Julie had taken UG to visit him in Chicago. He had quit his job there, saying that the income provided by his job kept him poor. Instead he became a high-level investment broker and made four billions and was on his way to making the fifth. His place in one of the valleys in the Los Angeles area was hidden away. We had to drive down a long driveway which had several signs warning, "Armed Response!" He had two ferocious dogs and lived alone with a whole lot of booze and vitamins and a huge TV screen with almost a thousand channels. He looked like a lonely man.

We later went to another place of his where he was having a huge house built with big lawns and bronze sculptures on the lawns worth hundreds of thousands of dollars. There was a separate annex being built which he was offering to UG to live in. But UG wasn't too enthusiastic about it as the place was located in a remote area not easily accessible for people who might want to visit him.

While I was in Hemet, Wendy mailed a copy of the book of Vemana's verses (*Selected Verses of Vemana*) translated by me into English which had just been published in India. UG immediately got hold of it in the car and started reading from it as we set out to go on one of our "malling" trips.

At one point, UG was making arrangements to go with Mario to the airport in Los Angeles from where Mario was leaving for Europe. Mario was to drive there, I was to go with them and then drive UG back to Hemet. UG suggested that we visit my daughter Shyamala after dropping off Mario, as she lived nearby in Santa Monica. We called her, offering to take her out to lunch. She asked if she could invite a few of her friends to meet UG. That was fine with UG, so it was arranged.

When we arrived the next morning at the airport, I had to get help from Mario even to start the car – needless to say, I was nervous to drive in the busy city. But I did anyway, and drove UG and myself carefully to Shyamala's apartment. Kash, her boyfriend (now her husband), was there. Shyamala didn't have any coffee or cream in her kitchen; so she had to send Kash out to get some, and then we had some coffee. Meanwhile, about ten to fifteen of their friends, mostly interns and residents from various medical specialties, including ophthalmology and psychiatry, gathered there (Kash was in medical school at the time). One of them offered to go to a nearby South Indian restaurant and bring us all some lunch. By about noon, the coffee table in the apartment was filled with a feast with all kinds of goodies, and we had a great communal lunch, instead of just taking Shyamala out! And UG, in his usual fashion, charmed all of them with his answers to their questions and with his one-liners, anecdotes and jokes. UG's magic at work again! After a couple of hours, UG and I drove back to Hemet.

On his next visit to the US, UG did change his base to Palm Springs.

In 1995, I and my family all visited UG in Gstaad. On this trip, our family also went to Heidelberg, on our friend Rima Holland's invitation, to spend a few days there. One event I remember particularly is the following:

UG asked Julie and Mario to take our whole family on a trip to Italy. They did. We stopped in a border village after passing through the big tunnel going to Italy and had a six-course elaborate lunch, (and we weren't allowed to pay – Julie paid for everything) including aperitifs, digestives, wine, portabella mushrooms and what not. It was so fancy. I realized that the Italians (exemplified by Mario) were just as picky as the French (and the Brahmins) about eating.

We took the freeways (which are toll ways in Italy) and went to Milan. We went into some stores and shops, had coffee in a shop that also sold ice cream, and went into a big cathedral where there was a dress code (you had to wear shoes and a shirt). There was a big water fountain in the huge plaza in front with lots of pigeons and people. We took some pictures there and headed back to Switzerland.

On the way we stopped by in Stresa, a resort town on the Italian-Swiss border, where UG had spent a couple of months with Valentine many years ago. Obviously, UG must have asked Julie and Mario to show us that place. It was on the Lago Majore, a big and beautiful lake. The place was very touristy. We walked around on the cobbled lanes and went into shops, stopped in a restaurant for a delicious pizza and in an ice cream place across the street for a fancy ice cream.

It was after dark when we left to head back to Gstaad. We drove through another long tunnel. After the tunnel, we stopped to pee under a magnificent full moon. And it was just beautiful. It was so fantastic driving through the magnificent high mountains on a moonlit night with Mario driving effortlessly and perfectly all the way. It was around 2 AM when we got home.

Palm Springs: December 1998 -- January 1999

The final event I would like to write about here is my ill-fated visit to see UG in Palm Springs at the end of 1998 and beginning of 1999. That December-January, I had a falling out with UG in Palm Springs. That was the same winter when he gave $10,050 to Kiran for both his grand piano and drum set.

I traveled to Palm Springs first and then about a couple of weeks later Wendy and Kiran joined me.

At first, UG fixed a place for me in a condominium (in a fancy gated compound called Whitewater) to share with Mahesh. I was doing the cooking there for Mahesh and myself. Once UG asked me to feed Bob and Paul as well, and then when they came along with him into the condo, UG started his talk about how he didn't like the stink and stench of an ashram. I was just about ready to punch him for his contradictory messages.

A week or so later, after we were moved to another apartment, UG asked me if I could feed Mahesh for the next ten days. I said fine. But I wasn't cooking just for him; occasionally the whole gang would come in for lunch. And I had to make something special for UG. I was making mashed canned garbanzo beans or something for him. I would take about an hour or so to prepare the whole lunch. UG was watching over all this. He didn't like my getting so involved with cooking. I should have seen it coming.

Ten days later, Mahesh left, and Wendy and Kiran came. We were all put up in one room in the main house next to the cottage where UG lived. Chandrasekhar and his wife Suguna were also there, as were Lisa, who lived there, the Guhas, who were eating there but staying elsewhere, and Julie.

I was supposedly to share the kitchen with Chandrasekhar and Suguna. I quickly made some garbanzo beans with a few spices and lemon for Kiran. I didn't take more than about 10 minutes. Meanwhile, UG was sitting there outside the kitchen watching and at one point he said, "Get out of there, they have to do their own cooking." By that time I had finished and told him that I was just getting out. Then a minute or so later, he said again to get out of there. I got furious. I was already out of the kitchen. I said, "UG, I am out of there! I'm done." He realized that I was really done and he couldn't say anything further.

After a while, I continued on, "I won't get into the kitchen! The three of us will eat outside from now on." UG replied, "You're guests here. I don't like your eating outside." I said, "Why are you sentimental about it? This is a decision I came to after thinking about the practicalities. After all, I am earning my own living. It's not a problem for me." His speech faltered and became weak. It was clear that he was disturbed.

Here is a quote from Chandrasekhar's notebooks (*Stopped in Our Tracks* – Series III, published on UG's website) about UG's reaction:

> UG faltered in his speech and his voice was weakened, reflecting the disturbance in him. "You haven't eaten anything? Why is your voice like that?" asked Moorty. UG had already cooked his oats and eaten them.
>
> I then went to UG's room. "Why should Guha and their family eat here? Why should Julie eat here?" he said. But it was he who wanted them to stay.
>
> I can't wait to see how far this saga of eating will go on today. "I am not going to have any more meetings or talks from now on. I never invited the Germans. They can do what they please," UG said. He turned to Larry and said, "America is finished. This is also the end of the Palm Springs chapter. I am not even going to India." Then he turned to Lisa and said, "Why do we have this big chair here? It's a waste. Return it to the owner. I must vacate this place by the end of January. I'll tell Lynn. There won't be any more meetings. There won't be any talking."
>
> He talked like that, rather incoherently, for a while. This incident is proof that he too reacts to situations by being sorry for what happened and being hurt. Although he says "I never question my actions," it's clear that he is affected by what happens in such contexts. The principal actor of the

drama, Moorty, however, sat quietly like a cool cucumber. The three of them ate after we finished.

Then I stopped using the kitchen. I told Wendy to take care of the cooking. I got my food and ate in the living room for a couple of times, and then I figured it would be better if I ate in the Lucky supermarket at the end of the street. This went on for about three days (just before New Year's Eve. On New Year's Eve, Dr. Lynn, Lisa, Wendy and I had a celebration with expensive champagne).

In one of the gatherings in the house, I said to UG, "I know when I am not wanted." He answered, rather disturbed, "You are very much wanted. If it comes to that, all these people, Chandrasekhar and all, can go." Although surprised by the reply, I wasn't too convinced by it. The fourth morning, I was telling myself in the bed that I had to leave the place. I was finishing up putting Chandrasekhar's *Stopped in Our Tracks* in a book form in Word Perfect. I was still struggling with the headers and footers. As UG entered the main house, I announced to him that I was leaving that afternoon (Wendy and Kiran were leaving that day to go to San Diego). UG looked very nonplussed, turned to me and said, "Why?" I said, "I don't feel very happy here." And that was it; there was no further conversation.

I went to his cottage to wind up the computer business and put all the files Chandrasekhar needed on a floppy disk to give to him. Meanwhile, UG walked in, and I said that he didn't owe me anything for whatever I did for him, that I did all the web business because I didn't make any distinction between his work and mine, and that I would look after his web page until he found someone else. UG replied that he wasn't concerned about that.

I told Wendy I would get a ride with her to the bus station that afternoon; she could drop me off there and move on to San Diego with Kiran. I would take a bus to Los Angeles, then to Salinas and Monterey. I said at the bus station to Wendy, "It's my life. You have to let me do it this way." The operator didn't have change for a hundred dollars. But he let me in and I bought the ticket at the next stop. I paid $70 not knowing that there was a cheaper fare; the sales clerk didn't tell me about it. In the L.A. bus station, I had a sandwich for dinner and sat there watching people while I waited for the bus. I was quite impressed by how a black woman treated another homeless person. That was quite moving. She was so compassionate. There were two buses; I took one of them knowing full well that it would arrive in Salinas around four in the morning.

When I got off the bus in the Salinas bus station, there was no immediate connecting bus to go to Monterey. I walked with my bag (and pillow) on the streets for at least a mile in that cold weather (it was 30 or

40 degrees) until I found a breakfast place. I ordered some cereal with milk and went and washed in the bathroom. I asked the waitress for directions to catch a bus to go to Monterey. One of the fellows there told me where the bus stop was, but advised that I should go back to the Greyhound station instead of to the bus stop nearby, as it was dark and not safe to wait there. I walked back to the bus station and waited for another hour or so. Then I took the bus to Monterey; I was dropped off in Seaside at Fremont and Ord Grove streets.

After eight days of internal turmoil, I did finally break down and call UG in Palm Springs and apologized, saying, "I'm so sorry, I made such a mess of things." UG said, "No need to apologize," and quickly started making arrangements for Chandrasekhar and Suguna to spend a couple days in Seaside.

Later, UG and I met many times, but the air between us was never very clear again. I did visit UG again in Gstaad in the summer of 2000. (That's when I edited Bob Carr's autobiography). The question came up in my mind, more than once, what in the world was I doing sitting there, day in and day out.

The next summer (2001), UG extended the same invitation, even offering to send me a ticket for my travel, saying that I didn't have to spend a penny. But I turned down the invitation. He said that it was terribly disappointing. I said, "For a long time I thought that no one understood me better than you." He enthusiastically replied, "Yes, that's true." I continued, "But I don't feel that way anymore." He then said, "Come over here, we will thrash things out." When I declined, he said, "Give it some deep, serious thought." He called me twice in this context.

I didn't go to Gstaad again until the summer of 2004, although I had been seeing him off and on in the US in various places, including my own. In 2004, I heard that he fell in the bathroom and was hurt. Being concerned, I called him a couple of times. I told him I planned to go to India for one last time to say goodbye to everyone. UG said that if I was going, he will be there too. The second time I called him in Gstaad, he said, "Why don't you come and spend some time here." I accepted the invitation and went to Gstaad to spend six weeks with him. That was when I also made arrangements to spend four weeks with him in Bangalore along with Wendy and Kiran at the end of the same year.

He did come to see us in Seaside in the beginning of 2006. But after that, he never visited the US again. My last visit to see him was before his death. The story of that visit of mine is recounted in the following chapter. You will notice that in spite of the air between us not being cleared, there was still that same friendship, affection and mutual respect between us as there had always been.

A Few Other Travel Memories

Sleeping Arrangements

On one of the trips to Gstaad, in the big room upstairs we were given to stay, I needed a separate mattress as Wendy and my little boy Kiran were occupying the big bed. UG was told by the landlord that there was an extra mattress in the storeroom. Before I knew it, I noticed UG climbing up the stairs carrying the mattress singlehandedly! I couldn't bear watching a 75 year-old man carrying a heavy mattress. I was so sorry I asked him. But it was too late. That's UG. When the occasion demanded it, he would throw his whole weight into the situation.

It was probably on my first visit to UG in Palm Springs, as usual, I was asked to sleep in UG's living room. There was a couch on which I was supposed to sleep. I told UG I had trouble sleeping on the couch as it was too uneven and soft, and that I would rather arrange the pillows on the floor and sleep there. He said he would rather that I slept in his bed and he would sleep on the sofa. I said, "No such thing." He then brought sheets and pillows from his bedroom and arranged the bed on the floor himself. I remarked to him smiling, "UG, you are doing everything short of taking me to bed and singing lullabies!"

Once Guha told me that UG said to him that only two people could sleep on the couch in his living room (referring to Chalet Sunbeam in Gstaad), that is Mahesh Bhatt and Narayana Moorty.

One night in Palm Springs, UG was sleeping in his room with his door locked and the heater turned way high (probably around 95 degrees). I in the living couldn't fall sleep -- it was so hot, plus I had to pee. But I couldn't get into the bathroom as you had to go through UG's bedroom to get to it. So, I went outside and peed in the plants. The next morning I told UG about it, and he said that he hardly ever slept at night and that I could easily have gotten him up.

Later, I started getting picky about where I slept.

On a visit to Lake Havasu, I was to stay in UG's hotel suite and sleep in the living room on the couch. There was so much party noise from downstairs that I suggested to UG that maybe we should look for another room for me. And with Larry's help we went around looking, but didn't find anything satisfactory. So I ended up in UG's living room again, with ear plugs this time, loaned by Larry.

I think from then on UG changed his policy. On my further visits to Palm Springs he never asked me to sleep in his studio apartment. He arranged for my sleep in others' places like those of David and Maria, and Lisa and Gary.

Children, Movies, and Censorship

It was in Chalet Sunbeam in Gstaad, I believe. We were watching a movie every night to pass time. The movies were either brought in by Julie from the US or rented locally by her. Sometimes the movies had much foul language (the four-letter word used hundreds of times), violence and explicit sex. But UG never disallowed children to watch the movies (the children present at this time were Shilpa and Sumedha, Guha's daughters, and Claire, Susan's daughter). "They will be exposed to them later in their lives anyway," was his justification.

A most touching time was when we were watching a movie on Larry Flynt, the "Hustler." The movie was quite painful to watch at moments, as Flynt's girlfriend was suffering from drug addiction. It was dark in the room, except for the light from the movie. Everyone was absorbed in watching the movie. But I looked at UG's face, and I could see distinctly tears rolling down his cheeks. Who could say that UG never cried?

Memorable Car Rides

I had the most memorable car rides while I was visiting UG. UG always made sure that I sat in the back of the car he was in (he always occupied the front seat by the side of the driver, and there were usually multiple cars following behind).

In California, the ride to Idyll Wilde was very interesting: The road up the hill was windy and the climb steep. Larry, Susan, Mario, UG and I and some others all went there looking for a house to stay while we were still in Hemet and UG was looking for a "base." It had snowed there earlier and was rather cold. We parked the car at the main intersection of the town and got out. Everyone else was shivering, but UG got out with not even his hands in the pockets of his thin jacket. There was sludge on one of the streets. UG was more sure-footed than I was, so he gave me a hand when I stumbled crossing the street. When they looked at a house on another street, I went with them inside and remarked while UG was toying with the idea of renting it, that he and others could stay there, but I would stay outside under the tree, and if I died in the cold, they could drag me out and throw me away! That probably poured cold water on any enthusiasm he might have had.

While in Switzerland, I remember going on such fantastic trips with UG and others that I doubt if I will ever have such experiences again. One was driving through Villars, the place where J. Krishnamurti had lived a long time ago with his brother. I remember stopping there and having coffee with Larry and Susan and whoever else.

3. Notable Travels and Visits

A second trip was to Lugano and the Italian borders where we saw Lago Majore. The views were phenomenal.

A third trip was when we all went to the Lichtenstein Principality. The small town was bordering on three countries, Austria, Germany and Switzerland. We stopped to have lunch in the local MacDonald's. I treated everyone to veggie burgers. We circled around the palace where the ruler lived. On our return trip, I was with UG in a car driven by Vibodha. We drove back on the Upper Alps and the views of the mountains and valleys were so breathtaking that I will never forget them. Vibodha was such a perfect driver. Mario, I think, was driving the other car. He too was a great driver, and also (contrary to UG's denunciations) a great cook.

Finally, even as recently as August 2004, we went in a two-car caravan to Chamonix, France, to see the glacier coming down Mont Blanc. The river from the glacier waters flowed through the town. Not only were the views there phenomenal, but I never saw water flowing so fast in a river.

4. My Last Visit with UG

In the beginning of February, 2007, when I heard (from Julie Thayer and Paul Arms) that UG had fallen again in the bathroom in his apartment in Italy, I was concerned about his well-being. I was told that this time he had been badly hurt. (He was hurt once before in 2004, falling in the bathroom.) I called him. UG told me he was doing OK and expressed his wish to see me. I called again a week later. Larry answered the phone this time and said that I should come and see UG. I told Larry that I would try to come in the summer. He said, "No, no, you don't understand. It's rather urgent; you should come now." UG picked up the phone and said, "I have to see you before I die. If I don't see you, I'll have to die in great pain!" I replied, "I will come soon. Let me look online and find a flight. Then I'll let you know." The phone went back and forth between UG and Larry, and I could hear UG saying in the background, "Why should he pay? I will pay for his trip." Larry repeated that to me. Later UG asked Sarito and Mario to arrange for my travel as well as for an apartment to stay while I visited UG in Vallecrosia, Italy.

I left Monterey, California, on the morning of February 14 and arrived late night of February 15, in Nice, France, to be picked up by Mitra, a friend of UG, and driven to Vallecrosia. Because of my missing an earlier connecting flight and some time-zone confusion Mitra had to wait for a couple of hours at the airport. He was so helpful in transporting my suitcase whose handle was broken en route.

The first morning after I arrived, Larry came to pick me up at the hotel where I was staying, after I had called UG's place using Mitra's cell phone.

When I entered UG's "cove" with Larry, UG was lying on the couch and sat up to greet me. He looked frailer than even the last time I had seen him at my home in California in January 2006. As I approached him to shake his hands after saluting him in the Indian fashion, I felt I was entering into a vast field of energy enveloping me. I sat down next to him, holding his hand. Then came that strange feeling I had had a few times before – I could feel no separation between him and me. It was the same energy in both of us. It was the same field in which everyone was engulfed. No wonder UG could bind so many people to him.

Just as I expected, the room was filled with people. There was a constant influx of visitors, some of whom would leave after staying a while. The apartment was heated beyond normal levels – we all knew that UG liked to keep his surroundings quite warm, almost hot. The heat had

4. My Last Visit with UG

the added effect of people not wanting to stay in the room too long. When UG had to answer a nature call, Louis would politely clear the room so he could assist UG.

UG expressed his appreciation of me: "You made me what I am today!" I replied, "Nonsense, UG, if anything, it's the other way round," knowing full well that he was exaggerating in his usual fashion.

Later, Guha told me that after I left the room UG had remarked, "Moorty played a major role in my life."

[On another occasion, while I was still in Vallecrosia, I was expressing my appreciation to UG and said that I was glad to have met him and spent almost a third of my life with him. I also said that he played a major role in my life. Then I started bragging about myself: I said that I had integrated death into my life and it didn't matter to me if I died the next day. He said that he was ready to die right then and there. I said, "Me too." And then I started bragging again about my integrating death into my life. UG sarcastically replied, "Sounds profound!" Served me right!]

* * *

Vallecrosia is on the Italian Riviera between the towns of Ventimiglia and Bordighera and is about an hour's drive from Nice, across the French border.

UG's apartment was built for him by his friends Lucia, Anita and Giovanni within their villa compound in Vallecrosia. It was right behind one of the main streets of the town and was an annex to the two-story main building. Sandwiched between these two were the kitchen with a dining ante-room with steps leading upstairs and a door which led to the back street. The villa had spacious gardens with a few lemon and orange trees and a grass lawn. There were reclining lawn chairs as well other chairs and a couple of tables. The grounds were periodically kept clean by the hard-working Lucia, the landlady. As you entered through the main gate, you went on a paved path through an arch to reach UG's apartment. Outside the apartment, you could see dozens of shoes on the stone floor. At times, there was also a black cat hanging around.

In the ante-room there was a window overlooking the grove, a table and several chairs, and places along the walls for people to leave their belongings. Even here people always left their shoes outside. They put their computers and other paraphernalia on the table. For the computers, there was a slow and temperamental broadband connection which could only handle a couple of laptops at a time. People sometimes had trouble getting on the Internet, but with Mitra's and others' help they sometimes had better luck.

A glass door let you into UG's apartment. The red curtains to the wide glass windows on the walls were almost always closed to prevent the intense daylight from bothering the resting UG. On the right of the entrance was UG's bedroom, with his bed and his few belongings such as clothes, "archives" and other papers.

The living room was rather small: it had a fireplace and good light fixtures which shed plenty of light when needed.

On the left was the entrance into the small bathroom and a cooking place with a microwave, a stove and a refrigerator.

* * *

My hotel apartment was on the sixth floor in an apartment building with a pizza restaurant and shops on the first floor. It had a grand view of the Mediterranean from my bedroom and another spectacular view of the Mediterranean as well as of the beach road with tall buildings on one side and tall lampposts with double-hanging-lights, on the other.

* * *

After I arrived, I learned the details of UG's fall in the bathroom which had happened about five or six weeks earlier. According to his own account, as UG fell in the bathroom, his head hit the sink and began to bleed, and he fainted. He had also injured his leg, When he regained consciousness, he heard knocking at the door in the living room. It was around 5 in the morning. He slowly crawled on the floor to the door and was somehow able to open the door. It was Avner making his early morning call. He saw UG's condition and helped him to the couch.

Since then UG had round-the-clock caretakers, the most constant of whom were Louis and Melissa[12]. But many others were at his beck and call, performing sundry chores: minding the fireplace (Avner from Israel), taking care of accounts (Sarito from Germany), cooking and feeding (Melissa, Trisha, Larry and Susan, Anandi, Lakshmi, Kathy from Hungary, Lucia, Golda from Australia, Paul Arms and Viresha, and so on), outdoor chores such as transportation, airline bookings, finding places to stay for people who visited (Sarito, Mitra and Mario), and last but not the least, photo and video shooting (Lisa, Avner and others). People took turns to cook. There were some phenomenal gourmet meals, all of them vegetarian, especially from Melissa (her great soup!) and our hostess, Lucia. Golda made her famous *chai*. It is thanks to Lisa and Avner that we have a record of many of the happenings around UG in his last days. The recording abruptly stopped because, for one thing, Lisa had to leave with me on March 9, and for another, about ten days before he breathed his last, UG asked Mahesh to go out of the room and announce to everyone to "go back to where you all came from, and not sneak around in corners trying to see me."

In spite of the looming tragedy, there was a sort of festive atmosphere in the air. (It must, however, be mentioned that at the times when UG was resting, you could notice that people sitting around him looked quite solemn and somber.) People were joking around UG and

4. My Last Visit with UG

UG never quit his ranting and raving, teasing and scolding people. His hyperboles, particularly about himself, knew no bounds. In the anteroom next to the kitchen, in the kitchen and outside on the patio, people were chatting away, e-mailing, chatting on the Skype, transferring videos, and photos they had taken on to their computers, and so on and so forth. The place was abuzz from morning six till evening about 8 PM.

When Louis was drawn into the scene to be asked to read something or do some other chore, he would always add his irreverent humor to whatever he did or said: he would even rock UG in the couch by holding one end of the couch up. He would do his improvisations or mimic Larry lying with outstretched legs on the sofa, shaking his legs, and such. He would sing the songs he had composed about UG, mostly poking fun at him, or he would show his drawings or read from the book he was currently writing on UG. Whatever he did, he would sprinkle it with his creative humor.

Sometimes, Larry would be asked to do his standup comedy or read from Chandrasekhar's book or something someone else had written. Or UG himself would read either from the "archives" or from the Internet clippings collected by Lisa. Or, there would be an astrological reading by Nataraj. The cell phones would constantly ring with callers asking to speak to UG. And there were daily sessions of UG's pulse reading by "the doctors": Dr. Paul Lynn, Dr. Susan Nettleton (now Morris), Ramateertha, Doris and Vibodha. There would be periodic medical consultations about UG's condition, which were more in the spirit of entertainment than serious consultations, because UG never really consulted doctors in his later life.

One of the pieces of entertainment (there were many) was performed by Chin Meyer, a German standup comedian from Berlin. I saw several acts of his, of course done at UG's behest, all of them centering around UG's "Money Maxims" which Chin had translated into German. He would read the English version and sing his German translations. The Germans that had gathered there, particularly Nataraj, appreciated the translations very much. As I don't know German I couldn't appreciate them. Later, Chin showed me a video of his performance on the Internet and gave me one of his picture postcards. Apparently, he is well known in Berlin.

To add spice to the scene, occasionally Leonidas chocolates, specially brought by friends from Germany, or some other goodies would be passed around.

There were occasions when UG would ask that all his papers to be brought to him, and he would read from them, or ask Larry or someone else to read from them. Or, Vibodha would be asked to read a piece from the UG "archives" on the computer, UG constantly chiding him for not finding a piece quickly enough. Sometimes, a letter or two written to UG, would be read. Once Sarito was reading a letter from someone who mentioned how UG "touched me where no one else has touched before," and she broke down crying. Someone else had to finish the reading for her. She was actually crying for everyone there, for each and every one of us was touched in a similar fashion. UG had a special, albeit different, relationship with each one of us.

And in one of those sessions, UG started tearing up many of those papers and asked people to throw them into the fire in the fireplace. Included in those were Yashoda's funny "letters" from the Dalai Lama, Ramana Maharshi and other celebrities and Robert's UG-into-Marilyn-Monroe morphing photos.

*　*　*

No one could have served UG with so much devotion as Louis. It's not that others wouldn't have served him well. But he did it all willingly, with gusto and a great sense of humor. UG was always grateful to him for his service; he even bought him an Apple laptop with a printer at considerable expense and had them delivered there in Italy. UG would even say that he would give Louis the remaining three hundred thousand dollars of his money, if he would only "pack him off." But neither Louis nor anyone else would do any such thing!

You could sense that UG was experiencing pain, although he would not express it except in rare moments. His cardio-spasm was acting up too, as a result of which he was eating even less than normal, which was miniscule to begin with. A small amount of rice sticks, *idli* or *upma* or a few sips of orange juice or scalding hot water were all he was taking in. He would frequently throw up, mostly liquids. Paper or plastic cups and paper towels or napkins were always on hand to help catch the vomit and clean up. It was obvious he was losing body fluids. His energy levels were diminishing. At times, he would just lie down with his head on the arm of the couch, supported by a pillow and his arms thrown back, and practically gasp for breath. Sometimes, he would just doze off.

A couple of nights I thought his life energies were leaving him. Those two nights, I didn't see how he could make it through the night. But to my utter amazement he would pull through by the next morning.

I was encouraging him to get up and take a few steps, with support, of course. He tried to do that and was even able to walk a few steps across the room holding Louis's hands. He even pretended to make a few dancing steps, to everyone's delight. All that seemed fine until one morning there was a major setback: apparently, around 4 AM he was taken to the bathroom (he was normally transported to the bathroom by being placed in a chair and moved); he stood up and, according to Louis, Louis's attention was distracted momentarily when he looked at Melissa

4. My Last Visit with UG

trying to say something to her, and when he turned back to UG, he noticed that UG's eyes were rolling in their sockets, and UG fainted and collapsed on the toilet seat. Louis had to carry him back to the couch in his arms. As far as I know, UG never took another step after that.

* * *

On the second morning of my stay, just as I entered his room, UG put me to work in his usual fashion: "Why don't you make some *upma* for everyone today?" I agreed and immediately recruited Larry's and Susan's help. UG in his teasing fashion forbade Larry to cook. But Larry and Susan did go out to get the necessary groceries for the *upma*. Susan helped me with the cooking. I made a little *upma* specially for UG, as he doesn't eat food with many spices, particularly ginger, with a little extra salt, to suit his taste, and sent it to him with someone (I think it was Mario). Mario came back with UG's comment on the *upma*: "Why did Moorty put so much salt in it?" I sent Mario back with my reply, a counter-question: "Since when UG has started complaining about excess salt?" Apparently, when Mario relayed my reply, UG smiled.

* * *

Just to stay away from the heat in the apartment, as well as not to crowd UG too much, I would sometimes get out of there and sit in the anteroom next to the kitchen, doing this and that. I helped clean up Lisa's laptop since she was complaining about how slow it was. Soon, thanks to her word-of-mouth, I ended up doing the same for Avner's and Paul Lynn's laptops. I also made CDs on request, copying some of the Indian music I had played earlier to everyone in UG's room.

* * *

One morning, there was a talk of the "Swan Song" that UG had earlier dictated to Louis which was now only on Louis's computer. UG wanted me to edit it (one of his "chores" for me). It took me an hour or so to edit it. The English needed work and the piece wasn't all that coherent. I tried to make it a little better. I transmitted it by e-mail to Louis who printed it out on Sarito's printer. I think it was read to UG and the rest of the audience. The piece is now posted on UG's website as it is in several other places.

* * *

Another morning, UG was talking away and was trying rather unsuccessfully to remember a Sanskrit verse about Vedantins, Naiyayikas, Bauddhas and other philosophers. I told UG that it was possible to get the exact text of the verse from the Internet. He said "Do it!" I went into the anteroom and fished for the verse on the Internet. It didn't take long. I copied it in the Devanagari script and showed it to him. He said he would be more comfortable reading it in the Telugu script. So I wrote it in the Telugu script on another sheet of paper and he was able to read it with ease. I told him that the verse was written by Sri Krishna Chaitanya, the founder of the Chaitnaya movement; and I related the legend of the conversation between him and Raghunatha, the Navya-Nyaya philosopher who was his fellow student. Chaitanya apparently was also a good scholar in Nyaya except that he didn't believe that logic would help one to attain liberation. So while saying this, as they were crossing the river on a boat, Chaitanya threw the logic palm leaf manuscript he was holding in his hand into the river.

* * *

Mahesh Bhatt arrived about a week or so after I did. When UG was asking Mario to look for a place for him, I told UG that I had a room vacant in my apartment which no one was using, so why not he stay there. UG agreed and put him up there. The night Mahesh arrived, he kissed me on the forehead and thanked me for the fast editing job I had done for him recently (on his journal concerning UG). There was not much conversation between us. For the week or two he was there, (I would say about 10 days), I would make coffee for him in the mornings and offer him some cashew nuts or a little piece of bread. He would leave early in the morning to see UG and spend the rest of the day in the villa.

Mahesh had a central role to play around UG. He had a special relationship with UG. UG would let Mahesh touch his feet with his head, (or UG would rub Mahesh's head with his foot), kiss him on the forehead, make violent gestures (in jest) or crack crude jokes at him. He would chide UG saying, "You say you are dying, UG, but you are not going to die!" I too thought this was the time to put aside all my background and pride and prostate once and for all in front of the energy called UG. First, he tried to prevent me. But I protested saying, "You would let Mahesh do all that, why not me?" and forced myself on him. After he left once, Mahesh returned again later, at UG's behest, after I left Vallecrosia.

* * *

Usha, UG's daughter, arrived in the latter half of my stay, after being stalled in Bombay when her Italian and Swiss visas were delayed. Apparently, there was a screw-up in the bureaucratic process, thanks to the ineptitude of Mahesh Bhatt's travel agent.[13] Chandrasekhar and Suguna, who were supposed to arrive with her, met with a worse fate. Their Italian visa was not only delayed, but Chandrasekhar had to go through an interview at the Italian Consulate.

Usha's arrival was a major event. Everyone was, of course, glad to see her. (In her childhood she was UG's "darling daughter.") As soon as she came in, she sat next to him and started nursing him -- massaging his legs and feet with oil -- as a daughter would minister to her father's needs. She made some *upma* or *idli* for him. She wanted to give him a bath on a

4. My Last Visit with UG

stool (she was going to get the stuff ready for it), but UG would have none of that. (UG had not had a bath in a month or so. Yet, there was not the slightest smell on him! He looked clean as a whistle!).

I renewed my acquaintance with Usha. (I had met her before both in India and in the US.) She wanted lessons in computing. I gave her a couple, teaching her the basics of blind-touch typing on the keyboard, setting up and accessing e-mail, writing replies to e-mails, and such. Having been a teacher herself, she was a fast learner. When I left, I said she should continue her learning with the help of Chandrasekhar or someone else. I don't know if she ever did, because later, when I wrote her an e-mail, I got no reply.

* * *

As I said before, Chandrasekhar and Suguna weren't able to come with Usha. Mario and others were pressing me to stay on. I too was telling people how sorry I was that I wouldn't be able to see Chandrasekhar, having come that far. I had another reason to see Chandrasekhar: I had just finished translating the Third Series of his book *Stopped in Our Tracks* and wanted to give him a CD of the book personally and talk to him about both that and his Second Series. I had also finished translating the Second Series recently and brought a hard copy of it to present to UG.

People had already been reading passages from the Second Series to the crowd that gathered around. Guha apparently had read out the chapter on the Upanishads in that book. UG expressed his appreciation of the chapter and admired Chandrasekhar's scholarship. (I conveyed that compliment to Chandrasekhar later.) I mentioned to UG that the chapter following it, "The Upanishads and UG," was even more interesting and said that he should read it. I don't know if he ever read it or anyone read it to him. The book was being passed around and people were reading parts of it. UG's granddaughter, Kusuma, who was also visiting from the US, and Lisa proofread it and caught some typos in it. Lisa asked me to read the last chapter in the book, "A Prayer to UG." She made a video of my reading. As usual, the reading was interjected now and then with UG's exclamations and "editorial comments."

Finally, word got around to UG, and about the 26th of February, when I went to see UG that morning, he asked me, "Could we persuade you to stay a little longer?" I said fine. I extended my stay till the 9th of March. Sarito called the British Airways, and I talked to them and rearranged my flight.

* * *

Chandrasekhar and Suguna didn't arrive until the 8th afternoon. Mitra and I went to Nice to receive them at the airport. I only had that half-day to spend with him, as I was leaving the next morning.

When we arrived at UG's, as usual, there were a lot of shoes outside, and the living room was packed with people. I think first Suguna entered and then Chandrasekhar. As she went in, Suguna broke down crying, "UG, why is this happening to you?" in Telugu. Then you could hear UG answering in Telugu with his own crying voice, "Why are you crying?" That was most heart-breaking to everyone around. UG's affection to her was boundless. She is a pure soul!

* * *

One day, being tired of his talk, I asked UG, "UG, what prevents you from dying *now*?" UG replied, "I want to go, but the body doesn't let me!" He had made that statement several times before. I tried to interject, "If you care about what the body is trying to say, you should pay attention to it, nurture it and bring it back to full life, instead of neglecting it and letting it go!" But he reacted rather sharply, speaking of my "schoolboy logic."

One thing remarkable about UG was his attitude toward his condition: You might sometimes hear him groan in his pain or gasp for breath, but he always remained unconcerned about his health and well-being. He never, even once, worried about what was happening to him. I heard him roar once: "Do you think I care about whether I live or die?" He was never the "frightened chicken" that he accused people of being when they were afraid of disease or death.

After giving an account of the money still left with him, UG was constantly saying that he would give the remaining $300,000 to anyone who would pack him off. Then there were plenty of jokes about that. I told him that I would do that and he could give the money to me. He said, "No, you wouldn't do it." I said I could strangle him or give him "the kiss of death." Louis was doing his own part in the joking: he would say he could make minced meat out of the body of UG, make patties with the meat and distribute them to everyone, to put catsup on and eat. And so on. This joking would go on endlessly.

One morning, I prepared a scheme for a "mortal combat" with UG and was waiting for Mahesh to arrive on the scene so he could record the conversation. (Mahesh had been taking copious notes so he could write a book on his days with UG later.) This mortal combat would be a kind of answer to UG's repeated statement, "I want to go, but my body doesn't want to go." When Mahesh arrived, I was massaging UG's legs along with Usha (I wanted to try a certain massage, Bowen style, which I learned from Linda, my ex-wife). As I was massaging, I stood up and said "Here are the three terms of the mortal combat: 1) It's a combat of debating until one of us dies; 2) We debate strictly according to rules of logic and nothing else; and 3) No bullying on UG's part." I don't think anyone was amused by my idea.

4. My Last Visit with UG

My complaint to UG was essentially that if he treats his body as something separate from him (or even if it is the same as him,), he should listen to his body and do its bidding, since he often claims that the body can take care of all its problems. I said that he as "UG" was not letting his body take care of itself. (He did admit that "UG" was a nuisance.) If he did, he would listen to the body's demands. The body was demanding nourishment and freedom from pain, and wanted to get some help in that direction. It wanted to get well. I added: "It's 'UG' I want to kill and let his body take care of the problems. It's that 'UG' who is subjecting the body to all his diet philosophy and other kinds of 'crap' and screwing it up!" UG right away agreed "it" (the philosophy) was "crap"!

I don't think UG heard any of that. But that's how he is. In a sense he was right. He in fact told people later that "UG" was already dead. He was just waiting for the body to go. And he would give no encouragement (except the minimal food or elimination) for the body to linger or carry on. And that's precisely what happened: he let the body wither away slowly on its own. It took a long time and he was deteriorating day by day, until finally he gave up when no one was around. He made sure that the three who were attending him (Mahesh, Larry and Susan) were out for a short while for a cup of coffee and then he breathed his last.

Ten days before that, after everyone else had left the room, he asked Mahesh to go out and tell everyone to "go back to where you all came from and not sneak around in the corners trying to see him." Larry and Susan had also left, but when they arrived at the airport in Nice, they were called back. Usha was also sent away; so were Chandrasekhar and Suguna. (I believe that if I had stayed on, I would have met the same fate.) Mario and Sarito were asked (by Mahesh) to hang around in town to do any chores that were necessary. Guha came back, of course with UG's permission, after going earlier to India with Lakshmi and their children, saying goodbye to UG. He didn't have the heart to stay away, but when he came back he still had to stay out along with others. So he hovered around in town with his cell phone (every one of these people had a cell phone).[14]

UG gave clear instructions to Mahesh that there would be no funeral. And there was to be no ceremony of any kind. His body was cremated locally. Of course, Susan was on hand to take care of any death certification process that was needed, as she is a medical doctor. I don't know what happened to the ashes that were collected from the. cremation.[15] I heard that Mitra was asked to take the few of UG's personal belongings to Gstaad and I do not know their final disposition. I also heard that Sarito or someone else was left in charge of the "German funds" to be disbursed according to UG's wishes[16]. Mahesh was left in charge of the other funds, mostly to be given away to deserving young girls of Indian origin studying abroad. There was a will of sorts which UG had dictated to Mahesh and which was read aloud in some gatherings, but I don't think it will have any legal validity. As for the apartment in Gstaad which had already been paid for by UG till the end of August, UG invited any of his friends to come and stay there and enjoy themselves.

Sometime toward the end of my stay, Yashoda collected money from those present to buy a tree and present it to Lucia and Giovanni, the hosts, in token of the appreciation of the group that had gathered there for their gracious and wonderful hospitality. They would plant the tree in their yard in memory of UG.

* * *

The night before I was to leave, I gave a little talk addressing everyone present there: I told how I appreciated everyone taking such good care of UG, especially Louis. What Louis did for UG no one else could do, including myself, I said. Everyone worked together like a family, I continued, like an orchestra without a conductor: everything got done and no one was there to tell them what to do. I mentioned the names of various people from various countries and I also made references to some who were not present, particularly to Julie Thayer.

* * *

Why were all these people so attracted to UG? On the one hand, they considered him as their spiritual master guiding them in their lives. On the other hand, thanks to their belief in his "supernatural" powers, they were looking to him for help in worldly matters as well, to become successful in career, love or money, or for success in other areas. Some regarded him as an invaluable friend, who was always loyal to them and who couldn't be replaced by anyone else. Some were simply in love with him. Many of them regarded him as a father figure who gave them that love and affection which they received from no one else. Their respect, love and obedience abounded to the point that they totally disregarded any apparent abuse by him.

Nothing explains better all these relationships than the one crowning factor, namely, that UG represents to many the end of a search: you feel that with UG you have come to the end of the road. There is nothing beyond. No wonder he became such a reference point (to use Julie's expression) for many of us. Such was UG's magical spell on those around him.

UG did ask several people, including me, to visit him one last time before he died. But some he didn't. It's not clear what his logic was behind this. Whatever it was, it was clear that when people didn't come to visit him, he never showed any disappointment. You are always left with the impression that his invitations were extended to people for their

4. My Last Visit with UG

benefit, and not for his, just to give them one last chance to be with him.[17]

I cannot but be impressed by the mutual cordiality which people expressed to one another in this group. Not just respect, but affection and friendship. I know that at least some of them will remain friends with me even after UG's death. With the others I feel that I could renew my friendship any time I might choose or when an opportunity might present itself; then it would be like I saw them only yesterday.

* * *

The night before I left, I told UG and everyone present that whichever way he decided, whether he decided to "stay" or "leave," we would respect his decision. If he decided to live and carry on, I would be glad to see him again in Seaside. On the other hand, if he decided to leave, that would be his decision, and we would respect that.

I thought, in the back of my mind, that UG might want to ask me to postpone my departure further; but that wasn't forthcoming. And it wasn't so clear to me that UG was going to die; there was some possibility that he could kick back, as he had once before, a few years ago[18], and hang on. But, I didn't want to sit there on my own initiative to keep a death watch. For some reason, that didn't make much sense to me. For one thing, UG had said several times he wanted to leave everyone there in Vallecrosia and get someone to drive him to Gstaad where he would settle all his affairs and simply disappear.

On the eve of my departure, I said my goodbyes to all friends. I asked UG if he would be available at 5:30 in the morning to say good bye. He said, "Why 5:30, you can come at 5:00. I will be up most of the night anyway." Lisa was going to leave at the same time and travel with me to London where we would be going our separate ways, I to Seaside and she to Palm Springs. Mitra was to take me to UG's with my bags at 5:00 AM. I hardly slept that night. By the time we arrived at UG's, Chandrasekhar and Suguna, Larry and Susan, Guha, Golda and Lucia were present. So were Kathy, Avner, Usha, and several others. I said good bye to everyone once again. I prostrated one final time at UG's feet to show my respect.

* * *

I feel, and I am sure that he was not unaware of it himself, that irrespective of all my ambivalences and ambiguities, there is a fundamental feeling of non-separation from UG.

I can't say I really miss UG. Sure, he is gone. But the unity I felt, the identity, the energy, they are not gone. It's just like I always said, "Whatever is real there in UG it is here now!" I am not real, fundamentally. And what is real is always there with or without UG, and with or without me.

One could ask whether I feel the same non-separation between myself and other people as well. The answer is, in principle, yes. But most of the time it doesn't surface, because my conditioning and background keep operating and prompt me to react to what others say or do, thus creating a division between me and others. In UG's case, however, my reactive mechanisms were at least temporarily, on some occasions, in abeyance. There was no room for them to arise, at least for those moments. Then it's not that I actually felt that there were two non-separate people, but rather that I felt as if there was just that field of energy, which I could feel any time I moved outside of my reactive mechanism.

You could feel the same way in intense moments of love, when the separation between you and your lover is gone. Then it's not that you feel you two are united into one, but you touch on the underlying energy field which exists everywhere and in everyone, and in you and me. Of course, we can't remain there. The world has to go on and have its play and we are part of the play. We act and we react to other people. We get involved and then we get disengaged. But fundamentally there is only that energy!

Goodbye, UG, my friend!

Part 2: Essays on UG

5. Science And Spirituality: Any Points of Contact?

The Teachings of UG Krishnamurti: A Case Study

[Paper presented at the Krishnamurti Centennial Conference held at Miami University, Oxford, Ohio, U.S.A., May 18-21, 1995.]

The following paper discusses some issues commonly raised in regard to the relationship between science and spirituality. In particular, I wish to examine the issue of the apparent similarities (or symmetry) between statements made by scientists and those made by mystics concerning the unity of existence (or of the universe). I shall argue that the position of the scientists and that of the mystics are not comparable, and I wish to propose that the very premise that the mystic or the scientist has any sort of experience or knowledge of a state of unity, especially when seen in the light of the teachings of UG Krishnamurti, a contemporary teacher, is questionable.

I shall include in my discussion references to a few well-known contemporary scientists, e.g., David Bohm, Rupert Sheldrake and Stephen Hawking. In addition, I shall use some statements of UG Krishnamurti as a reference point, and I will raise some questions concerning his statements as well. I shall also discuss the issue of the survival of the soul after the death of the physical body and compare the views of Rupert Sheldrake and UG Krishnamurti. To complete my account of UG, I shall report some of his views which are more or less relevant to science and its methods and conclusions, as well as make some remarks as to how UG functions in day-to-day life without the burden of thought. I shall conclude my paper with some of my own remarks on UG and his teachings.

* * *

UG Krishnamurti (referred to in the rest of this paper as "UG", as that is how he is addressed by those who know him personally) is not only radical in his teaching, but he also makes constant remarks about the radical transformation he had undergone in 1967, when he was 49 years-old (he was 76 at the time of writing this paper), and about the altered way he currently functions in his day-to-day life. Whatever changes he went through at the time of his transformation made him free from the "stranglehold" of thought, and in some sense he is "self-less" or "mindless". His remarks about the way his body functions, the manner in which his perceptions, visual or otherwise, occur, and his remarks about other matters, are quite pertinent to the topic of this paper. Also his remarks about the possibility (or rather the impossibility) of understanding the universe or of having any experience of unity generally attributed to the mystics question many of our own assumptions in this area.

I

Religion, of which spirituality is considered an essential aspect, has in the past come into conflict with some of the theories and conclusions of science. Three major areas of conflict are: the time of creation, the manner of creation, and the constitution of the human being, particularly with regard to the question of whether there is anything in the human being, such as the soul, that survives the death of his physical body. The most conspicuous instance of this conflict is that between creationism and evolution. Most people, at least those who are not totally committed to the teachings of the Bible (or Koran), consider the conflict settled in favor of science. As to the first of these concerns, i.e., the age of creation, again, unless one is a total and literal believer in the Bible, one would have to agree with the current teachings of science that the beginnings of the universe lay in a much more remote past than 3000 BC.

* * *

Some religions, in particular Hinduism, Buddhism, and Taoism (and perhaps also Confucianism), have, at least sometimes, claimed to have no conflict with science, especially in the areas of the age, origins and manner of creation. Hinduism, for instance, is quite compatible with the idea of evolution, although it would allow that creation takes place out of some primeval matter at the beginning of each cycle of creation-sustenance-dissolution. It has its own version of evolution, which agrees with the scientific theory that evolution is from the simple to the complex and from the homogeneous to the heterogeneous. It would also rather vaguely agree that the age of the universe is, say, some billions of years.

In whatever manner these issues are settled between religion and science, there is another area of contact between the two which seems more attractive and amenable to mutual interest and investigation -- and that is the interface between science and spirituality. The points of contact here seem to be much closer and more intimate. René Weber, in her *Dialogues with Sages and Scientists*, maintains that both the scientist and the mystic seek unity in the universe or reality.

> A parallel principle derives both science and mysticism -- the assumption that unity lies at the heart of our world and that it can be discovered and experienced by man. (Weber, p.13).

While the scientist, according to her, approaches the question of unity through the scientific method and reasoning, the mystic approaches it through self-knowledge. While the methodology of science is quantitative and mathematical, the methodology of mysticism is meditational. (Weber, p.8). Weber admits, however, that there are other differences between science and mysticism: scientific method is cognitive and analytical; it studies the universe piecemeal. It claims its results to be objective and value-free. (Weber, p.8). The mystic's unity is experiential -- it is union with the infinite (for instance, the "Thou art that" of the Upanishads). (Weber, p.9). While the scientist seeks to unify, he leaves himself out of this "equation" (Weber, p.10), in spite of the fact that in quantum mechanics the observer and the observed are "admitted to constitute a unit." According to Weber, the scientific community has not yet caught up with the full meaning of this declaration. (Weber, p.10).

The search for the "singularity" before time, as in the physical theories of Stephen Hawking, is an expression of this search for unity, just as the "super-implicate" order in David Bohm is another such expression. Professor Bohm claims that the quantum-mechanical field theory implies some such notion as his super-implicate order. (Weber, pp.34, 37) In his view, the relationship between what he calls the super-implicate order[19] and implicate order is similar to the relationship between consciousness and matter. They are two aspects of one "process". (Weber p.38) Bohm disputes other physicists who claim that his theories do not have much scientific value because they do not yield any empirically predictable results. Yet he claims that his theory is not mere speculation but "is implied by present quantum mechanics if you look at it imaginatively." (Weber, p.37) But when he is asked the question of whether there is any super-super-implicate order, he answers:

> ...we can't grasp that in thought .... We're not saying that any of this is another word for God. I would put it another way: people had insight in the past about a form of intelligence that had organized the universe and they personalized it and called it God. A similar insight can prevail today without personalizing it and without calling it a personal God. (Weber, p.39)

Bohm observes that Sheldrake, a biologist, admits that the evidence for the latter's morphogenetic fields[20] is very limited and "requires a lot of experimentation." (Weber, p.96) His own and Sheldrake's theories are:

> "...about as testable as any other theories. There is no way to disprove a hypothesis of this level of generality, although it's possible to conceive of evidence accumulating which would make it look unlikely. As far as the

5. Science and Spirituality

implicate order is concerned, since that's even more general, it would be much harder to discuss evidence. The only 'evidence' I can present is that it's a way of looking at the subject which brings it all together. And I think it has a promise of being truthful..." (Weber, p.96)

Bohm disputes the scientific idea that the ability of a theory to predict and control nature proves its truth.

It merely proves that we can turn this crank and get the right answers in a certain area. If you restrict yourself to these areas, your theory naturally appears unassailable." (Weber, p.105)

In general, both Bohm and Sheldrake seem to embrace the idea that the universe ultimately developed out of some sort of consciousness or intelligence. They both deny that either matter or mechanism explain nature and the universe. They both believe that meaning (mathematics for David Bohm) and order are part of nature and that we can study that order through mathematics or scientific theory. And yet, Bohm clearly gives the idea that thought is incapable of grasping the ultimate origins of the universe, because previous scientists (like Poincaré, or Einstein) didn't know what the source of their mathematics was, and therefore they called it mysterious. (Weber p.147) It is Bohm's view that, inasmuch as he is studying the mathematical order of the universe, and inasmuch as mathematics is meaning and meaning is a property of consciousness, the scientist is ultimately, like the mystic, studying consciousness.

In some ways the pure mathematician is going into one of the aspects of consciousness." (Weber, p.149)

He says that although the scientist is

...inspired by the experience of matter, nevertheless once it has entered consciousness he is trying to find something that goes on in consciousness which has an order of its own." (Weber, p.149)

Physicists like Hawking, although critical of the speculative fancies of scientists like Bohm, do, on grounds that their theories are not falsifiable in Karl Popper's sense (Weber, p.210), admit that

...most of theoretical physics is connected with an urge to understand the universe, rather than with any practical applications, because we already know enough to deduce practical applications.

Hawking admits that the theories about the laws governing the four fields are not consistent, although they are all adequate "to predict more or less what will happen in most normal situations." (Weber, p.210) They differ at the level of predicting very high energies, energies much higher than we can simulate. We require physical theories to be consistent; thus we require nature to be consistent. Hawking also thinks that time and space and everything else are really in us. They are just mathematical models that we've made to describe the universe.

Consequently, Hawking says that the distinction between studying nature and merely our models of nature is not a meaningful distinction.

Thus it's clear from the ideas presented above that the difference between scientists like Hawking and scientists like Bohm is only a matter of degree, not of kind. They both would like to arrive at an understanding of the universe. And both are interested in arriving at a theoretical understanding of the universe which aims at unity. Both rely on reasoning and thought, even though Bohm, due to his inclinations toward mysticism, admits that thought is incapable of understanding ultimate reality. Both would go beyond merely experimental predictability. The difference between the two seems to be that Hawking would restrict himself to reconciling the conflicts in the various scientific theories concerning the fundamental fields, whereas Bohm would want to go further and try to understand the theories and achieve a unity beyond current physical theory.

According to Weber, the mystic, on the other hand, is engaged in "splitting his self-centered ego and the three-dimensional thinker that sustains it." (Weber, p.11) He, "in changing himself, changes the subtle matter within in some radical way for which no scientific explanation is at present adequate." (Weber, p.12) For the mystic, a theory cannot comprehend reality, for it puts limits on the unbounded. (Weber, p.14) The questions of the why's and the wherefore's of the universe lead, for the mystic, to the idea that the universe originates in consciousness. (Weber, p.15)

> Subtle matter gives birth to and governs dense matter, but all matter forms a continuum. ... At its most subtle and inward point (if there is such an end point) matter and consciousness become indistinguishable." (Weber, p.15)

Professor Weber thinks that this subtle matter can be "approached through non-ordinary states of consciousness" as experienced, for instance, in Tibetan Buddhism (Weber, p. 15). "A traditional meditation in Tibetan Buddhism enables the meditator to experience the unity of space, matter, and consciousness." (Weber, p.16)

Regardless of Bohm's and Hawking's statements that they only study models in physics, that, in other words, the physicist is merely studying himself (i.e., the mathematical models in his mind, rather than reality itself), it is clear that in some fashion the study does not, and in principle cannot, include the scientists themselves. It's not just that theoretical physics, as Weber claims, has not yet somehow come to understand the implications of quantum mechanics. It is not even that, as the "Copenhagen Interpretation" of quantum mechanics states, we do not actually study reality, but only our interpretation of reality. It's just that no matter what theory a physicist arrives at, it must, as a theory, preclude the person of the scientist as part of the unity. A theory is a thought, and as thought, it must preclude the thinker. It is precisely this separation that the mystic is trying to transcend. It is merely a concession on Bohm's part to mysticism when he says that thought cannot reach reality or that the physicist studies consciousness. These statements made by him are not consistent with his being a physicist, for they are not compatible with science or its method, particularly its rationality.

* * *

For a teacher like UG, on the other hand, what is problematical is not only that our theories of the universe, of space and time, of causation, or of evolution are merely our interpretations of reality, but also that the self (of the scientist, from the scientist's point of view) is itself a product of the putting together (in the mind of the scientist) of various sensations or memories through (his) thought. In that sense, the self or the subject who does the scientific study, and who is normally taken for granted, is himself an "interpretation."

The mystic, in his turn, inasmuch as he is a mystic, is more interested in what Weber calls union with reality. Such a union may result in transcending one's sense of separation, a transcendence which the mystic had been seeking through his methods of self-knowledge and meditation. However, the mystic's pronouncements concerning his experiential discovery of the unity of existence, of the universe, or of the Godhead are not in any way comparable to the physicist's theories of the universe, for the mystic's statements have no scientific, that is to say, publicly verifiable (or falsifiable) content, as do the scientist's.

It is true that in some sense both the scientist and the mystic do seek unity. Perhaps the very search for understanding is born out of a sense of separation which is caused by one's thought processes, and which presents, in one's consciousness, the clear division between oneself as the observer and the world (including oneself, inasmuch as one is aware of oneself as a being in the world) as the observed. But there is a fundamental difference in the approaches: the scientist is not satisfied with a mere "experience" of unity, whatever that experience may consist of, but seeks unification in theory. The mystic, on the contrary, is sure that no theory will ever result in a unifying experience. Furthermore, when the mystic does "experience" such a unity, the quest for unity will no longer be there. Not only the quest is gone, but the seeker is gone in a very fundamental sense. It is in this context that UG's teachings have relevance.

UG says that the basic questions concerning the universe or ourselves (or reality, if that's what you call it, and, we may add, questions about the meaning of life) *are* the self. And these questions try to maintain themselves as the self. And, moreover, they do not allow for any complete answer, for the answer would put an end to the questioner. In fact, the same thought process which created the original separation between the thinker and the world would endlessly keep asking further questions about whatever answer is given.[21]

Furthermore (and this goes quite contrary to many mystical traditions), UG says there cannot be any "experience" of unity or union with reality. According to him, a claim to any experience presupposes not only an awareness of the experience as an object, but also recognition of it as an experience. And these conditions are enough to destroy any possibility of there being a unity, let alone an experience of unity, because any recognition implies a duality or division between the subject and the object. How can there be an experience of unity where the subject is left out of the object of experience?

* * *

Is it possible that there is indeed an experience of unity, but when the experience occurs, there is no awareness of it, yet it could be recalled as such sometime later? UG denies that such a possibility exists, because, in order for there to be a memory of an experience, there has to have been an initial experience (or knowledge) with an awareness which implies a subject-object distinction. In other words, he denies that it is possible to have an experience without a subject-object distinction; were it possible to have such an experience, he denies that we could have a memory of it. When there is no such distinction (as should be the case with the so-called experience of unity), there can be no recognition of that state and therefore the state does not constitute an experience; and for that reason there can be no memory of it later.

Nevertheless, when UG describes his own process of "death" or a "thoughtless" state, he admits that there must be in that state some awareness of what was going on, or he would not be able to talk about it. This admission leads us to wonder whether, after all, UG is not concurring with scientists like Sheldrake and Bohm in their assertion that consciousness is the ultimate reality and is the "unity" of the universe. UG's admission would be somewhat akin to that of the scientists in another sense also, namely, that it is somewhat speculative (although perhaps not to him), for in the awareness of his own thoughtless state there must be some thought operating (according to his own admission, or else he would not be able to report about it), and his statement about consciousness being everywhere would, therefore, also be somewhat speculative. He may have superior knowledge (superior to ours) in this matter, but, to us, his statements expressing such knowledge must, like the statements of the scientists, sound speculative.

5. Science and Spirituality

Is it possible, then, that when the mystic talks about the experience of unity (say, his experience of Brahman or of Emptiness) there is just a unity of consciousness (let us say, just awareness) without any awareness of that consciousness (or a "minimal" or "implicit" awareness, as UG himself seems to suggest in his own case when he undergoes his experience of "death" or similar extraordinary experiences [*see below*]), and that a full-blown subject-object division comes into the picture when that experience is recalled and named? In other words, is it possible that, although in the mystic the continuity of thought is broken up in such a way that there is no self (the continuity of thought or experience or memory is what creates the self), there is still a physiological lingering or trace of a previous experience? And is it possible that, although there might not be any explicit subject-object distinction at the time of experience, a memory of it becomes possible later because the physiological trace is translated at that later moment as a memory experience, and as a consequence, one recognizes and names the experience (albeit calling it nameless)? It may well be that the experience now is remembered as one of formless emptiness or of energy or of ecstasy. In any case, it would be remembered as being free from any of the delineations of ordinary experience.

Suppose it is possible for the mystic to experience unity in such a fashion. In what way would this unity be compared to the unity posited by the physicist? Is it not possible to interpret this unity (or the experience of it) as just a subjective (although uplifting) experience of the mystic? Does this imply that there is unity (such as of consciousness, or whatever the scientist might be speculating about) in the universe as a whole? If there is any unity in the universe in the scientific sense, then it is not something the scientist can observe (for the scientist always has to remain outside of it as the observer). And if it can be observed, then we can't know if it is the unity of the universe or not.

Given such a paradox, it seems to me that the unity professed by the mystic and that professed by the scientist are not comparable. In fact, I think we got into the trap of comparing these only because of the ambiguity in the term "unity". The unity for the physicist has to remain a conceptual and objective unity. And unity for the mystic has to be an experience where there is no observer, and hence there would be no distinction between objective unity and the subjective experience of it.

II

For UG there is no such thing as reality; whatever our thought constructs as reality is all the reality we know or can know of. While the Copenhagen interpretation of Quantum mechanics says that what we know is only our interpretation of reality (including the reality of the scientist), the interpretation does not, however, doubt the reality of the scientist who makes such an assertion. UG, on the contrary, says that the thinker, you, me or UG, are all constructs of thought. That's all we can know. And this idea is quite consistent with the general tenets of mysticism. UG merely draws the consequences of this thesis consistently.

The above remarks also apply to our understanding of reality as being bound by the laws of cause and effect. Current physics (because of Quantum mechanics or of Heisenberg's principle of uncertainty) may revise our notions of cause and effect. UG, on the other hand, sees any attempt to relate events in terms of cause and effect, along with the attempt to "understand" reality, as part of the project of making the self. Causation is the self's means of controlling the world and of thus maintaining itself and its own continuity. It is more than an effective way of surviving in this world and decidedly more than a way of ordering events with a view to understanding "reality".

For someone like UG, then, the quest of science would reveal itself as a mere technology which delivers various products, rather than an endless attempt to understand reality. Science is valid to the extent of its results. Outside of that, according to UG, it is just an endless spinning of wheels for the purposes of the scientist's self-aggrandizement.

UG, in fact, does not separate the scientist from his science. As he calls the scientist's enterprise into question, he is also calling the scientist's person into question, inasmuch as he is exposing the personal motivation behind any scientific enterprise. Just as he does with people from other walks of life, he is attempting to frustrate the self-centered efforts of the scientist in the way of self-aggrandizement. He has no positive teaching of his own in this matter -- he only seeks to frustrate the efforts of the scientist, and he does not attempt to fill in that gap with any other suggestions.

III

Generally speaking, religion has problems in accepting the current hypotheses (and implications) of science concerning the constitution of the human being. While science does not explicitly deny any specific teaching of religion (nor is it interested in investigating religious claims), its investigations of the human being are limited to the physical, biological, psychological and social or cultural aspects of man. Science does not easily lend itself to a belief in anything else, particularly in a soul which may survive the death of the body. This -- the belief in a soul -- seems to be essential to most religions for a simple reason: besides a commitment to a belief in some supernatural being, religion is also committed to a belief in personal morality, with its implications of sin and

5. Science and Spirituality

redemption. Without the idea of salvation or liberation and some blessed state that would be associated with it, religion would probably not have much appeal. These conceptions of salvation and liberation, of heaven or nirvana, have to be correlated with the opposite conceptions of sin or bondage, or some state of suffering (caused by man's fallenness) from which he has to be saved.

Science is generally resistant to the idea that in the human being there could be a soul above and beyond the body, or some entity besides the body and its structures, an entity which survives the death of the body, for the fundamental reason that scientists cannot conceive of any memory or personality traits existing without the support of the brain or the body. Whatever is psychological (or spiritual) in man must seem to be rooted in the physical. After all, physics is the most basic of all the sciences.

Rupert Sheldrake, however, is one of the few contemporary scientists who maintain that such a survival of something beyond the body is possible on the ground that it is possible for memory to exist without the support of the brain. (And David Bohm concurs with him on this possibility.) Sheldrake argues that just because we do not know of any memory without the brain, it does not follow that there cannot be any memory outside the brain. For all we know, the brain can act as a conduit through which memory (or consciousness) manifests itself, much like the antenna and the wiring in a radio act as conduits for the electromagnetic waves to be manifested as sound. Thus, just as the radio signal can exist (in the form of electromagnetic waves) outside the radio with its antenna and wiring, memory can exist outside the brain.

It's clear that Sheldrake is speaking from a vitalist persuasion in biology, which is not shared by the majority of biologists. They think that his claims are not supported by scientific method and that hypotheses such as Sheldrake's are mere conjectures and have no predictive value. Sheldrake denies this. He thinks that his "hypothesis of formative causation [his morphogenetic field theory] is testable. It can be tested through experiments that I propose...." (Weber, p.78)

Let us compare these views with UG's views on the human being, particularly his views on memory and consciousness.

UG says that memory is not necessarily located in the brain:

> They say that memory is in the neurons. If it is all in the neurons, where is it located in them? The brain does not seem to be the center of memory. Cells seem to have their own memory. So, where is that memory? Is it transmitted through genes? I really don't know. Some of these questions have no answers so far. Probably one of these days they will find out. (NWO, p.161)

In UG's conversations, we can see that, for him, thought is somewhat akin to memory. Thought, memory, and knowledge are all ways in which our past experience operates on the present "input," by recognizing, interpreting, comparing data, and so on. These processes create our sense of time and also our sense of the self. If we ask the question, "Where do memories or thoughts come from?" UG answers it as follows:

> Where does thought come from? Is it from inside or outside? Where is the seat of human consciousness? So, for purposes of communication, or just to give a feel about it, I say there is a thought sphere. In that "thought sphere" we are all functioning, and each one of us probably has an "antenna", or what you call an "aerial" or something, which is the creation of the culture into which we are born. It is that that is picking up these particular thoughts. (ME, p.111)

UG seems to warn us that science may not be able to study consciousness or the field from which these thoughts or memories arise:

> All the experiences -- not necessarily just your experiences during your span of thirty, forty or fifty years, but the animal consciousness, the plant consciousness, the bird consciousness -- all that is part of this consciousness. (Not that there is an entity which reincarnates; there is no entity there, so the whole business of reincarnation is absurd as far as I am concerned.) That is why in your dreams you dream as if you are flying like a bird.... How it is transmitted, I don't know, I can't say, I am not competent to say. But this seems to be the means. There must be some means of transmission...much more than the genetic: the genetic is only part of it. Consciousness is a very powerful factor in experiencing things, but it is not possible for anybody to find out the content of the whole thing -- it is too vast. (ME, p. 114)

About phylogenetic memory UG says:

> I can make no definitive statements about the part genes play in the evolutionary process, but at the moment it appears that Darwin was at least partially wrong in insisting that acquired characteristics could not be genetically transmitted. I think that they are transmitted in some fashion. I am not competent enough to say whether the genes play any part in the transmission. (NWO, p.171)

There seems to be some parallelism between Sheldrake's morphogenetic fields and UG's field of consciousness of which human consciousness is a part. Racially and individually, we seem to be "tuning" into that field. Of course, neither Sheldrake nor UG is clear about the specifics as to how this takes place. UG (much like the Dalai Lama) leaves the matter to the scientists, although he is skeptical that they will ever be able to study consciousness as such. Sheldrake, being a scientist, hopes his theories will be verified by experimental methods someday. But, at the moment, neither Sheldrake nor UG have any confirmation from science for their views, and, as such, these views remain speculative. UG may be more certain of his ideas than Sheldrake, but to his audience, the veracity of his statements remain just as speculative as Sheldrake's.

IV

While UG frustrates all of our attempts to understand human consciousness, he, at the same time, describes the way he functions and what happens to him in a thoughtless state. These descriptions pose a challenge to science. Not that he would let scientists study him. (At times he does, but that depends on the scientist he is at the moment talking to):

> I am simply making a statement, not selling a product. (MM, p.146) There are no persons and no space within to create a self. What is left after the continuity of thought is blown away is one disjointed, independent, series of interactions. What happens in the environment around me, happens in here. There is no division. When the armor you are wearing around is stripped away, you find an extraordinary sensitivity of the senses that respond to the phases of the moon, the passage of the seasons, and the movements of the other planets. There is simply no isolated, separate, existence of its own here, only the throb of life, like a jellyfish. (MM, p. 145)

> ...It [the death process] defies description. But I can mention that in this death state, the ordinary breath stops entirely and the body is able to "breathe" through other physiological means. Among the many doctors I have discussed this strange phenomenon with, only Dr. Laboyer, an expert in childbirth, gave me a sort of explanation. He says that newborn babies have a similar way of breathing. This is probably what the original word *pranayama* meant. This body goes through the death process on a daily basis so often, in fact, that every time it renews itself it is a given a longer lease. When, one day, it cannot renew itself, it is finished and carted off to the ash heap. (MM, p.145)

> ...After the breath and heartbeat come to almost a complete stop, somehow the body begins to "come back." The corpse-like appearance of the body -- the stiffness, coldness and ash covering -- begin to disappear. The body warms up and begins to move and the metabolism, including the pulse, picks up. If you, out of scientific curiosity, wish to test me, I am not interested.

> This whole process of dying and being renewed, although it happens to me many times a day, and always without my volition, remains very intriguing to me. Even the thought of self or ego has been annihilated. Still there is something there experiencing this death, otherwise I would not be able to describe it here. (MM p.146)

> When the separative thought structure dies, these glands and nervous plexi take over the functioning of the organism. It is a painful process, for the hold of thought over the glands and plexuses is strong and has to be "burnt" off. This can be experienced by an individual. The burning or "ionization" needs energy and space to take place. For this reason the limits of the body are reached, with energy lashing out in all directions. The body's containment of that energy in its limited form brings pain, even though there is no experiencer of pain there. (MM, p. 147)
>
> This painful death process is something nobody -- not even the most ardent religious practitioners and yogis -- wants. It is a very painful thing. It is not the result of will, but is the result of a fortuitous concourse of atoms. (MM, p.148)
>
> How all this fits into your scientific structure, I do not know. Scientists doing work in this field are interested in these changes, if they are described in physiological rather than mystical terms. These scientists envisage this kind of man as representing the end product of biological evolution, not the science-fiction superman or super spiritual beings. Nature is only interested in creating an organism that can respond fully and intelligently to stimuli and reproduce itself. That's all. This body is capable of extraordinary perceptions and sensations. It is a marvel. I don't know who created it. (MM, p.148)
>
> Scientists in the field of evolution now think that the present breed of humans we have on this planet probably evolved out of a degenerated species. The mutation that carried on the self-consciousness must have taken place in a degenerate species. That is why we have messed everything up. It is anybody's guess as to whether anyone can change the whole thing. (MM, p.148)

Speaking further of how he functions without the domination of thought, UG says:

> Then, the senses become very important factors; they begin to function at their peak capacity without the interference of thought except when there is a demand for thought. Here I must make one thing very clear: thought is not self-initiated; it always comes into operation on demand. It depends upon the demands of the situation: there is a situation where thought is necessary, and so it is there; otherwise it is not there. Like that pen you are using -- you can write a beautiful piece of poetry or forge a check or do something with that pen -- it is there when there is a demand for it. Thought is only for the purpose of communication; otherwise it has no value at all. Then you are guided by your senses and not by your thoughts any more... (ME, p.110)

The way UG functions is as a natural living organism, without the "stranglehold" of thought -- he functions efficiently, from moment to moment, without any urge to be or do anything other than what he is or what he is doing at that moment. He explains how, in him, there is chaos

5. Science and Spirituality

and order simultaneously in every moment of attention; how his visual perception is two-dimensional; how one picture of whatever is occurring is replaced by another, totally disconnected picture as soon as some other thing in the environment captures his attention; how (for him) there is no connecting link between one event and another; how music can be mere "noise;" how, as an occasion demands, all the knowledge relevant to it is brought to bear upon it, and when the need is gone, then he is back to the "meaningless" or thoughtless state.

There is no way for another person to understand all this. To try and understand it, one would have to put it as information into one's own mental and conceptual framework, and then there would always be questions about this information springing from one's own experiences, prejudices and expectations (concerning oneself and one's life). Or, one could live like UG, in which case there would be nothing to understand, as the need to understand will have disappeared.

UG does make some startling statements about genetics, rebirth, disease, and so on. Some of these statements are hard to make sense of, because our present-day science has not investigated them, or they may sound false, because science sometimes seems to conflict with them. Examples of such statements are:

> For those who believe there is such a thing as rebirth, there is rebirth; and for those who do not believe in it, there is no such thing. However, "objectively speaking" there is no rebirth -- for what is there to be born again? ...

> All chronic disease is genetic.

(Here he seems to believe in some kind of physiological karma - there is nothing you can do about it, except bear with it and, if necessary, temporarily palliate it.)

> To experience pain you have to link one (momentary) sensation with another through memory and thought. Pain is necessary to the healing process -- if you let it be, the body will find its way of absorbing or integrating it.

> The body never dies; it is only recycled -- our (non-existent) self is the only thing that dies. If left alone, without the influence of thought, the body functions most sensitively, efficiently and absolutely peacefully.

> We don't want to be free from our problems, for to be free from them is to put an end to ourselves.

V

The most immediate question that might come to a reader's mind when he reads the above discussion of UG is: how does UG know whatever he is saying about himself (and his thoughtless state)? For all normal and practical purposes he seems to use his knowledge and thought like everyone else. Either he is in his thoughtless state and he does not know it; or he knows his thoughtless state and he is not in it.

In ME (p. 46), UG describes his state as a state of "not knowing;" knowledge only comes into the picture when there is a demand for it. Once the demand is met, then he is back again in the state of not knowing. On the very next page (p. 47), speaking of the "tremendous peace that is always there within, that is your natural state," he says, "...This is volcanic in its nature: it's bubbling all the time -- the energy, the life -- that is its quality." Then, UG asks, "You may ask how I know. I don't know. Life is aware of itself, if we can put it that way -- it is conscious of itself." Nowadays, UG would express the thought somewhat differently by saying, "Knowing and not knowing exist in the same 'frame.'"

In looking at this "tremendous peace," If we substitute "unity" for "peace" we immediately notice the paradox: on the one hand, we cannot experience "unity," for to experience it is to recognize it; and that can only be possible when there is a duality or division. On the other hand, to make a statement that there is unity (or peace, in the above context) implies knowing it. And to say that unity (or life) is conscious of itself seems to be inconsistent with the previous statement. How can we understand this paradox?

I think that when a person is freed from the "stranglehold" of thought, in some sense the person (or the subject) does not exist as a continuing entity any longer. Not that the entity ever really existed before -- only the illusion of it was there. Now that the illusion is not there; knowledge operates for a moment, answers the demands of the situation, and immediately and automatically slips back into the background.[22] When UG answers his audience's questions, he responds in words. His audience tends to make sense and meaning out of these words, and is tempted to apply the same rules of logic that are normally applied to discourse. But as there is no "person" in someone like UG, there is no division (or sense of separation) within him; and whatever "unity" is there is expressing itself without the normal logic of "consciousness" or "experience." Even UG's responses to our questions have no meaning for him. It is not that they are meaningless. There is no consciousness of "separation" or of anything (or anyone) as being separate from himself. Hence, it would not be appropriate to call statements of UG expressions of "knowledge," at least in the ordinary sense of knowing. Words, meanings, music, sounds, objects and such appear for a moment and then in the next moment (or "in the same frame") recede into the background and become mere noise, two dimensional space, irritations or 'blobs". We, however, "interpret" the sounds coming from UG as meaningful and try to apply truth values to the statements coming from him. But, for UG, these ideas do not have "meaning", or truth or falsehood.

If such is the life of a person free from thought or the self, we could call it a state of "unity," but there is no one to realize or experience that unity, nor is there any knowledge or experience of it in the usual sense of the terms. UG tries to express this life in a fashion peculiar to himself. To his audience who try to measure whatever they hear with their normal yardsticks of subject-object, meaning-object dichotomies, such a life, however, must remain a mystery.

At this point UG's audience is tempted to ask:

How do we understand such seemingly nonsensical utterances of UG? Why should we even be interested in such "nonstatements" of UG? Why should we pay any attention to UG or his teachings at the expense of disregarding the testimonies of the many mystics of the world making claims to knowledge (or at any rate an experience) of unity?

I think the answer to these questions lies in the epistemological challenge UG poses to both the mystic and the scientist. If the critique he makes of both mysticism and science is extended to his own statements, it is true that we are led to some puzzles and paradoxes. But then, what if the above is the only possible way a man who lives in an undivided state lives, and traditional mystics did not always realize its implications?[23] Although UG's utterances make no "sense" to UG (it is not that they are nonsense either), his audience cannot help but try to make sense out of them, for they are using the activity of making sense as part of the project of making their selves, in the sense that they relate his statements to some project (epistemological, spiritual or some other personal project) in their lives. UG, on the other hand, can operate in this world without having to fall into the dichotomy of sense and nonsense. To us, he appears to be a man like any other man, living, and carrying on in this world. UG, however, has no sense of who he is. He has no concept or image of himself, and hence even the question of whether he is alive or not-alive does not arise for him. He may momentarily answer our questions with counter-sounds or utterances. The problem of making sense, attributing truth or falsehood, or looking for the facts "behind" the words, is our problem, not his.

In view of the above discussion, then, shall we say that UG's thoughtless state is a state of experiencing the unity of the universe? As UG in some sense does not exist as a continuing person (subject, self), there can be no knowledge (which is a temporal "state of mind") of such unity; and in such a person there is no awareness of unity, or its opposite, viz., disunity or division. Unity and division are concepts which presuppose continuity in consciousness. For UG's audience, on the other hand, any such unity must remain a concept, for as far as they are concerned, they will never know what is in UG except as a concept, which always necessitates its own opposite. For instance, the audience might be tempted to theorize that when UG is in a thoughtless state he is experiencing unity and that when that state is temporarily disturbed, there is disunity or division. But how can they ascertain the truth value of such statements?

Bibliography and References

(Abbreviations of UG's works referred to in the text of the paper are as shown below.)

1. Sheldrake, Rupert, in Doore, Gary (Ed.): *What Survives?* Tarcher, Los Angeles, 1990.

2. Krishnamurti, UG: *Mind is a Myth*. Dinesh Publications, Goa, 1988. (MM).

3. _____: *The Mystique of Enlightenment*. Akshaya Publications, Bangalore, India, 1992.(ME).

4. _____: *No Way Out*. Akshaya Mudrana, Bangalore, India, 1992.(NWO).

5. Weber, Renee: *Dialogues with Scientists and Sages*. Routledge and Kegan Paul, London and New York, 1987.

6. *Thought, the Natural State and the Body*

Phenomenological Deconstruction of Spirituality in UG Krishnamurti

[Paper presented at the 17th International Vedanta Conference on September 21, 2007 at Miami University, Oxford, Ohio.]

UG Krishnamurti (known to his friends as "UG") has been teaching across the world for some 40 years, ever since he had undergone what he called "calamity" in 1967, in which his life processes ceased for about 45 minutes (he was brought back to life by a phone call from a friend) and he was cleansed of all his past experiences. The continuity of his person had been broken into pieces; gone was any central coordinator or a reference point. Since then, to quote Terry Newland in his Introduction to *Mind is a Myth*:

> What is there is a calm, smoothly functioning, highly intelligent and responsive biological machine, nothing more. One looks in vain for evidence of a self, psyche or ego; there is only the simple functioning of a sensitive organism.(p. 12)

UG passed away on March 22nd of this year (2007). With his radical approach to philosophical questions and issues of living, he left an indelible impression and had a deep personal impact on many of the people who had met him.

After having known UG for over 25 years, it is now time for me to put together my thoughts on his teaching. In the following, I will not only summarize his views on thought, the natural state and the body, but will also present, in the last two sections, my reflections on his teachings and make some conjectures based on my own personal life. The last two sections are somewhat tentative. Because this paper is mainly exploratory, it should be viewed as "work in progress."

* * *

UG was not a systematic philosopher in any technical or academic sense. As a matter of fact, he abhorred technical jargon, especially psychological jargon. He did not leave behind any theory or body of teaching. It is doubtful that one could extract any consistent and coherent system of ideas from his teachings. One could aptly describe him as "a teacher without a teaching." What he taught came in short discourses, dialogues and one-liners, most of which have been published in several books and in a biography of him by Mahesh Bhatt.[24] In the following, I have organized UG's teaching into a number of topics.

The uniqueness in UG's teaching lies in his demystification of spirituality. While discounting all spiritual experiences, he provides a rather naturalistic explanation of spirituality in terms of what he calls the "natural state." He maintains the impossibility of attaining the "natural state" through search, effort, seeking or any other strategy employed by our thinking process.

Spiritual experiences are, he says, like any other experiences, only more glorified. They do not solve the problems of duality or suffering. There is no such thing for UG as a non-dual experience: it is a contradiction in terms. In order for you to know non-duality as an experience, *you* must somehow be there. That means the experience is not truly non-dual.

None of the means which tradition has handed down to us to attain such a liberated state of non-duality delivers the goods. Meditation, renunciation, prayer and worship are all practiced with an ulterior motive and can never free you from duality. You are always there measuring your progress. As long as *you* are there, you can never be free.

Thought: The "you" is thought-generated. Thought is memory, your cultural and individual past, operating on the present situation. Each thought splits itself, as it were, into two: the object thought about and a fictitious, non-existent subject. Thought creates the illusion of the subject, the thinker. Since there is no thinker as such, we can never know the thinker. The thought is the thinker. There is no other thinker.

Thought cannot understand reality. Reality and life are constantly changing. Thought, being dead and static, can never understand or know them. We know or understand anything only through experiences molded out of our past. If thought cannot understand reality, nothing else can, either. You can never know anything directly without the mediation of thought or knowledge. If we could, then there would be no need to understand anything.

For UG, thought is only useful for communication. The structures that thought produces, its theories and hypotheses are only useful in producing technological tools and gadgets. The theories and hypotheses are mere fictions created by thought.

Thought superimposes itself upon the biological organism, creating a parallel world, the world of thought, which consists of all the things we strive for, our pleasures and pains, our knowledge and values.

The Cultural Input: UG says that all typically human problems arise out of the values that the society or culture around us has imposed upon us -- what he calls the "cultural input." Our desires and goals are all passed on to us by the culture around us. This culture wants us to become

6. Thought, the Natural State and the Body

the "perfect man." It induces us to emulate the models which history has produced, models like Jesus and the Buddha, or to strive for utopias such as the Kingdom of God or Nirvana that those models have presented. The cultural input gives us the notion that by living this way we will gain permanent happiness.

Thought is the mechanism which enables the experience of the past to repeat itself through images and words by creating a future, which is only a modified past, and prompting us to strive for it. Ideals thus projected into the future falsify our present condition, making us feel as if there is something wrong with it. We are in a constant conflict between what we think we are and what we want to become. We feel restless, inadequate and unfulfilled, and we constantly search for a meaning in life to fulfill us.

Thought presents us with various goals and prompts us to strive for them to gain permanent happiness without a moment of pain. But permanent happiness is an illusion; it does not exist. In our attempts to realize our goals,[25] especially spiritual goals, we begin to transform ourselves. Furthermore, the process of seeking self-fulfillment is endless, resulting in suffering for the individual and destruction in society. Our seeking leads us to a search for security, power, wealth, sex, love or spiritual liberation. As we strive to attain our goals, we have conflict, fear, jealousy, exploitation and war. These are generated by what UG calls the self-protectiveness of thought.

Instead of a peaceful living organism, we now have an individual torn by conflict, stressed out, competing, conflicting with other individuals and groups, causing suffering for himself and for the society. As long as we are driven by thought and its goals and structures, our problems are inevitable. The problem is that we take our thoughts and goals to be too real. They are all fictitious and generated by the society around us. Since the goals conflict with each other, we are constantly in conflict. "We want all this and heaven too," to quote UG.

Then we ask how we can become free from all these goals. The "how" is a mischievous question; it implies another goal, this time one of "thoughtlessness" or absence of goals. All our effort is utilized to strive for goals.

To become free from the "stranglehold of thought," to use UG's expression, all effort must cease. A clinical "death" must occur. But you cannot bring it about. If and when it happens, the organism will function smoothly without the interference of thought and its artificial goals. Thought then falls into its place as an instrument of communication and problem-solving.

The Body: For UG, the human organism is unique. No other organism is like it. It is unparalleled in nature. UG maintains that the body is a tremendously intelligent organism capable of living in the world without any help. It does not need any of our knowledge, education, goals, pleasures and happiness. It does not care to achieve anything or to improve itself. The only needs of the body are survival and reproduction. The body has no need for transformation or liberation. "There is nothing there to be transformed," UG says.

The body is always in a state of peace, not a dead peace concocted by thought, but a living and dynamic peace. Through our conditioning we constantly seek pleasures. But the body is not interested in them. Pleasures take it away from its peaceful harmonious state. Pleasures are indeed pains, in that sense. For that reason, the body constantly tries to get rid of them.

According to UG, the body has the needed intelligence to take care of any problems, such as ill-health, that it might confront. It has the needed resources and the power to recuperate and renew itself, given a chance. When all else fails, it will die gracefully. Medical science only prolongs the agony of pain; it does not cure it. In a sense, the body is immortal, because at the time of "death," its atoms may be reshuffled and recycled, but the body is always there in some form or other.

UG calls the mind the "interloper" or "squatter". He says that through its pleasure-seeking movement, it constantly interferes with the functioning of the body and disturbs the peace and peak functioning that are already there.

UG holds out as a possibility that when one becomes free from the stranglehold of thought through some "calamity", which might happen not because of any of our effort but in spite of it, the body falls into its natural rhythm; then thought functions harmoniously without creating a surrogate life. Such a body is in the "natural state." According to UG, when one falls into this state, the body and the senses will resume their full function and sensitivity.

UG at times spoke of the body as being put together by thought, much as space and solidity (the three-dimensional view of the world) are put together by thought. In those contexts, he might appear as though he is saying that body is not part of the basic furniture of the universe. I think this can easily be reconciled by saying that UG takes different points of view at different times. In this context, he is speaking of how thought puts our world together, including our body; whereas in other contexts, as for example, when he is speaking of "calamity" in biological terms, he is taking an "objective" or scientific point of view, to try to make sense of what happened to him to others, especially to the scientists he is addressing.

Means: UG does not supply any specific method to become free from the stranglehold of thought. Instead, he wants us to see the futility

6. Thought, the Natural State and the Body

of striving for all our goals for self-fulfillment. He asks us to find out what we really want. If we are free from all those fictitious goals and realize that there is no such thing as permanent happiness and no meaning in life, our lives become simple and easy. Otherwise, we are wasting our life and talents in futile pursuits. As UG says,

> You are not ready to accept the fact that you have to give up -- a complete and total surrender.
>
> It is a state of hopelessness which says that there is no way out...
>
> Any movement in any direction, on any dimension, at any level, is taking you away from yourself...
>
> It hits you like a ton of bricks. (*Mystique of Enlightenment*, p. 21)

With UG, there is no talk of mysticism or mystical experience, oneness, nonduality or such. Rather, he speaks of returning to the natural state where there is no conflict.

Teaching Process: UG was a teacher who constantly operated from a state of nonduality: his actions were not born out of calculation or premeditation; they were spontaneous. His dealings with people were directed constantly toward drawing them into the vortex of nonduality where there are no distinctions between bondage and liberation, or indeed, even between life and death. UG did not distinguish himself from others. He was not trying to achieve any results, nor was he trying to change anyone. Yet, his dealings had that effect on people, *viz.*, they were constantly prodded to question their belief structures. His only aim seemed to be to destroy the mental structures people had so carefully and assiduously built for themselves, without attempting to replace them with any of his own. He would say, "You can walk, you don't need any crutches."

Reflections (A): Ground Zero: **1.** Does UG's teaching not leave us dry and empty, without any hope? Doesn't it seem to advocate that we have to give up all our goals? If so, why live? If there is nothing we can do to achieve the "natural state," then why even talk about it? UG may have deconstructed spirituality, but hasn't he deconstructed life itself, leaving it dry and empty?

Is UG asking us to revert to the state of the animal, to start at the beginning, as it were? To be sure, he says there is no going back. In fact, his own life after "calamity" was much more than survival (albeit without reproduction).

He says that whatever you are, you have to live in this world. Living in this world requires that you develop and utilize your talents, that you make a living of some sort, and that you live with some sort of arrangement with your society. You have to compete with others, make money, work at a job or whatever else you have to do. But UG never tells us, of course, what to do. You cannot derive any "directive" from what he says.

Then what *is* he saying? Why did he keep talking to people until the end of his life? What did he hope to accomplish?

I don't think he intended to achieve anything. The nature of his being was such that he always talked; he always commented on whatever was happening around him. Of course, his talking might have had the effect of disillusioning some people about the goals they had been pursuing, making their lives less burdened, but that was a consequence which just happened. He didn't plan anything.

2. So, what role do thought and thinking play in daily life? I have to use thought to solve problems for sure, to plan ahead and to organize my life — in short, to lead a successful life in this complex civilization. If I don't, I would be reduced to an animal state. Then, in precisely what sense do I have to become free from the "stranglehold" of thought?

The answer is: only in terms of being free from the religious or spiritual goals (or other goals for self-fulfillment) — that I have to have this, or that I have to become that, or that I have to seek this pleasure or avoid that pain.

But if I have pain and I want to solve the problem of pain, would I not be using thought to solve it? Wouldn't that be the same as avoiding pain? UG never made this very clear — on the one hand, he encouraged people to go see a doctor ("You can give your ailing body a helping hand"); on the other hand, he said he himself would never see a doctor and encouraged people not to take any medicine or see a doctor for their troubles. I don't think he was very consistent on the matter. However, one must admit that he was mostly consistent with himself about his own life, in the sense that he never saw doctors. He said pain is a great healer. You have the problem of pain, he said, only when you link two sensations (of pain) through memory and then say to yourself, "I have pain."

3. Even toward the end of his life, UG seemed to believe in the basic status of the body. He would say something to the effect, "The body doesn't let me go," or "The body is not ready to go." If the body and its solidity are put together by thought, it's not clear how he would take the body as basic or real.

Of course, he could say that these statements too are just interpretation. Or, more appropriately, UG's statements could be taken to mean nothing more than preventing you from believing anything as real; his statements are just teaching tools to demolish our mental structures

4. To act outside the self-centered framework is to act outside the framework of thought. But we don't know if such action is possible except when we act impulsively, habitually or reflexively, or in situations of emergency. UG, on his part, said his actions were not based on thoughts or ideas. He never told us how they arose or how they were possible. He said none of his actions were initiated by himself. They were always prompted by something "outside," a person, circumstance or a thought. It is as though he was simply drawn into action by a situation. What he says reminds us of *wu-wei* in Taoism.

5. Somewhere, we must find peace and fulfillment without having to seek any goals. Of course, I can't solve any social or political problems or problems of the world. Then what good am I without contributing anything to the world?

A counter question here would be, I didn't create all those problems, why should I bother to solve them? Who asked me to? (As UG would say, "Who gave me the mandate?") On his own part, he said that he was perfectly at peace with the world. Given the way we are, the world "couldn't be any the different."

All this discussion is based on the question of how to live in this world or what policies of living we should have. The answer is that there is no answer to that question. We don't need to know how to live in this world. We are actually living.

6. The virtue of UG's teaching is that through the process of his questioning he unburdens us not just from our cherished beliefs and prejudices, but primarily from our goals. Whether or not we are completely free from them is up to us. When we are, we can live in peace.

Reflections (B): One Blind Man's Elephant: 1. UG hints at a life which doesn't involve symbols, meaning and interpretation. This living is in contrast to the life of striving for goals and fulfilling ourselves through them. If we let all our goals (for self-fulfillment) go, then perhaps we could view everything, including ourselves, as a unitary energy — that we are the energy aware of itself in a non-dual fashion.[26]

2. Let us say that I am disillusioned[27] about all these goals that I seek to fulfill myself. And when I am free from the goals, I am also free from my attachment to things and therefore from my fears as well and the consequent self-protectiveness. Thus when I can let go of everything, including life itself, I can land in that state of total peace (energy). Then hopefully I would not be causing the problems which are generated by my striving for self-fulfillment.

Of course, theoretically I may still be a problem-maker in the world, but that is something for the world to judge and respond to. Also, perhaps, in the heat of the moment, I could be acting rashly or emotionally; but I would have no grasping nature nor would I accumulate property beyond my needs or protect it with all my might.

3. When you let go of everything, you are the Energy. This letting go of all concerns may occur through various means which have been known to tradition: passive awareness, "contrary" (or "opposite") thinking (as in Buddhist meditation and stoicism), looking at the situation more objectively, reversing roles, going behind or stepping out of feelings and experiences, and so on. Yet no seeking is necessary and nothing needs to be changed. There is this state of just being awareness or an organism, an awareness or being whose energy may last only a moment. And the energy released thus vitalizes the body. It may not affect the individual organs in any specific manner (like in acupuncture); but it certainly refreshes the body.

4. Suppose we let go of everything: then, as I said before, we will recede into the body or, rather, into an energy field where there are no distinctions or divisions. But that too, as I was suggesting above, is only a temporary state. At least, just out of the sheer necessity to respond to the needs of the body and of the world, we have to engage in thought and then again we become involved in a state of duality.

So becoming free from the stranglehold of thought must just amount to becoming free from the goals that thought generates for self-fulfillment. This does not preclude us from using thought in solving problems of day-to-day living.

As UG would say, life would then become simple and easy. One is not involved in anything except for the moment. Goals and meanings (including the meaning of the world, things and people in it, as well as values and points of view) are only temporary and tentative. When you are not in the world of meaning, then, as UG often said, thoughts are mere noises in the head and time ceases to be.

5. Now we can see how when a person is in this Energy or awareness, he (or she) could be passively watching things, persons and events in the world as a passing show; or, he could be merely aware of his memories, images or sounds come and go. And for one split second, he could become one of those memories, images or sounds. Then, the world of meaning and all that is associated with it would again exist for the person. Yet, he could once again withdraw from that world and recede back into the field of energy. It's interesting to note here that when we are in the world of meaning, we often confuse our mental realities, which are mere symbols with meaning attributed to them, with actual realities, and respond to them as if they were real.

6. This being "in-and-out" of energy occurs in full awareness; there is only periodic disengagement. When the present context is finished, when the "me" is no longer needed, then there is disengagement and the "me" is gone. The ending of the context happens in many ways, as for example, when a person visiting leaves or when a task is accomplished. Then one is back at ground "zero". There is no awareness that one is even living. Nothing matters. When a need occurs, such as having to mail a letter, or being hungry, or having to go to the bathroom, then the particular thoughts and images come into play, and the self is temporarily involved again. But, since there is no desire to continue, there is no conflict in either "being in" or "being out;" there is no duality here.

7. But there is a fundamental difference between the disappearance of the ego temporarily and one becoming an automatically-run organism where the will simply has withered away permanently. But such a thing is not in our hands. There is nothing we can do to make it happen. We can't even "wait" for it. All the strategies, even to passively wait for it to happen, are thought-generated and willed. Yet, that's what true liberation is: to be totally and permanently freed from the ego. Unfortunately, there is no protocol for it, no program and there is nothing anyone can do to achieve it. Yet, from what I can see from my time with UG, it seems to be a possibility.

References:

1) *Mystique of Enlightenment.* Edited by Rodney Arms, Sahasranama Prakashana, Bangalore, India. 2001.

2) *The Mind is a Myth.* Dinesh Vaghela, Goa, India, 1988.

3) *UG Krishnamurti, a Life.* Mahesh Bhatt, Penguin Books India, 2001.

* * *

Postscript 1: Each thought is from a certain point of view. As long as a point of view is there you will keep thinking. The point of view is itself another thought. When you can trace the thought to the point of view and question the point of view, the thought is gone. The point of view may be just any hang-up or hook-up (or attachment of some kind).

Playing the Skeptic: The big skeptical question is that this whole approach reduces one to ashes. One might claim that something might take over and that might act in some fashion. But the plain fact of the matter is that you won't be there to know it, or experience, enjoy or suffer it. Take enjoyment, for instance: What I notice is that if the experience only lasts a split second and then something else is there in its place, you can't even use the term "enjoyment" anymore.

And when you recede into the awareness, an awareness with no point of view, it looks like everything in life is falling apart, and people, actions, events, relationships etc., don't make any difference. Then I could as well be dead!

Then what is the virtue of all this teaching? Just that I'll supposedly be free from suffering? To be sure, psychological pain is pulverized, being broken up into pieces. But physical pain is always there drawing your attention to it. You are never going to be free from it. It doesn't even matter if you don't concatenate different sensations into a state of mind which has continuity, or if you do.

Postscript 2 -- Answer

These skeptical questions are based on a point of view, namely, that life must have some value and that it must amount to something. In other words, the skeptic is not willing to just go. If he does, there is no problem remaining.

7. Being with UG -- His Teaching Process

UG's teaching process cannot be separated from his person. With that in view, in the following I report mostly how UG related to people around him as a way of demonstrating his teaching process.

It's not possible to make any generalizations about either UG or his teaching, as for each generalization one makes about UG there are bound to be many exceptions. At best one can paint on a broad canvass a mosaic of many concrete instances from one's own experience and dealings with UG.[28][29] Others undoubtedly will readily come up with their own different experiences. I wouldn't even bother to mention here the many instances in which people experienced UG's healing of their pains or saving them from accidents or illnesses or other dangers, as they are not only countless, but they are entrenched more in the realm of the subjective.

Being around UG: To be around UG can be quite a challenge. UG always maintained that wanting permanent happiness without a moment of unhappiness is the source of our misery. In his own life, things constantly changed. If you spent a whole day around UG and went along with all the changes he went through or put you through, you would emerge at the end of the day totally exhausted and wiped out. You wonder how anyone could live through so much change in a day without ever looking back. I have not seen another person like UG who could do that. Being around UG and moving with him were in themselves a great learning experience.

UG's Teaching Process: [*This paragraph is mostly a repetition from the previous chapter. I am doing it to provide continuity.*] UG was a teacher who constantly operated from a state of nonduality: his actions were not born out of calculation or premeditation; they were spontaneous. His dealings with people were directed constantly toward drawing them into the vortex of nonduality where there are no distinctions between bondage and liberation, or indeed, even between life and death. UG did not distinguish himself from others. He was not trying to achieve any results, nor was he trying to change anyone. Yet, his dealings had that effect on people, *viz.*, they were constantly prodded to question their belief structures. His only aim seemed to be to dismantle the mental structures people had carefully and assiduously built within themselves, without attempting to replace them with any of his own. He would say, "You can walk, you don't need any crutches."

UG was not aware of any distinctions: yet, he appeared to make all kinds of distinctions: he seemed to punish, praise, brag, exaggerate, play games with money, challenge, and so on and on. He even seemed to act through various conditionings and prejudices of his own.

After his "calamity," the question did occur to UG how he should talk to people or relate to them: he decided, "I will tell it like it is; I will talk about the way I operate." From then on that became his talking mode of teaching. Sometimes, he talked constantly about himself and his past experiences. He often spoke about himself and his Natural State. He spoke of how it was being constantly in peace and how there were no problems there.[30]

He used this approach until the very end of his life, although later on he mixed in details from his past, his encounters with J. Krishnamurti, and other talk about himself. This served the purpose of pulling the minds of his audience away from themselves. He would often talk for hours, to the extent that people would doze off intermittently, and their minds would be dazed after he finished. They were temporarily removed from their daily concerns, thoughts and worries. As a result, people might have been, at least for the time being, cleansed of their past.

UG talked about his main ideas concerning thought, self, conditioning, liberation, meditation, calamity and so forth. He would engage and answer people's questions. On some of those occasions, he sounded as if some ancient teacher was speaking in a strange voice across centuries of time; and you felt as if you had heard him in another lifetime as well as this.

UG taught during all his waking hours and perhaps when he retired too, as you never knew what happened when he went to bed. He used to say he lay awake in bed most of the time so as not to disturb others in the apartment or house. What things might have transpired in that bedroom! We used to joke about UG saying that he ruled the universe from his bedroom (while everyone else was asleep!).

UG left no holy cow unslaughtered. If he even as much as sensed someone being hung up about a tradition, a country, a religion, a nationality, a spiritual tradition or a teacher, idea or belief, he would pour his verbal abuse and sarcasm on that subject. Many people who gathered around him were former followers of J. Krishnamurti or Rajneesh. Most of his verbal attacks were on J. Krishnamurti and the next frequent victim was Rajneesh. He added Ramana Maharshi, Sri Ramakrishna, Jesus, Buddha, and others later on to his list.

7. Being with UG -- His Teaching Process

UG also left no demons buried. He poured out praise for people like Hitler: his famous one-liner was: "Only two good things came out of Germany: Hitler and Cambazola cheese!"

In spite of all the vituperation he showered, UG never showed any malice. After everyone left, there were many times when I was alone with him. Never once did he mention the topic of abuse after everyone had left. In fact, there was once an occasion when he talked to me appreciating J. Krishnamurti.

After watching him over many years, I am convinced that his attacks were intended to unhook a person from his hang-ups and dislodge him (or her) from his fascination for a certain guru, or his or her uncritical repulsion to evil.

There were also times when he threw *koan*-like questions at people: he would ask you, "If someone asks you, 'what does UG say?' or 'what is his teaching?' what would you say?" Then, without waiting much longer, he would answer the question himself: "Any answer you give, any movement your thought makes in any direction, is a false answer."

* * *

In later years, he resorted to reading a passage or two from one of his books or "the archives," consisting of letters people had written to him and newspaper and magazine reviews, or what someone else had written about him (Mahesh Bhatt's *UG Krishnamurti – A Life*, for instance). Or, he would ask to play a video or audio tape or CD. He did not play them just to entertain people, but as part of his teaching. This had the added benefit of giving him a bit of rest from his constant talking.

Astrology, Palmistry and Nadi: UG was notorious for his seeming interest in astrology, palmistry and *nadi*. If he noticed that someone could read palms or horoscopes, he would right away extend his arm to the person to read his palm or ask them to interpret his horoscope. His pet questions were always about money and travel. Many times, the readers would also talk about how long he would live or where he would die, and so on. A whole book of these readings has been put together.

When astrologers made predictions about UG, for instance, that he would face a certain danger on a certain day, he always brushed aside what they said and did whatever he wanted to do anyway. Those astrologers then claimed that the planets had no influence on him because he was a liberated man.

In my opinion, his interest or belief in these matters was perfunctory. He was more interested in the astrologer or palmist than his reading. I witnessed how he once involved an American astrologer in such a deep discussion about his horoscope that the astrologer not only noticed his own shortcomings but was at his wits end to respond to UG's technical remarks.

When UG himself read someone's hand (which he did -- he had learned palmistry in his youth from Julie, former secretary of the famous palmist Cheiro in Chicago), his readings were always vague and general, like, "Nothing comes easy for you; you have to work hard for things," "You have a pot of money hiding somewhere," or "Where are you hiding all that money?" "You will live a long, long life," etc.

Sometimes I suspected that he might even have influenced the astrologer so that the readings would come out the way he wanted. But, of course, I can't prove any of that.

Care and Compassion: On occasion, a grieving person would come to him, having lost a dear one recently; or, upon hearing the news of the death of someone, UG himself would go and visit the grieving person or family. Typically, UG would not say many words to comfort the person, but would sit silently with him or her. Once, a woman came to visit UG for a week, having just lost her 11 year-old son, and sat in the room with him each day. To everyone's relief, within a week, she was comforted and healed and left for her home with a smile on her face.

I had just had a cancer operation. (I consulted with UG before and he advised me to go through with the operation.) After the surgery, I called him from the hospital room in Stanford to tell him how the operation went. When I returned home a couple of days later, UG and Mahesh took a plane from Palm Springs and came to see me in Seaside. UG made sure that no others visited us (as they normally would) at that time. When they came, I went into the living room and sat on a high stool talking to them. After a while, I felt exhausted, still suffering from the after-effects of surgery, and said, "You guys keep talking. I am a little tired. I will go and lie down in the bedroom." And after I lay in the bed, UG came into the bedroom and sat by my bedside for a length of time and chatted with me. I was so touched!

Later, after he returned to Palm Springs, UG wanted me to go to Switzerland to his place and get a good rest there. He cashed his frequent-flyer miles and a first-class ticket and got me a business class ticket and Wendy and Kiran tourist class tickets and told Wendy, "You drop this guy off in Gstaad, and then you can return to Seaside." Of course, Wendy and Kiran stayed with me the whole time and we spent two months in Gstaad as UG's guests. I was kept busy translating Chandrasekhar's notebooks at that time – that's some kind of rest! But UG's care and compassion were boundless.

I had heard of an occasion when UG encountered a paraplegic in a parking lot as he was walking toward Bob and Paul's restaurant in Larkspur. The man was obviously suffering from cerebral palsy, I was told. Upon noticing UG, he apparently stretched out his arms towards him. For some mysterious reason, UG went toward him, held him by his arms, almost hugged him, and then quickly walked away. You never can tell with UG what transpires between him and those who come to see him.

Severing Connections: UG on occasion did interfere with people's lives and unsettled them in their beliefs or make suggestions about their specific problems of living. There were times when he even meddled with people's lives rather intimately, sometimes to their annoyance and reluctance; but ultimately many of them were grateful that he had. He actually tried to sever some relationships, which he must have thought were destructive or otherwise untenable.[31] Sometimes he would advise people, depending on the person, either not to meditate (and take ecstasy instead!), or to teach meditation, or make more money, find a girl, do something useful with their lives, and so on. He was not, however, always successful in breaking up an unhealthy relationship or changing a person's life in a basic way. His or her problems remained in spite of his best efforts and despite his radical "ill-treatment" of that person. It's hard to assess his influence on people, as much of it is unspoken and intangible, or the effects would only manifest themselves years later. But many individuals were surely affected and benefited by his paternal care.

He gave advice to people on practical matters of money, work, relationships, and so on. Some thought he was not competent to give advice on money matters; but in my opinion, he was very astute in practical matters and those who didn't listen to his advice might have lost out.

UG insisted that people take advantage of and exploit their natural talents, whether they be beauty or intelligence or some other virtue, talent or advantage. He wanted people to succeed in this world, and he always chided people who were wasting away their time in "useless" pursuits, not doing what they could to utilize their talents. And he would be all praise for those who made a good buck in the day.

UG often remarked: "All problems result from wanting two things at the same time. If you just want one thing, you have no problem." And he sometimes added: "There is nothing you can't get, if you just want one thing."

Personal Problems: Most of the time, UG refused to give private audience to people, even if they begged him for it. In general, he would not even respond to requests for advice, but there were exceptions: sometimes someone would ask a question or bring a problem and he would respond in such a way that the answer would be quite appropriate to the person's problem and would even contain a suggestion: generally to "accept" the problem or to do such-and-such or do nothing. Sometimes UG would analyze the problem in such a way that the analysis would expose hidden agendas of the person that were the source of the problem.

At other times, UG would simply maintain a prolonged silence, which lasted as long as a whole hour. Then something got communicated and the person would leave in peace.

And if the person didn't mind speaking out about his or her personal problems in front of others, UG might discuss them: (Of late, he was wont to say, "You don't have a problem.") I remember on one occasion, he discussed a couple's problem of the wife's mother staying in their house. (I was the only other person present in the meeting.) He summed up his discussion, "You don't want her to stay with you, do you?" He made the couple confront their own resistance to the person. Yet he didn't point any fingers. He was very calm and non-judgmental in his remarks. After they left, he asked me what I thought about the discussion: I said, "You made the problem very clear to them." That's what he did. I was a witness to many such occasions.

UG was a master at laying bare hidden assumptions and motivations in people's psyches. No wonder people often shuddered to stand in front of him as they felt they were being stripped naked with his looks. They felt that UG's "truth serum" was at work.

When a friend of UG's was is in dire need or crisis, often they reported that they either got a call from UG or he visited them at their place on some pretext. I myself remember the time when someone suggested that I eat a bagel to take care of the problem of hypoglycemia, which turned out to be a serious mistake: I almost fainted. Then my phone rang and there was Guha's voice on the phone telling me that UG wanted to know what my plans were for the following summer. Of course, this could have been a sheer coincidence. Or it was not!

UG's ways were indeed mysterious. No one could fathom them.

* * *

Reflecting People: UG physically reflected people: I always felt that he could not only read my thoughts and feelings but he could feel what was going on in my body and even arrange a situation which would address that problem. Here is an example: once in Palm Springs, because of sitting on the floor in front of a computer for a number of hours, my back was in utter pain. I didn't say anything about it. But UG took us all out on a "window-shopping spree." After browsing a little in the Sharper Image store, he left me with one or two others, saying he would be back in about twenty minutes. Waiting, I sat in the massage chair for those twenty minutes and turned it on until UG returned, and most of my back pain was gone. Of course, it could also be a coincidence. But knowing UG for so long, it's hard to believe that it was merely that.

At other times, he so reflected people and their problems that he would actually worry for them at that moment. When we went with a couple of others for car-shopping in Seaside, California, he and I were sitting in the lobby of the car dealership while the others went into to the office to bargain for a car. UG kept watching a sales woman pacing back and forth in the lobby, and he started worrying about her: "What will happen to her? What will happen to her?" (Meaning how she was going to live that style of life.)

I noticed, on another occasion, while in Gstaad, Switzerland, he was pacing up and down the room worrying about a friend's credit card problems: "How is he going to pay for all that? The bank will be after him." This went on and on for a whole hour that morning.

Once, UG and I were waiting for a friend in a restaurant in Berkeley. The man was a few minutes late. Meanwhile, UG started worrying about him, looking out the window repeatedly to see if he was coming yet. He did worry about people's welfare.

Outbursts: UG is known for his unexpected, almost "irrational" outbursts of anger: (He never found his anger to be a problem: he always called it an expression of "energy".) His outbursts could be on some social or political issue, against a government or its policy, or against a politician, or against a person in the gathering. The outburst wasn't always intended for the person whom UG was addressing; many times it was directed obliquely at someone else in the group whom UG didn't want to address directly. There was a time when I actually felt that UG was dealing with me and my hurt while he was yelling at someone else. In a few minutes, I could feel my hurt simply erased![32]

Yet, although he was often in totally foreign places among foreign cultures and peoples, he would not criticize people's ways of living: he would always fend off others' criticisms by saying, "That's their way."

Power: Few knew the role of power in human relationships as well as UG. He pointed out how relationships are mostly based on each person getting his or her way. Many times he himself was an absolute monarch, but only when he had a say or choice in the matter. (He had the manner of a prince dealing with his subjects. That was so evident when he gave gifts to people -- children or adults.) Even then, he would sometimes yield to people's desires and pressures, and some other times he would be as friendly as anyone could possibly be. It all depended. Often he pointed out how if you don't care about what the other person (or authority) could give you or do to you, you could not only be fearless, but free to do precisely whatever you wanted to do. He always dictated his terms and encouraged friends to do the same.

One good reason why he stayed away from institutions, governments and people who held high offices was that he kept his freedom and didn't have to compromise with their rules and regulations. But there was another: institutions breed power and power-mongering. He did not allow any organization to be built around him just for that reason. (No one then could claim exclusive rights over his teachings.) He did not let himself be subjected to any scientific research on him, because he bemoaned the probable outcome of the results of that research being exploited by businesses and governments for money and power. The Internet served as a suitable medium for publishing books on him or collections of his dialogs, because there they were released free of copyright and other commercial strings. He never voted. His argument, if I remember right, was, "I don't have to choose between two evils." In fact, he never paid taxes, as he didn't stay in any country long enough to establish residency. His passport was Indian, and of course, he had to have it to be able to travel.

UG's own energy was such that you could never take him or your relationship with him for granted. When he (or "It") was dealing with you, he ("It") knew nothing personal. (And as I said before, there is no "person" there in UG.) He could attack you viciously or even throw you out.

Debates: They could happen in the context of answering a question or responding to what someone said: there would be a heated conversation, usually ending with UG abusing the other person, pointing out the flaws or fallacies in his argument or attacking in some other fashion. But sometimes the other person would attack UG back in a personal fashion or the debate would end in a stalemate. And UG never shied away from "wrestling in the mud" with any interlocutor. UG would say, "You say that and I say this. Where do we go from there? You take it or leave it." If someone asks, "Why you do talk?" UG would answer, "I talk because you are here, because you ask these "idiotic" questions. I didn't ask you to come here. You can as well leave." If the person says, "You have invited me to come," UG might even answer, "The invitation is withdrawn; now you can leave."

There was a time when UG was visiting at our house and someone phoned and asked if he could come. After he came the person talked to UG rather confrontationally for a few minutes. UG must have sensed something going on in the man's mind. He said abruptly, "Now you can leave." My wife had just given the visitor a cup of coffee which he was sipping, and she said, "Please finish the coffee before you go." UG said forcefully, "No, no, he can leave now." The fellow was simply shaking in his pants; you could hear the rattle of the cup in the saucer. He put down the coffee cup and rushed out of the house.

I saw many contexts in which UG got involved in verbal wrangling with people: the argument would go on at length, UG working hard at breaking down the defense structures of the person he was dealing with, and he would not quit until the point of capitulation, like in arm wrestling. He would yell at the top of his lungs, (once, in the middle of it he turned to me with a twinkle in his eye and a smile on his lips, as if it was all a big joke), pouring insults and abuse on his victim. At times, UG himself had to pay a heavy price for a confrontation: there was a physical drain from which he would not recover for a few days (a guy who routinely hardly slept for more than forty-five minutes at a stretch would not get up from bed until late the next morning). Unfortunately, you couldn't tell what was really at the bottom of such encounters.

There were times when people would be at loggerheads with UG in argument; they would get furious and leave the scene. One of those persons, a Sufi teacher, called me back the next day wondering what had happened. He came once again later to be clobbered again. His Sufi philosophy was under attack. He never returned after the second time. When I saw him later in the supermarket, he remarked that UG seemed to represent some dark, evil force!

If UG was cornered into a contradiction of some sort, he would become helpless. He would say something like, "What do you want me to do?" or "What do you want me to say?"

On the other hand, his genius would manifest itself on some rare occasions. For instance, I noticed his discussion with a biologist once in Chennai. For a minute or two, I could follow their discussion. But then the exchange between them went so fast that I completely lost track of the discussion and the biologist himself was dumfounded. He probably never expected such a challenge from a non-scientist. I don't know if he ever returned.

There were, however, times when his professional audience, in this instance, scientists and professors from Oxford gathering in Australia[33], weren't all that impressed. In this video I was watching, I noticed one of them saying repeatedly, "It's absurd...." The man was obviously annoyed by UG's assertions such as "There is no such thing as matter...."

Money: When people are told about UG, a frequent question they ask is, "How does he get his money?" Some complained about UG's money-hustling deals, but few doubted his integrity in money matters. There was a time once, in the early years of his coming to California, the friend who was taking care of UG's housing needs, asked me to contribute some money toward paying extra rent to pay for the few days before UG arrived so he didn't have to forfeit the place. He made me promise not to reveal the matter to UG, as UG would never approve of people raising money for him. I agreed and never told UG until recently, years after my friend's death. UG's integrity in money matters, in my opinion, was impeccable.

Nevertheless, he always pointed out to people that money and food were their deepest attachments. He knew that people treated money as an end in itself and amassed it beyond proportions. As for himself, money was as a mere instrument, although he constantly claimed that "money is at the top of my list and food at the bottom...."

In later years, he changed his ways. Although he never directly asked people for money, his dealings with them bordered on hustling. (He did this only to a few people: you could feel that he was teasing them and also testing their attachment to money.) I know the reason: in the early years, he collected and saved people's money for them in a Swiss bank account and the money was later returned to them intact. On the other hand, the money people gave him as gift whether on his birthdays or on other occasions, and the money he "hustled", went to funding children's education or as gifts to the needy or to friends and relatives, but little of it went toward his own expenses. He himself lived rather frugally, in spite of the fact that he traveled in luxury class, paid for by his friends. People gave him expensive clothing, which he would in turn give away, replacing it with newer pieces of clothing given by others. Sometimes the clothing was passed on unused.

When he was young, he sold off the property he had inherited from his grandfather for a discount to the farmers who leased the land and cultivated it. Ever since then, he never owned property except once for a few months by mistake[34].

Nothing Personal: UG would constantly test people. No one could take him for granted. Sometimes he would extol what a person did for a living, but the next moment around he would be critical of the same person. He might be the chummiest person at the moment, but at the next turn he might attack viciously. He didn't spare anyone. In that sense, he had no personal relationships. He was loyal to many of his friends, but not all. Some broke away and never saw him again, and some just veered off and remained distant to him without openly breaking up with him.

It must be mentioned here that UG had a way of making everyone around him feel special. That's a unique experience people had when they tried to relate to UG.

UG also tested strangers: Of late, he didn't make it easy for people to see him. When they called to see him, he would put them off giving some excuse or other, or ask them to call later and so on. But there weren't many who were serious and persistent that did not succeed in seeing him. UG was making sure that they were earnest.

On more than one occasion, he would draw a person into a discussion by asking for his response: He did this with me several times. It surely was something he used to communicate with the audience (he wanted my "moral support" he sometimes said), but also as a way of teaching me by drawing me out, as I didn't always readily come forth with my views.

7. Being with UG -- His Teaching Process

To my mind, UG had not only a sharp intellect, but astounding artistic creativity: I didn't realize this until I saw him giving his suggestions about the biography Mahesh Bhatt was writing in Carmel, California, near where I live. At a critical point in writing the biography, there was a discussion about how to proceed: UG was going on so fast with his ideas, I completely lost him after a while. Mahesh Bhatt, after hearing his suggestions, protested, "UG, I can't write like that!"[35] The gist of UG's idea was to show how he, after his Calamity, had no life of his own and that he only lived in the lives of the people around him. That perspective would have been impossible to convey in a book.

* * *

One thing I can say for certain: I have never seen another human being who could metamorphose so suddenly and completely that you felt as if you were seeing a totally different person before you. No matter how strange or difficult the situation was, or what had happened in the past, if the situation demanded it, UG would throw in all his resources into resolving it. I remember an occasion when he planned to spend the night in Seaside in a motel and even paid for the hotel room. But something changed all that; a Polish fellow was driving to Los Angeles in his old beat-up car, and UG suddenly changed all his plans and drove away with him to Los Angeles. Of course, he had to forgo his hotel rent, as it was too late to cancel the reservation. Forfeiting the rent meant nothing to him.

Getting Physical: In his last years, UG started getting physically demonstrative. Before then, I thought he was physically shy: I knew many men, including myself, from my culture as being shy in that way. I had noticed the very first time I met UG in my house that he had shied away when I tried to put my arm around his shoulder. The most he would ever do was to pat on someone's shoulder or shake or touch someone's hand (his touch was actually one of his means of communication). He would joke with his friends when they were parting, asking them, "You want some energy transmission?" and shake their hand.

But all that suddenly changed a few years ago when I noticed that he had gotten quite physical with Louis. He would get physical to the point of hitting him and beating or pouring stuff on him (making him eat and drink all kinds of weird concoctions – handfuls of sugar or chocolate, for example). He would not only beat him himself, but would ask people like Nataraj to hit Louis on his (bald) head with a split stick (which wouldn't really hurt as much as an unsplit stick). Nataraj would obey and beat Louis on his head with the stick, keeping the beat while singing a song. Or UG would ask a child, a son of one of the visitors, to beat up Louis. And the kid would do that, rather viciously, to the point that I would protest, saying "Stop it UG!" or I would leave the scene – I just didn't want to sit there and watch. UG would remark to everyone: "Narayana Moorty can't take it anymore; he is leaving." Louis had to admonish the father for not intervening.

You could notice the uneasiness in those who were watching. You would wonder what UG was trying to teach in such situations.

Releasing Aggression: But this procedure was not limited to Louis. I saw UG prompting a kid to beat up his own grandfather. First, I thought it was just all part of UG's teaching through entertainment; now I am sure it was more than that. I didn't realize that until the same child hit me very hard with a ring of keys while I approached his mother, who was holding him, to say goodbye. I then saw that UG was dealing with the aggression in the kids by giving free expression to it and releasing it (of course, under his supervision).

I again wonder what sorts of things were being dealt with in Louis!

Taking Breaks: After all his talking during the day and after everyone had left, UG would collapse in a sofa and instantly fall asleep. He worked hard like this day in and day out for so many years. There were times when he took breaks from this routine: then he would not have any meetings ("No shop today," he would say), but would go on car trips to different places, sometimes visiting people, or just going around shops in downtowns or riding in cars for long distances without any specific destination.

UG's "Driving Tests:" Sometimes his car trips became his method of teaching: There were times when he would subject the driver to highly risky situations. His driving "tests" thus became famous. He would expose people's fears and confusions to themselves. Except for a couple times, people never got involved in accidents. Even when they were, they were never injured or killed. I know at least a couple of people who felt grateful to him for saving them from serious accidents just by being in their car.

While driving, the driver would be asking UG for directions or other instructions as he didn't have a prior knowledge of where precisely UG wanted to go. UG would say, for instance, "Turn right," and just as the driver was about to make a right turn, UG would say, "I think you should go left here," as if he wasn't sure himself which way to go. Then the driver would make preparations to turn left. But by then UG had already changed his mind and he would say, "I think it's the next exit." This changing of directions would go on endlessly to the point that the driver would begin literally to freak out. No wonder the seat next to the driver in which UG usually sat was sarcastically called by some the "death seat."

Of course, sometimes the driver would get lost and stop and reach out for a map in his glove compartment. But UG would have none of that: "You don't need any maps; you use your eyes;" "Don't think, just

7. Being with UG -- His Teaching Process

watch;" "Don't use your head, use your eyes" – were his normal admonitions. If the driver complained and said "We lost our way," UG would reprimand, "You are never lost; you are always somewhere; keep driving."[36]

The more the driver would fret, the more pressure UG would put on him or her, to the point that at the end of the trip, UG's "blessings" would always be waiting for them: "You can be sure that he makes mistakes. He doesn't use his head. He's a dunderhead. He took the wrong turn," and so on.

It's not clear what anyone would learn from all this haranguing, but I think UG's main concern was not so much to get anyone to the right place, or to plain abuse anyone, but to expose us to our own reaction mechanisms and push us to deal with them. And of course, the point may also be to make the person lose his bearings (in all respects)! I don't know if he ever succeeded.

One more thing should be mentioned here, to be fair to UG: With those whose driving he wasn't "testing," UG normally never interrupted a person's driving with his criticisms or compliments until after the trip was completed. Then he would come out with his comments. His "driving tests," on the other hand, were a different matter!

* * *

This happened not too long ago: Just as UG's birthday was approaching, as was his wont, UG unplugged the telephone (to avoid being inundated with phone calls) and took a bunch of people (including three children) in three cars to travel, practically day and night, moving from one country to another, through France, Germany, Belgium and Switzerland. People were huddled together in the cars, sometimes being hard-pressed even to get to the bathroom or get a decent meal or sleep. This went on for three days, and then they finally returned to Gstaad after the harrowing journey. Some birthday party! Only UG knew what was behind this trip, or what, if anything, it accomplished. Of course, no one dared to question UG or complain.

* * *

There were occasions when UG would take a set of people with him looking for a place for a lengthy stay (a couple of days to a whole month). He would investigate different places, collect people's opinions and their conveniences, and finally find a perfect place to the satisfaction of everyone. UG was never afraid of the unknown.[37] Although people were a bit tense about where they were going or what they were getting into, they had implicit trust in him, which always paid off.[38]

When UG went out, most of the times he ate with many others: he would always ask, "Who's going to pay?" Someone or other would volunteer. I did notice however, of late, when he sensed that this became a burden to people, he would allow them to go "Dutch". His own meals in a restaurant were extremely simple, limited to a piece of bread (with butter) and soup or *rosti*, or some such ridiculously simple and small meal. He always had hot water after every meal to wash down the food.

Going Along: UG never directly opposed people's fixations or tried to change people's ways: instead, he played them up. For instance, the oblique way he dealt with people's attachment to money was to make them more money-minded, to encourage them to make more money, and to "talk-up" money practically all the time. (Notice how his *Money Maxims*, which he dictated in about 45 minutes, has become so popular among UG circles.) At the same time, he made people shed money freely, including giving it to him (which he in turn gave away to children). His dealings with people's attachments remind us of the traditional Tantric ways of dealing with energies by going along with them consciously, instead of opposing them.

I remember an occasion when he once arranged for a drinking session between me and Mahesh Bhatt (Mahesh was drinking at that time) in his hotel room; he never criticized either of us for it. After a couple of drinks, of course, we all went downstairs to the restaurant for a meal. On the way to the restaurant, in the hotel corridor, I noticed UG staggering a little. I couldn't help joking: "UG, this is not fair. We do all the work and you get the effect!"

Mahesh later quit both his drinking and smoking when he was aghast at how his little baby daughter shunned away from the strong smell of smoke and drink when he drew close to her. He never touched either habit again. UG always praised Mahesh about that. "If you quit a habit, it should be like that -- at once, not promising or practicing to quit little by little," he would say.

UG Never Questioned Facts: Before something happened, UG might sometimes plan for this or that, or ask someone to come or not to come, and so on, but when things actually unfolded, whether by design or by accident, he always accepted the outcome. I never saw an exception to it.

Once, I was traveling with UG and others in a car driven by Major Dakshinamurti, and on the way to Mysore City, the car had a flat tire and it stopped. UG's reaction was merely to ask, "What do we do next?" Of course, the Major changed the tire and we continued on our journey.

* * *

In Carmel, when Mahesh's biography of UG was being put together, there was a couple who visited him for at least a couple of weeks. They had a garbage-dump-like truck that they parked in the driveway. At night they crawled into a barrel-shaped black-painted shell on the back of the truck to sleep. The man was some kind of a guru, but also technically savvy (a drop-out graduate student in computer science). They were on the run from the law, I don't know for what reason. The man and his mate (who was a young woman who seemed to be under his influence and a disciple of his, and was mortally afraid of him), had not had a bath in at least a month or two! They stank. Sarcastically, I was referring to the couple (in their absence, of course) as "Mr. and Mrs. Stink!" The sofa on which the man sat acquired some of his odor and the living room was filled with the smell. But UG wouldn't say a word about the smell. He let the couple be (they even used his kitchen to prepare food) as long as they were there. When they finally left, he went into his room, brought out a couple of incense sticks, lit them and put them up at the fireplace. That's UG!

* * *

The UG "Treatment": This is a common experience to many. First, UG would be very enthusiastic about a certain person and extol him or her to the skies. But then things would start to cool down and UG would gradually start pointing out problems in the person's behavior. Then, if that person came too close to him and did some "unwanted" things, like making repeated mistakes in what he was asked to do, or did something contrary to his specific instructions, or was dishonest in some way, he would take the person to task. A huge harangue might ensue. It could go on for hours. There was a time when he even ordered a pick-up truck to haul a person's belongings out of his apartment to be delivered to her apartment at her own expense. In another instance, he even pushed a person out of a moving car for her alleged misbehavior. There is no doubt that UG was giving the harsh treatment to drive home the person's problems and weaknesses to himself or herself.

But then, at the next moment, the person would be treated normally until there was another occasion for a flare-up. You would never get the feeling that UG had ill-treated that person earlier. Of course, the person would be mortally afraid that UG was keeping a watchful eye on her, and that would lead to more mistakes and more harangues. It could become an endless saga. Sometimes people around him felt that this treatment went beyond limits. Who knows what the final outcome had been or would be?

I know UG verbally belittled, abused and condemned more than one person for their superficiality, dishonesty and inability to exploit their own talents. He would continue to taunt them each time he saw them. And at times he would throw them out. But these same people would swear by how touched they were by UG's love and affection.

Perhaps this was part of the UG "training process."

But if you didn't come close to UG by being friendly with him or trying to do him favors, if you were just a visitor or remained distant otherwise, he would not touch you. Of course, visitors could provoke his ire when they challenged his actions or ideas; or a hot exchange might result when he had to attack their ideas. It all depends.

I also know that if he sensed that you were feeling hurt for some reason or other, he would make sure that you felt better (without your even knowing it) before you left. I am remembering one occasion in Vallecrosia during my last visit with him, when a young woman was leaving. UG sensed she was hurt. Her feelings were indeed hurt as some people there had been critical of her ways. As she was leaving she said something to the effect, "I won't be a bother to anyone anymore." UG said goodbye to her saying, "Everyone liked you."

He did praise people, but not directly, but only by saying that everyone had liked what she wrote or did or said.

Pleasure-seeking: Although UG seemed to enjoy himself when he was going places or having conversations or playing with children or being outdoors, in all my acquaintance with him, I never saw him being a pleasure seeker. He didn't crave for any foods or experiences or anything. If someone performed music in front of him, he practically paid a deaf ear: you could detect absolutely no reaction in his face. If he seemed to like a certain food and you offered it to him again, he would say, no, and comment: "Just because I liked something doesn't mean I want it again." He used to say that he wouldn't know what something tasted like the moment it went down the gullet from his tongue.

He was always proud to show off his refrigerator to people. Unless someone else was also using it, it was always bare, with little else than a can of frozen pineapple juice, a container of heavy cream and perhaps a bowl of leftover oatmeal.[39] He would always quote someone who said, "People don't need even a sixth of what they normally eat." When he was alone, he said, he would eat the same small meal (like oatmeal, cream and pineapple juice) four times a day.

As I said before, UG attacked people's attachments to money and food. When he went to someone's place for lunch, he frequently admonished, "I don't like the stink and stench of an ashram." Yet, when there were several people around who hadn't had lunch or dinner, he would ask whether there was enough food for all of them and make sure there was, even if it meant that someone had to cook.

When he went shopping for food, UG never bought anything more than what was needed for that day. He also discouraged, sometimes rather strenuously, others from buying excessive amounts of food and hoarding it "for the morrow." There was an occasion in Palm Springs when he ordered all the excess foods in the kitchen be collected and thrown in the garbage!

7. Being with UG -- His Teaching Process

The Shepherd: I was visiting UG in Switzerland with my family. That morning I was still in bed. UG walked upstairs where we were staying and walked into our room. I sat up and greeted him. At that time or later, I remarked: "UG is checking his wares!" UG was constantly checking to see if everyone around him was OK.

Champion of Children: I remember an occasion[40] when Chandrasekhar's family had just returned from a wedding, and their two children conked out in the living room, having been deprived of sleep the night before. UG stood guard at the entrance that whole afternoon and prevented anyone from entering the room lest they would disturb the kids' sleep.

He not only played with children wherever he went, he would give them money from his pocket and encourage their talents. Some children had great affinity for him. Yet, he would not hesitate to expose them to foul language, violence, sex or pornography in films. His reasoning is that they would have to deal with all that in later life anyway. Why protect them? Once, I did take him to task when he was encouraging a child to rebel against her teacher. I said, "What's the girl going to do when she gets out of school without education, if she is thrown out of school?" I think UG got my point.

Indeed, a similar point was driven home by a Korean monk who was in one of UG's meetings at my home: UG was attacking educating children in religion. And the monk asked, how are the children going to grow up without any guidance or education? I think UG saw his point and conceded.

"Virus Research:" With people giving him money, particularly for his birthdays, he accumulated enough to give it away to kids. He decided to give it to girls of Indian origin studying abroad, as compensation, he said, for all the persecution which Indian women were subjected to by men for centuries. He now had a fancy idea of establishing a fund for research to discover a virus that would wipe out the whole of humanity! He wanted to establish scholarships for girls to be educated abroad to do such "virus" research.

Guha and I discouraged UG. One fine morning, Guha and I stormed into UG's room in Palm Spring. I told him that what he was doing was not any different from J. Krishnamurti establishing foundations and schools. Guha and I told him that the girls would already be rich enough to be able to come to the US anyway, and that they wouldn't, in that case, needing his help. Moreover, his intention of establishing a scholarship fund anonymously would not succeed, as legally his name would be there, albeit under the surface: anyone who dug deep enough could discover it. UG immediately tore up the papers of his correspondence with lawyers in Stanford and called Chandrasekhar in

India right away and asked him to cancel the plans relating to setting up the fund. Later, Aruna in Bangalore chided UG about the same plan: "UG, we're just starting our lives. Why do you want to us to do things to end them?"

In this context, UG called Aruna and me "my gurus." He ultimately did give the money away to girls of Indian origin for their education and arranged to give much of what remained at the end of his life to deserving girls who were yet to be discovered.

* * *

Response to Reports of Experiences: Different people at different times related their personal experiences to UG. There were times he not only agreed with the person, but he even elaborated or commented on what they said. Some other times, he pooh-poohed them. I can mention a couple of my own experiences here:

1) I caught myself falling asleep once. Later, in the car, I said to UG, "Nothing seems so important, even what UG says doesn't seem to have any value." He replied, "No, what UG says has no value."

2) During a conversation I said, "...all this is shit. And I don't know when all this will end," or something to that effect. I remember UG shooting back with a resounding reply, "If *that* is not there [meaning if you don't compare this with something else], this is *not* shit."

3) Another time, I remember my bragging to UG, "I have seen..." UG cut me short while everyone listened, "You haven't seen it...." I grumbled something in reply, but I dared not challenge the authority with which he had responded.

4) One of the first things I learned from UG is not to attach any importance to experiences (no matter of what kind). Since then my oft-used motto has been, "experiences are a dime a dozen."

5) One morning in Hemet, I was sitting alone in silence after getting up early in the morning. Noticing that I was sitting idle doing nothing, he commented teasingly, "Meditating?" I asked whether he was objecting to my meditating because it was "pleasure-seeking." He answered, yes.

6) On a rare occasion, I was asking UG a question about what he meant by "knowledge". He turned to me and looked at me in a certain way. I will never forget it. I could hear his voice changing and his compassion flowed from him to me, as if it were some sort of fluid. It was almost physical. His answer was, knowledge was "whatever you have learned in the past as to what gives you pleasure or pain." But his compassion was worth a million answers. I know many people were bound to UG through such a flow of compassion.

It was brief conversations like these that really drove some points home to me.

7. Being with UG -- His Teaching Process

Mountains of Energy: Some of the conversations which friends had with UG were so memorable that they made permanent imprints in their minds: these occasions were not only noteworthy for their absolutely profound discussions of various topics, but also for the mountains of energy that would be generated during these discussions. The atmosphere would simply be electrified, as if there was a great celebration unfolding! Unfortunately, many of these discussions were not recorded, as placing a recording device in their midst would have simply ruined the process. In fact, although the moments are unforgettable in their intensity, most of us have hard time even recalling the details of those conversations.

Meaning of Life: UG often asserted that there is no meaning to life. Yet, when people were around him, he would assign various tasks to them just to prevent them from mentally chewing on themselves. Many women became familiar with his "sweatshops". Each time one of these women came to see him, he would give her some kind of sewing job, to fix a button on a shirt, to cut off a collar on a sweater and sew the edges, and such. If there wasn't a job ready, he would create one. He would act as if he was ripping a tag off a sweater, shirt or pants, and there would be a tear in the clothing (I wonder if it wasn't done purposely). He would then complain that he had torn the garment and ask the woman to mend it. He would of course get his royal haircuts from some of these women (although at other times he would go to a barber). He would also assign various chores to men. With people who were knowledgeable in other areas like computers, he would ask them to do some chore or other on the computers. I remember his asking Kiran in Gstaad to transfer all the addresses and phone numbers in his address book to an organizer.

In Palm Springs he once led a whole expedition of two or three cars going in a caravan to hunt for rubber sandals for me with bumps on them. We had looked for them earlier but hadn't found a single pair to my satisfaction. I had protested to UG that it wasn't really so important to find those sandals. But he would have none of that. He said that it would give everyone something to do!

"Malling": His shopping (and "malling") trips were similar. He would go with a bunch of people into different stores, particularly clothing stores, and browse as if he was looking for a specific something. Meanwhile, he was watching everyone's movements (and thoughts, too, I would imagine). The shopping trips were never for the entertainment of the people. They were part of his teaching – except no one really knew what they learned out of them. Indeed, UG's teaching was mysterious.

When he seemed to be interested in some piece of clothing, be it a silk shirt, a cashmere sweater, or an inexpensive pair of pants, there was always someone to buy it for him, although at times, he refused the offer. When he accepted, it was more for the sake of the gift-giver than for himself. In fact, much the same can be said about all the money gifts he accepted from people, particularly for his birthdays.

Las Vegas: UG made several "caravan" trips to Las Vegas from Palm Springs with a dozen or more people parceled out 4 or 5 to a car. They would all rent hotel rooms and stay overnight. UG would let everyone else (except the children) play at the machines, but would never gamble himself.

Once he was short of $25 for his room rent, I heard. Mario and someone else were at his door knocking. He opened the door, gave Mario a quarter and pointed to a slot machine at the end of one of rows and told him to put it in the machine. Mario did and got exactly $25 out of the machine and gave it UG. When Mario handed the money to UG, UG quickly snatched the money and shut the door.

When someone lost money in gambling, that was his own loss. But when he or she won, all that money would go to UG. And of course, UG would give it all away to the children in the group.

The Supernatural: All sorts of supernatural powers have been attributed to UG. It's part of the nature of the subject matter that it doesn't lend itself to any objective assessment. UG has been credited with telepathy, clairvoyance, clairaudience, precognition, psychokinesis, miracle healing, and the seeing of ghosts and departed spirits. I personally had several experiences when I felt that he knew not only my thoughts, but the current state of my body. When I was once talking to Julie I felt he was listening in from his place in a hotel. I then joked aloud to Julie: "UG, it's rude to eavesdrop on people's conversations!" He seemed to be able to forestall coming dangers and prevent them from happening. And more often than not people claimed that their lives were saved either from a serious illness or from an accident either by UG being next to them on the scene or by their thinking of (or praying to) him. Unfortunately there is no way to objectively verify any of this, for we simply lack the tools. I just mention these to complete the picture.

UG sometimes joked around, asking someone who was saying goodbye, "You want some energy transmission?" and then would shake his hand. There were times, when he would say, "I have powers, you know." At other times, he would say, "How would I know?" or "There are no powers." But I do know that he had his ways of taking care of people through his physical touch: He would, for instance, have Nataraj sit next to him and shake his hand frequently.[41] Nataraj credits him with not only knowing what was going on inside him, but with "saving my life." I have heard others who said similar things about UG. I know at least one instance in my own case, and I saw it several times with others, when I was in a certain state of mind and shook his hand, he withdrew quickly it saying, "Ouch," or something to that effect. He truly was aware of what was going in another person's body.

Sadly, however, I must report of at least one instance in which a friend of mine who was severely ill hoped for a miracle from UG and it never came. Eventually he died. In fact, UG told him more than once to go to a hospital, see a doctor and get himself tested. It was just in such contexts UG would say, "There are no miracles, go to a doctor!" In fact, as another example, one could cite his own son's death from lung cancer in Bombay while he was there.

Sometimes he would say that one should "give a helping hand" by taking medicine.

Of course, he never followed his own advice: he always believed that pain is a healer and given a chance the body has the power to heal itself. (He would, however, add the caveat: "If the body cannot heal itself, it will go gracefully.") In his later years, he never visited a doctor or went to a hospital. But he wouldn't advice others to do the same, he said.

Conclusion: UG always attacked conventional morality, religion and politics. He said that our legal, political and moral systems are all corrupt. He did not believe in any moral rules; but he said that one who is not moral can never be immoral, will never do anything to hurt others. He said, although he criticized laws, he would not himself break the law.

UG had always warned us not to be fooled by appearances; yet we don't and can't know what the reality of UG is. We can't but feel that we are somehow affected by having been around him. I have seen people who would even kill themselves for him. He touched them, in their minds, as no one else in their lives had touched them.

UG sometimes made what seemed like scientific statements, and say, "One day scientists will confirm it (*viz.*, that consciousness is everywhere, for instance)." But immediately he would add disclaimers like, "I am not a scientist."

For UG, freedom of the will is a myth. "You can never be free from conditioning," he said, "Conditioning is intelligence." Nonetheless, UG encouraged people to make money or to be successful at this or that.

UG would tell all these gloom and doom stories, and yet he said that things couldn't be any different from what they are because of the way we are and we live. So there is nothing one can do. So, one might ask, "Then should we or should we not do such and such? Should we or should we not meditate?" Neither conclusion follows. You cannot derive any "directive" from what he says.

UG would use anything and everything in front of him as a tool for his teaching process and then simply discard it and walk away. He didn't have a specific means or method of teaching. He said once, long ago, "I could as well be reading out the numbers from a telephone book; it would have the same effect."

And you can't grasp his teaching in your hand and say "this is what I have gotten from UG." You don't know what you have gotten.

UG himself said repeatedly that people who listened to him over the years would not find any such thing as enlightenment, for, according to him, there is no such thing, but they will find their burdens (he meant the mental "baggage" we carry from our past) becoming lighter. And I know many a friend who listened to UG who would attest to that.

8. *Further Remarks About UG*

"**UG is not Real**": Once I said to UG, "UG, at a certain level, I feel as if none of this is real; even UG is not real." UG replied, "Yes, UG is not real."

UG not a person: The first time I had a clear inkling that there is no "person" inside UG was when I was visiting him in Corte Madera, California, in the early years of my acquaintance with him. It was a rare moment when I looked into his eyes, inside the pupils. What I saw was startling: it was a vast impersonal energy. No sign of a person and nothing which would recognize me as a person, either. I can never forget that deep inside those eyes what was moving was not anything I expected such as a reflection of me or something which would look at me and recognize me. It's no surprise that people often characterized UG as, "Nobody home!"

Now, when I look deep within myself, I see nothing but surging "energy" (I don't know what other term to use). Even the images and sounds I talked about in my recent paper[42] are just waves surging from this energy. I don't exist there! That must be why I felt at times when I was close to UG physically that there was no separation between us. It's not that I am in that awareness or energy most of the time. But I know what the "bottom-line" reality is.

UG asserted more than once that the "division"[43] which is millions of years-old, keeps recurring, bringing "UG" into the picture and that it will never go away. It's that UG we saw from time to time, the "UG" who reacted to people and situations, sometimes through his own conditioning.

The Lion's Den: I was always a bit suspicious of and annoyed with UG's statements like "There is no such thing as matter," "There is no space," and "Thought interprets reality." I felt that UG's talk of everything being an interpretation is like the Advaita Vedanta's assertion that "The world is Maya". "Interpretation" is a like a huge lion's den into which everything went and out of which nothing came.

I tested UG once on this: while I was visiting him in Palm Springs, I asked him: "UG, please raise your arm." First, he was reluctant to comply, even after several requests. Finally, he did. I said, "See, I made some sounds, and you raised your arm," meaning neither his raising the arm nor my instruction that he should do so is just an interpretation. (Of course, he would have said that my instruction was a mere noise.) He replied,

"Your seeing of my arm being raised is also an interpretation." Then I said, "I see what you did," and didn't say anything further. His reply confirmed my suspicion.

Further on the Body: As Mahesh and others have understood (I may have missed this point when I was debating with UG about the body), UG, in his last days, neither tried to end his life, nor did he do much to prolong it. He merely let it take its own course. In fact, this should throw a good deal of light on how he viewed his relationship with his body, particularly when he said, "The body does not want to go."

"This is a Dog barking:" UG would conclude many conversations by saying, "This is just a dog barking," meaning that he is merely making sounds and the meaning is all made up (by thought). His statements about his body and people's responses to him are all just noise at a certain level (or from a certain point of view). Underneath, there are not even noises. No one is saying anything and nothing is being said. Not even consciousness or energy or waves, or noises and images. And of course, there are no bodies. There is no wakefulness, no dream and no sleep. There is no life or death either. It's a vast ocean of peace.

On the surface, it seems like UG was talking about living and dying, the body not wanting to go, and so on and so on. But that's all an appearance. There is a place where none of this is real, UG is not real, his living or dying is not real, and neither is ours. There is just this vast ocean of peace. You and I are part of it.

This morning I was lying in bed feeling all this. I also felt that *I* wasn't breathing. "It was being breathed." The body is a surface phenomenon.

PHOTOS

Moorty and UG in Mill Valley, California, 1981 (first visit to UG)

UG in Moorty's home, Seaside, California, November 1988

Chandrasekhar, Terry Newland, and Sajid Martin
in Seaside around 1988

Chalet Sunbeam, Gstaad, Switzerland

Gstaad, viewed from Chalet Sunbeam, 1986

UG and Moorty on the path going down from Sunbeam

Shyamala (Moorty's daughter), Moorty, UG, and Chandrasekhar in the dining area of Sunbeam, 1986

UG making a point to Paul Sempé, sitting outside of Sunbeam, 1995

Moorty, Unknown, Bodil, Julie, Nataraj, Sushma, UG, and Harry

UG in Gstaad, summer, 1995

Behind "Sunbeam", Gstaad, 1996

"Command Center", Sunbeam, 1996: Larry, Moorty, Julie, UG, Kiran (Moorty's son), and Lisa

Part of a large group having hot chocolate in the Palace Hotel, Gstaad, 2000: Claire, Sumedha, Kiran, Shilpa, and UG

Bangalore, India 1986: Raja, Moorty, UG, Smita, and Shanta

Chandrasekhar, Julie in mirror, UG, and Valentine, Bangalore, 1990

Brahmachari, Chandrasekhar, UG, and Moorty in Bangalore, 1990

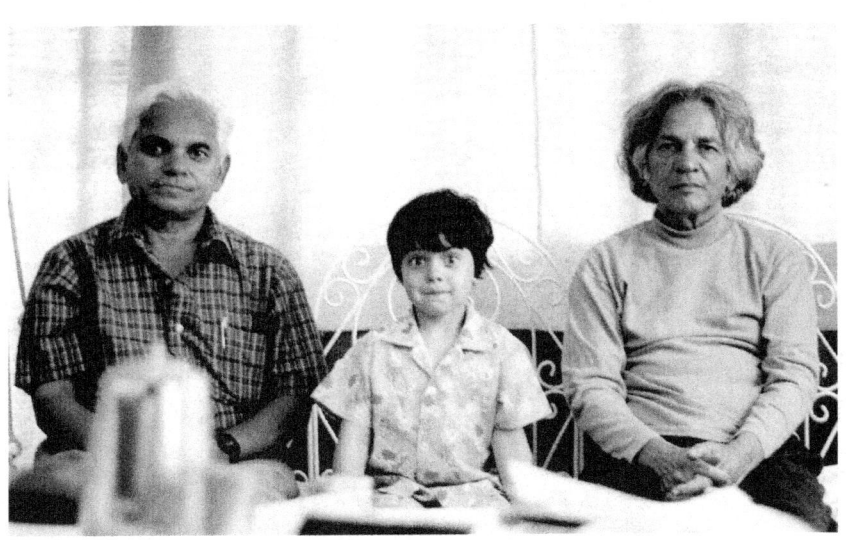

Moorty and Kiran with UG in Bangalore, 1990

Nartaki with UG and her adopted son, Tambi

UG with (counterclockwise): unknown, Ramesh, Chandrasekhar, Moorty, and Dinesh, Yercaud, 1994

Mahesh and Moorty at work editing Mahesh's biography of UG, Carmel, California, 1991

Mahesh and UG discussing UG's biography, Carmel, Fall, 1991

UG, Julie, and Moorty, Point Lobos, south of Carmel, 1994

Walking the path along the ocean cliff at Point Lobos, 1994

UG shopping in Monterey (near Seaside), 1992

Something's funny: UG and Douglas, Seaside, 1992

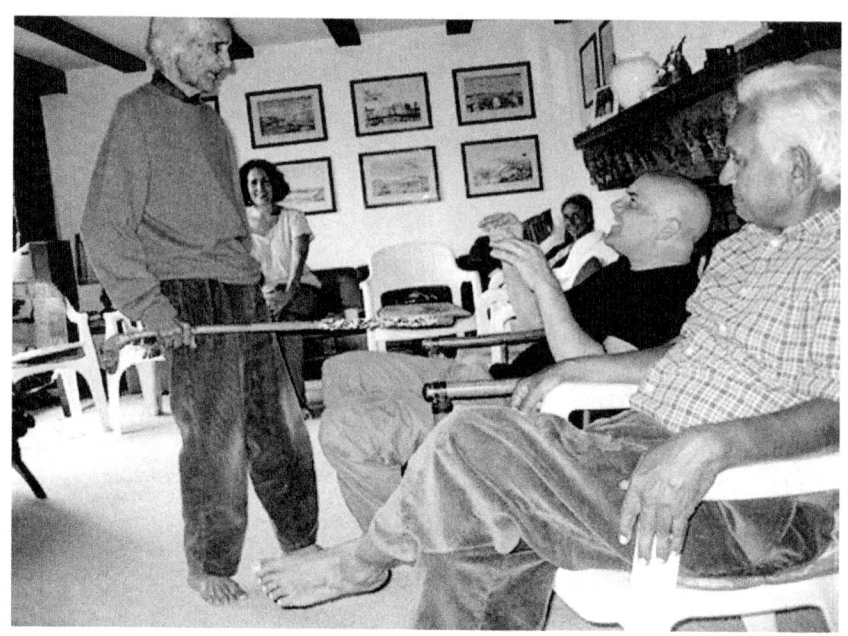

UG engaged with Louis, Gstaad, 2004

UG and Moorty outside the Farm House near Bangalore, 2004

Gathering in Chadrasekhar and Suguna's house, Bangalore, December, 2004

Seaside, January, 2006: Larry, UG, Moorty, Melissa, David, and Maria

Annex in Lucia and Giovanni's villa in Vallecrosia, Italy, where UG spent his last days (d. March 22, 2007)

The Medical Conference, February 2007: UG, Ramatirtha, Susan, Doris, and Paul

Gathering around UG in Vallecrosia, February, 2007: UG, Lisa, Yashoda, Sarito, Giovanni, Trisha, Larry, and Golda

Moorty, Golda, Viresha, and Suguna sitting with UG

Larry and Susan

Guha and Lakshmi (in back against the wall)

Melissa and Lucia

Louis and UG

Usha, Suguna, and Chandrasekhar with UG

Moorty and UG, February, 2007

Part 3: Being

9. Thought, Thinking and the Self

Preamble: In the following, I am not so much interested in what scientists have to say about thought and thinking, their scientific studies, which generally involve establishing correlations between thought processes (or other mental phenomena like perception, feeling, emotions and dreaming) and various brain centers or electrical and chemical processes, as I am interested in understanding thought from my own point of view in a commonsense fashion. The problem with scientific studies is that they don't leave us with much we can do anything about. And they eventually can and probably will lead to commercial or political exploitation.

Beginnings of Thought: We all use the words "thinking" and "thought" without ever being conscious of what the words mean. I think the thinking process has its roots in consciousness which in turn has origins in the very simple activities like responding to stimuli, recognition and various stages of remembering. Response is evident even in the world of inanimate matter, as for instance, when iron filings respond to the presence of a magnet, or a gas heater or toaster responds to a set temperature in a thermostat. In the biological world, response takes place in the form of reacting to stimuli, whether internal or external, even at the level of ameba or other primitive organisms. Here we see the beginnings of what we can term "consciousness." Responses become more and more complex as life forms become more complex and heterogeneous, forming the senses and their sensations, which serve an organism's basic survival and reproductory needs. Some animals respond to stimuli even when they are not in front of anything in the present: an animal like an elephant is said to be able to dream. Dogs are known to be able not merely to recognize their masters but remember where their homes are and get back to them, sometimes from hundreds of miles away. Whales and birds migrate thousands of miles as their instincts and other internal and external stimuli prompt them. And bees can communicate to other bees with precision the location of a source of nectar.

Internal stimuli too cause responses of various kinds. But most important for our discussion is the idea of image making. Images are said to exist in some primitive form in animals, particularly in elephants, chimpanzees dolphins, and gorillas, and perhaps even in cats and birds. They miss their partners when they are not present for a length of time.

The grieving process and dreaming caused by fear (such as nightmares) presuppose some sort of imagery, however primitive and isolated it might be.[44] Images are representations of objects which may or may not be directly present. Concepts too are representations, but they are more abstract and represent, at least initially, classes of things. In this sense images can be construed as concrete concepts, although they may often be non-verbal.

Consciousness: When animals respond to images in a primitive fashion, they are conscious, but only in an incipient sense. An explicit consciousness, as when we are self-conscious, requires the division between the self and the other mediated through thought, whether it is verbalized or not. Therefore, we cannot say animals are conscious of images or of their own responses to them. We too were probably like them before self-consciousness developed in us. Words, like images, are vehicles for concepts and physiologically they exist only in the form of sounds (which we notice in our sub-vocal speech movements).

Self-Consciousness, Reflection or Introspection: Then what is self-consciousness? I think the roots of a typical thought processes must be sought here. Self-consciousness must involve some consciousness of oneself as part of the feeling of being conscious of whatever it is that one is conscious of (say, a sensation, an object or a situation in the world, or a feeling or an action). Self-consciousness does not take place in a vacuum. It is not a mere nothing, nor is it just a consciousness. It involves an object, something we are aware of, and the subject which is aware of that something. The subject is not a mere nothing. It is perception, thought, feelings, reactions, plans and so forth, which are all based on the background knowledge one has acquired over a lifetime. It is the ground on the basis of which we are aware of the objects. All perceptions (and recognition which is implied in them) and our reactions to objects as subjects occur by means of the past knowledge concerning the object. The subject, as subject, can never be the object of attention. It is only evident indirectly through the inner dialog that goes on in the mental processes. The knowledge we have acquired represents to us the world we live in. And the knowledge reacts through its known methods. There is no perception without such a reaction.

Although self-consciousness is an aid in the process of learning a new skill, as it helps us in monitoring and putting together through memory various details one has to learn, it can also hinder us in the smooth performance of a skill once it is acquired. Much intellectual thinking as well as problem-solving occurs in the field of self-consciousness in the form of a dialog one carries on within oneself.

Reflection is a form of self-consciousness; it too necessarily involves the subject-object division and is an awareness of a previous perception, feeling, emotion, memory or thought. Since it involves the subject, it is still the thought process operating upon our mental contents; and since the viewing of the contents is from a point of view, it must be itself be a thought. Thus reflection necessarily perpetuates the thought process. In this context, I am using "introspection," "reflection" and "self-consciousness" rather synonymously.

Knowledge and Valuation: Our reactions are manifold and add to the edifice of knowledge and hence of the world we make up for ourselves. Perception first of all implies recognition of objects. Recognition is an implicit thought process. And the very recognition of the object is at the same time an evaluation. Also, the reaction to the recognized object or situation or person is simultaneously an evaluation on the basis of a scale of values one has built for oneself over time. The values reinforce experiences positively or negatively. The evaluation process is simultaneously also a process of becoming something other than oneself, something which will resolve a perceived shortcoming, difficulty or problem, and steer one toward goals which presumably imply an improved situation. The process of the self (which I will describe below) is a process in time. Evidently, without the movement of thought, there is no past, present or future to the conscious mind or self. Thought is very much involved in this process. Now, what is thought?

Recognition and Judgment: Thought is not only the process of recognition, but of judgment. More often than not, judgment implies an evaluation and a projection into the future. Images, concepts, as well as language, are implicated in the mental processes of judging, evaluating and projecting into the future. Some sorts of intuitive problem-solving, particularly those that involve creativity are beyond the reach of conscious thought, or, at any rate, they are best carried out when conscious thinking is not present. Once the problem is solved, then the solution is thrown into the realm of conscious thinking and then the thought process can work out the details of a solution.

Intelligence: Intelligence includes many skills such as problem-solving, scanning, assessing, evaluating, estimating, hypothesizing, drawing consequences from an idea, systematizing, comparing, organizing, analyzing, synthesizing, abstracting, projecting into the future, and so forth. Thinking is a function of intelligence that draws upon all the above. Animals, of course, have a lower level of intelligence as they lack the capacity to envisage in thought (or even in imagery) a situation in its absence and manipulate it consciously.

The Notion of the "I" Thought implying a division between the subject and object already implies the subject as the self. When one becomes conscious of one's thought, one automatically has the notion of the "I" or the self. The notion of the self becomes enriched and filled

9. Thought, Thinking and the Self

with content through further thinking and experience, as one's knowledge grows with experience and is added to the content of the subject. In the division between the subject and the object, as one's attitude is determined by one's past pleasant or unpleasant experiences (i.e., knowledge), one either desires or tries to avoid the object. In the process of desiring what a person feels he or she lacks, she creates for herself the need for fulfillment which is really a filling a need or lack. However, once the need is fulfilled, other needs take its place, for the very awareness of a fulfilled need generates a further need or want, either to secure the result or continue it or to achieve something else. Thus the person is set on an endless travel to realize the ultimate -- ultimate happiness, pleasure, meaning or resting place for the self. The self is also a process of seeking permanence and security, and this is where the self-protectiveness of thought comes in. While every thought we think is geared to reinforce the self in some fashion or other, it is doing so by means of the structure it has already built for itself.

While, on the one hand, thought seems to seek something other than itself, on the other hand, its search is always limited to the known. We have no clue as to what we seek if we don't already have an idea of it. The seeking serves to further strengthen the self that is already there.

The self is not only the world we build for ourselves, but it is also a fictitious center which holds the world together and acts as its center. All the feelings, experiences and thoughts, as well as achievements, worries and projects are referred to this center. We feel as if there is a unitary entity that acts through all these mental processes and governs the body as well as our dealings with the world.

Mental States: As I mentioned above, the awareness of an object, a sensation, an image, a feeling or a thought is simultaneously a reaction to it. We are hardly ever aware of something without reacting to it. But then the reaction itself becomes an object of awareness and of further reaction. This happens particularly when we rehash an issue approaching it from different points of view.

This constant action-and-reaction process linked through memory creates what we might call mental states. A state is something we ascribe to ourselves as, for instance, when we say to ourselves, "I am angry; I am depressed," and so on. This ascription is itself a thought and is more often than not mediated by body awareness. Notice how we reinforce this feeling or awareness by clasping our chest and by being aware of our speech muscles or of tension in other parts of the head or the rest of the body. This ascription to ourselves of a thought or a state or a feeling, associated with a certain body awareness, is what generates the illusion of the "I". In each of the specifics (thoughts, body sensations, for instance) there is no "I". But through the process I mentioned above, you get the feeling of 'I', the feeling that "I" am thinking, "I" have pain, "I" am the agent of my actions, or "I" am what is being referred to by other people as "great", and so on. This illusion is perpetuated through repeated ascriptions linked through memory. In other words, I remember for example two such ascriptions from my past, and in that very recollection, a feeling is generated that I have such a quality as anger, for instance.

Mental States Have Continuity: We contribute to the continuity of mental states by reacting to them either positively or negatively. We are strengthening our state through our reaction. If we stop reacting, the state ceases to be when it loses its momentum. Thus states have an inertia of their own, and they tend to persist because of our participation in them. When we participate in a state, we are within a tunnel, as it were. This inertia resists change and indeed any interference from outside. And within the "tunnel," the states have a tendency to perpetuate themselves either by building on themselves or keeping a fight for or against something going. These states, or what I might also call mental tracks, include fear, loneliness, depression, pride, inferiority, superiority, or a belief or knowledge system, and such. For instance, when we are watching a movie, we are within the track of watching the movie, and as such, we are identified with the characters and situations, and as a consequence we experience the joys and sorrows expected (or not expected) of us as spectators. You can only stop the process of involvement by stepping out of it, "snapping out" of it, as it were. Then you don't have the illusion any more. Reality sets in; the movie has become a mere show without any effect on you.

Our normal states of mind are similar. We are within one tunnel or another, and we labor hard trying to get out of them, particularly when we feel one is undesirable. But that's a futile struggle, for we labor on the basis of a certain base identification (even if it is only a negative one) and cannot extricate ourselves. When we can get down to the base identification and question it from outside of it, as it were, then there is a chance of truly distancing ourselves from it and eventually becoming free from the entire state.

We Must Think About Something: Without something to think about, the mind (or consciousness) is in an unstable state. It keeps wanting to chew on something. It tries to achieve stability and grounding, if necessary by harping on the negative, as when negative memories impinge upon our consciousness and we react to them by building on them, just as we react to positive memories by building on them. We tend to think of the worst outcomes when we are in an uncertain situation, as that gives us more grounding and security ("It can't be worse than that," we say to ourselves) than turning to positive ones, which are always questionable in regard to their future occurrence (they might or might not happen). One way to solve the problem of sinking deeper and deeper in a negative state is to let the negative state be and if necessary focus on something innocuous, as one would in meditation, and "rise above" the state. Or, one could break up a mental state by interspersing it with self-consciousness, i.e. being aware of what we are doing as frequently as possible and breaking the state into pieces. By "pulverizing" the state, the continuity of the state is broken up and the state loses its hold on us. This will at least temporarily remove us from that state of mind. Habits are like states of mind and they too will tend to become weaker by the same processes. More lasting freedom, however, can only be found in becoming free from the source identification(s).

We can superimpose states upon states, say, guilt upon anger, and make them multi-layered. Also, we can suppress them to a subterranean level beyond the reach of the conscious mind. We can become conscious of the states, but as I said, such consciousness only reacts to the state from a point of view, generally the point of view of identification with something and tends to reinforce the state. Normally we don't just let the state run its course, say just be afraid and let the fear run its course and die its natural death; we keep reacting to it and then react to our reactions, and so on, ad infinitum.

States add to the notion of the continuing self: Go through a few of these states, you get the feeling that there is one constant "I" running through them all. The more organized my memory is, the stronger is my sense of "I", or you can say, the bigger is my ego.

To sum up: States of mind continue through memory. Each thought or feeling we have is "linked" to other thoughts or feelings relevant to it – it may be the same or similar thought or feeling we have had in the past or something connected to it. This connectivity, association or linking is what gives rise to the notion of the continuing "I".

Once the notion of the continuing "I" is established, every thought we think is used to reconnect us to the relevant past and further support the continuity. Although we can never find a specific beginning for the "I", we believe in the history of the "I" with some beginning, its current life and an end.

In the process of organizing our world we arrange our goals in order of priority and look for ultimate goals. And when these are waylaid and unfulfilled repeatedly, and we confront frustration, we struggle hard to find meaning in our lives. Until we become involved in some other search we become bored with life.

Whenever we perceive and relate to anything in the world, we do so by placing it in this mental world of ours, which has the "I" as its center. The world of the "I" is intimately bound with ourselves, because at the bottom, it is nothing but a multitude of identifications interconnected. We feel that whatever happens to each of these things in the world happens to *us*. Our interests, values and goals are bound with these identifications, determined, of course, by our earlier exposure to them.

Psychological Survival: Our instinctive biological struggle for survival is now translated into a struggle in the mental world. But these two types of survival are completely different because our idea of psychological survival is embellished by our imagination, which is one of the functions of thought. It can imagine a fictitious future and fear my non-continuance. Each thought thinking thus about the future is my future that I think about and fear. Our mind can thus generate insecurity and fear of death even when our physical survival is presently not threatened.

Dialogue Within Ourselves: The constant dialogue within ourselves is what provides us with the illusion that the "I" exists at the center of all my thoughts. I wonder if we would have this idea of the "I" without the inner dialogue. What does the dialogue imply? When the sounds (thoughts) go on in my head, there are subtle speech movements. I am always aware of myself as thinking these thoughts, and also of the person who has experiences and feelings, and is the author of his actions. With each such awareness, there is a feeling that "I" am thinking those thoughts. With this feeling I link those thoughts and memories. Hence the feeling that there is an ever-present "I" behind all my present thoughts and experiences that I remember.

The same is true of our memories: as memories impinge on our consciousness we become aware of them and in that very process a reaction to them is generated and then a response to the reaction, and so on and so forth. This is partly how the inner dialogue is generated.

Features Of The Self

1) The Self Is The Center Of Our World: The self is our self-image or self-esteem which is a result of the process of constant evaluation. We are quite sensitive when a remark is made about us as we are constantly on guard as to how others look at us. We worry about ourselves, worrying about every little thing that happens to us; we evaluate it; relate it to the rest of our lives and react to it until we are satisfied that the problem is solved. Notice how the same problem-solving skills of intelligence are exercised here to work out the problems of the self. Of course, our worry can easily turn into an obsession or a phobia and we can create panic and a literal hell for ourselves as we continually build on our worries. This is evident even when we notice a slight change or ache or pain in our body and react to it by panicking thinking that we might have a mortal ailment.

We divide our world into the positive and the negative, into right and wrong, and good and bad, pleasant and painful, happy and miserable. We pursue the positive and try to avoid the negative. We constantly reflect on and evaluate our lives, figuring out the direction in which they are going, and are satisfied with our progress or disappointed with the lack of it or with our failures. We have now a life constantly focused on becoming, a life where there is no rest or peace.

2) The Self Is Meaning: What we experience is interpreted through our past experience and thus the new acquires meaning through the old. When an experience acquires meaning, it becomes part of the world. The world we make up for ourselves is not just our world; in some sense I am the world, because the things, people and situations in my world are things I am identified with, either positively or negatively. In fact, language itself, the words and sentences we hear, have meaning to us only because of the associations they have with our past experiences. They, as well as anything else that has meaning to us, must invoke our past in some sense in order for them to have meaning for us. Or else, they would remain as mere noises or marks on paper, or, if they are things, as mere nondescript objects which have no interest or meaning to us. In our perception those things would recede into the background as having no significance.

3) The Self Defines Itself Through Comparisons: The process of self-evaluation is mediated often through comparison – comparison of ourselves with others, our present state with a possible future state, our actions with our own scales of values or others' values, and so on. The process of evaluation creates feelings of elation, depression, self-congratulation, importance, pride, inferiority, superiority, sense of power, dominion over others as well as anxiety and fear about the outcome of a given situation. Insecurity is built into this process. The uncertainty generates anxiety and creates an unending search for security.

4) The Self is also Self-image: Self-image is something we build on the foundation of our notion of the self. We fill it with various projects we have, our desire structure, our estimates about ourselves, our achievements and failures, our sentiments and beliefs, and so on. This structure is held together by the center of the self. Not only is each thing that occurs in our world related to the self via the self-image, but it is interpreted and reacted to through the image. The reaction in turn reinforces the self and its self-image.

We constantly build and rebuild our self-image by feeding it with various reinforcements, particularly those stemming not just from our opinions about ourselves, our qualities and actions, but from what we hear from other people, and also from what we think other people think about us. This is a constant process which keeps building and revising our idea of ourselves.

5) The Self Uses Thought for Its Protection: This indeed is where we can notice the self-protectiveness of thought. Thinking does not take place in a vacuum. It takes place within the process of the self, within the context of the self, maintaining and continuing the self and its self-image. In fact, we are only interested in those things that are directly or indirectly connected to the self and its image of itself. Even our physical perceptions not only select but seek those that are relevant to our interests. We seek those self-enhancing things and consciously or unconsciously ignore the rest of what is given in the field of our perception. As they say, "You only hear what you want to hear." Our reactions to what we perceive reinforce our self-structure. We become sensitive to anything that is seen even as remotely threatening to this structure, and we not only take a mental note of it, but do everything to eliminate it, fight it off, erase it or diminish its importance and strength.

Anything that is seen as possibly threatening, say, a disease symptom, a pain, an insult, or anything which could possibly hurt our self, raises at least a minor disturbance, if not a storm, in the mind. We don't rest until the storm is quelled and equilibrium is restored. All our thinking and emotional process is utilized in this direction. When we say we want peace, normally, it's this kind of peace we seek.

Many mental processes are carried out by means of thought and all have the self at the center. **A) Desiring, striving, goal-seeking and pleasure-seeking:** Anything which is perceived as attractive or desirable or pleasurable on the basis of one's background experience is automatically turned into a goal that one seeks and becomes part of the desire process. **B) Emotions and feelings:** In the process of responding to the various situations, including successes and failures in our attempts to deal with the world, as well as to the self-evaluations that we constantly make, we undergo many emotions and feelings. More often than not, these emotions and feelings are verbalized and as such exist in the form of thought – for instance, thoughts of envy, jealousy, anger, fear, elation, depression, and so on. Without the verbalization and thinking these emotions and feelings lose their identity and reduce themselves to diffuse energy.

6) The Self Creates a Sense of Time: Our sense of time is created in the process of seeking. There is no time without thinking. Although our striving implies time, with its future, past and present, there is also something interesting about our dealings with our self: when we seek or avoid, of course, there is time, because the distance between what we seek or avoid and ourselves implies time. However, within the elements of the

9. Thought, Thinking and the Self

self, however, there is no time. It's as if everything is frozen there in time. Take, for instance, our memories. I was in love with a girl say forty years ago. But my fantasies or reliving my past experiences with the girl hardly ever take into consideration the changes in time that have probably taken place in the girl or in myself over the last forty years – perhaps she is an old hag by now, or even dead, for all I know. I myself have become old and perhaps have no ability even to perform sex. But my mind knows no such age. In some sense, it acts as if it is ageless. It's immortal!

What's interesting is that our dealings with life are based on this notion of our "frozen" self. We act, strive, accumulate wealth, and protect ourselves, our health, and our good name as though there will be never an end to us. At the same time, time is very real to us, as that's what is implied in our striving for our goals and whenever we are involved in thinking consciously about anything. Although in some sense time is frozen within individual experiences, as a continuing self I am very much aware of time; and in spite of the fact that I know of no beginning to myself in time (I cannot even imagine it except through concepts and someone telling me about it), I am mortally afraid of my life not continuing. Also, it is impossible for me to imagine myself ending. No wonder as human beings we create fancy notions such as a "Kingdom of Happiness," a heaven, immortality, and life-after-death as pure Consciousness, and so forth. All these notions are our lame and ineffective attempts to combat our fear of death. None of them, of course, can be sustained when faced with a seed of doubt.

Combine this sense of time with our constant attempts to reach goals and our seeking to restore our mental equilibrium; we can then understand what UG says about man seeking only one thing, namely, permanent happiness. A resting place where is there is no further need of seeking is indeed what counts for man as permanent happiness.

7) The Self Is Not Always Aware Of Its Workings: Thought processes do not always take place at a very conscious level. We are not always aware of what's going on. When we seek a goal or fend off an offense, we are not always aware. When we are aware, the awareness only takes place by means of another thought. In other words, we are not merely aware but we react. We don't know much about a thought until it surfaces in consciousness. We don't even know that it exists. Say, we bear a grudge or resentment against someone. Our behavior, including what we say to the person, might show it. That may be evident to someone else. But until our grudge is formulated as such in thought, we don't even know that it exists. We may have subtle inklings about such and many other things. And in fact, even much of problem-solving takes place subconsciously. If we include these inklings, the field of thought becomes vastly expanded and enriched.

And there may be layers and layers of these mental processes. Part of the challenge of either psychoanalysis or self-analysis would be to peel off layer after layer of these processes to lay bare the root -- say, the thing that we are primarily afraid of or the person we resent.

8) The Self Moves In Mental Space: When we think, whether in a goal-directed fashion or in order to solve a problem, we move in a "mental space." Sometimes we find gaps in the mental map we lay down in thinking which we then try to close to solve a problem. And at other times, the space is traversed in an uncharted territory as when we create, as in science, music or art. When we understand or we think we know, there are flashes and clicks in this mental space. In relationships also we feel a mental distance -- we may want to close it (as in a relationship we like to have) or maintain it (as with a student in a classroom or with a stranger), as the case may be.

9) The Self Is Prone To "Tunnel Vision": There is such a thing as a "tunnel vision" in thought: The point of view or prejudice or belief governs our thinking process. Of course, we could become conscious of these points of view, but generally we are aware of them only from another point of view. When it is possible to become merely aware of them without reacting to them, then the process no longer has any hold on us. For instance, take fear. When we get to our fear at its basis and can face it without reacting to it, that is, without trying to escape from it or justify it or build up on it, if we can face it without resistance, then the fear no longer has any strength. It simply dissipates. In doing so, we are dissolving the duality or division that has hitherto existed between ourselves and the object of fear. We become one with the fear, as it were. The same is true of our other mental states such as anger, depression and loneliness.

10) The Self Covers Up Our Emptiness: All feelings of insecurity, loneliness, as well as our fears cover up our emptiness, the vacuum which is pure consciousness or awareness or energy or whatever you will. In point of fact, it can also be said that all thinking is a way of covering up our emptiness. We sense that emptiness as nothingness and are terrified by it, and start covering it up with all kinds of activity, information, knowledge, and achievement, knowing full well that we can never completely succeed in doing so. But that knowledge doesn't prevent us from trying. In other words, the whole mental edifice, the edifice of the self and of thought in general is built upon this emptiness. Yet, we struggle so hard to maintain the structure.

11) The Self Is A Mechanism of Desire: Thought and desire are intimately related to each other. As UG would say, to think is to want something – if you don't want anything, you don't need to think. I once expressed this idea to UG (and later to others) in these terms: every thought we think is an attempt to change the given. It's an attempt to become something other than ourselves. This is part of the movement of the self in which our very awareness of something as other than our self automatically reveals our own lack of it, and that in turn sets off a reaction mechanism which tries to change the given situation into a more settled one. All such desiring processes are means of self-fulfillment, as we feel inadequate without the object. Our inadequacy is further enhanced through the process of comparison which goes on all the time. And our desires and reactions always take place against the backdrop of our background, past experience and knowledge.

12) The Self Takes Itself Seriously: We sometimes are interested in helping others, and undertake various social work activities, charities and so forth; or we carry on intellectual activities, pursue knowledge, and practice art. In all of them, the self is at the center and those activities are basically part of the projects of the self. There is one simple way of testing this theory: when a conclusion we have arrived at or a long-cherished fundamental belief or project of ours is attacked, of course we buttress it with various justifications; but more often than not, we feel that the very ground we stand on is taken away from us; we do not rest until we quell the opposition, even at the expense of qualifying our belief or abandoning the project and taking up another ("I shall return!"). We resent and bear a grudge against the person attacking our belief, in spite of our ostensible attempts to appear impersonal and objective. We do all this because we identify ourselves with the project (or belief) – the success of the project is our success; its failure is our failure. In fact, if there is a series of these "failures," then we feel that we ourselves are a failure. That's a disaster that can set us on the course of a prolonged depression.

13) Relationships Are Movements Within the Self: Although seemingly occurring between real people, relationships in fact take place in our mental world between the self and others who are part of our perceived world. And these relationships, no matter how much we whitewash them in the name of love, affection, unconditioned love and so forth, are part of the projects of the self. We desire a person and try to have a relationship with him or her for various reasons: it may be sex or companionship we want; or we are simply identified with the person to the degree that the person's welfare or accomplishment become our welfare or accomplishment. I am not saying we don't do anything for other people just to benefit them. Of course, we do. But when we do, our self is in some way or other involved in it. We do not simply know how to act selflessly. When things fail in relationships, of course, as UG says, "'Love' is our trump card:" we blame the other person claiming that he or she does not love us.

14) Thought Is Capable Of Creating Illusions: Thought always seeks a state where there is no striving anymore and where all its desires are fulfilled -- the utopia; the kingdom of permanent happiness, *moksha*. But such things are all based on illusions. As long as thought is there, there is no end to striving, for the two are synonymous. And it cannot find a state of total fulfillment as long as it keeps seeking it, for seeking presupposes a sense of a lack of fulfillment. Also, seeking presupposes that we are an independent entity capable of a destiny. And apart from the set of thoughts and experiences we have created for ourselves, there is no independent "I". The "I" as the contemporary philosopher Daniel Dennett puts it, is a "gravitational pull." We can never directly see it. As Sartre puts it, "We can only see it with the corner of our eye." In other words, it only appears to be there when we are not directly looking at it. When we look at it directly, it's not there. Yet, it is for this fictitious "I" that we strive and struggle so much. Knowing all this, thought "thinks" that it might even want to end itself. And that's the grandest of all illusions. An ending of thought cannot be achieved by thought. It cannot be achieved by will, which in turn is thought. Of course, when we physically die, our thoughts will die with us.

15) No Self?: If the thought process is suspended for any reason, or put in abeyance because it is utterly frustrated, having exhausted all its resources, or because it is disillusioned by all its goals, it collapses. Then there are no problems. At that moment, the body knows how to handle itself. You are in the field of pure awareness. But this cannot be contrived. Nothing we do or can do can make it happen. None of our methods of spiritual realization actually work, because they all take place through thought and the self's contrivances as their means. We constantly look for and calculate the results.

But unfortunately, we, as conscious human beings, don't know how to live without thought or what to do with the pure awareness. We just don't know.

10. Reflecting on Reflection

In the article above, I made "reflection" sound like a mental process which is bound to perpetuate the self, which it surely does. But there is another type of "reflection": a reflection which is aware of all this, aware of this process of generating goals and being bound by them or continuing through them, and which in the very process of being aware of them, dissolves them by letting them go. We can call this "meditative reflection."

Such reflection is a continual process. Not that it is done through volition; it's something that happens rather automatically. In the flame of awareness, goals burn away and therefore with them all the rubbish that is generated from pursuing goals. And instead of building on themselves, thoughts dissolve themselves.

Reflection may be generated by the awareness of the pursuit of a goal and therefore could itself be called a thought, but once it is generated it dissolves the process instead of strengthening it.

Of course, there may be a motivation behind reflection, the motivation to be rid of the pursuit of the goal, with the further motivation of being enlightened, and so on. But as long as such motivation doesn't generate further goals and seeking, it doesn't matter if it exists. Meditative reflection is a movement of releasing, letting go, letting everything go, including attachment to life, and letting even reflection go. It's done in full awareness. It's not a movement of one thought chasing another thought, like a dog pursuing its own tail.

If, on the other hand, this reflection perpetuates the self by generating a sense of pride and achievement (of "enlightenment!"), which may well occur; hopefully, the pride too will happen in the field of my awareness and be dissolved. If I am deceiving myself in all this, that's life. I let it be, assuming I can be aware of it too..

Then I land in the body awareness or awareness in which thoughts, images or sounds may come and go.

I may later be dragged into action or pursuit of a another goal. But then through reflection I can drop the pursuit of the goal whenever I find that it is complicating my life and binding me further. Again, I may be playing games with myself. But that's the best I can do.

11. On the Division between Spiritual and Worldly Goals

In the essay in Chapter 6 (p.90) I made a distinction between the goals necessary for day-to-day living and goals for self-improvement and self-fulfillment – goals which involve the "self" in some fashion or other. While the former set of goals are temporary and cease to be once they are achieved, the latter persist in our consciousness and cause endless striving. Indeed, the continuity of the "self" is perpetuated by our contemplation and striving for these goals.

My friend Vito Victor raised a question about this distinction:

> But in your essay you also talk as though the rational mind has its legitimate place in solving "practical" problems. As you put it, "I have to use thought to solve problems, for sure, to plan ahead and to organize my life – in short, to lead a successful life in this complex civilization." But what is it that requires us to "plan ahead," and what is to count as a "successful" life? When I retired, with a monthly pension of $1,500, our financial adviser thought we were nuts. The definition of 'financial security' is itself another thought product.
>
> Do you see what I am getting at? I think that the dichotomy of spiritual-practical (goals) may be shaky. It may be that everything is thought, that the mind entirely pervades human functioning and we can't get rid of it.

And my friend Elliot Roberts-Ruchowitz (see below) had similar concerns. Now is the time to discuss this issue:

1) Is this distinction that clear-cut? When my goal is to make money, does that not also involve my "self?" When I make money, I feel elated; when I lose it, I feel lost. Will I ever stop making money? Then isn't that a spiritual goal?

A typical goal of wanting to go to some place just disappears once we arrive there. But it's not so simple with other goals. Many of these wants are generally part of other wants, means to other goals. When the bigger ones are satisfied we find ourselves going after other wants or more of the same (better food or more of the same food, for example.) In this same vein, of course, when you finish cooking a meal, the desire to cook that meal comes to a stop. But a similar desire is instantly formed from the success of it; *viz.*, I must cook something like this again, or cook a different thing. Or if the cooking is not successful, I say I must cook it again, this time a bit better. Desiring, based on goal-formation, is something, as Hobbes says, which only ceases in death.

11. On the Division between Spiritual and Worldly Goals

2) There is a constant restlessness in us which continually prompts us to seek goals, wanting us to become something other than ourselves. On the one hand, this seeking is based on our awareness of what we are at the moment, an awareness which evaluates the present condition and posits a goal to make the condition continue, or make it better, and so on.

On the other hand, we also have a restlessness which looks for anchoring, seeking some foundation. Notice this condition when we have nothing to do, when for just a moment, the mind is blank. Why does it have to go anywhere, become anything else or do anything?

It seems, therefore, that in the ultimate analysis, all goals are spiritual goals. They all want to make you better, change you into something other than what you are.

So where does that leave us?

3) Pleasure-seeking, goal-seeking, becoming something other than oneself etc., must all amount to the same thing. They are all goal-seeking behaviors. In other words, whatever we do directly or indirectly involves goal-seeking or pleasure-seeking.

Still, when Elliot asked me the question whether money-making is worldly or spiritual, I said that it is worldly, as long as you can quit it when you have as much as you want or as much as you think you need ("need" defined by you). In other words, money can be worldly or spiritual depending on whether you can let go of the goal once you have fulfilled it, which, of course, presupposes that you can arrive at such an assessment using "worldly" measures. That doesn't mean you are free from all pleasure-seeking goals. If not money, you will be seeking something else.

To stop the movement towards goals means you have to "die"! When for just a moment the movement stops, there comes a strong impetus to go after something, to think about something, to become something. It's a very unstable situation. You have to accept death and be disillusioned about all goals. Then you will probably recede into the body and be a mere awareness, at least temporarily.

And when you are drawn by some situation into action, then you can just do what's needed for the moment and return to mere awareness.

4) Then there is the factor of thought complicating the issue: More often than not, thinking is not such an innocent function. Most of the time, it is used to perpetuate or continue the self in some fashion or other. That means, there is a goal-seeking, pleasure-seeking activity going on whenever you think. At times, the mere recognition of an object is enough to judge and evaluate and therefore to seek a goal. Perhaps there are moments when you get tired of the whole thing, and go into a mode of mere being.

5) But what is reflection? Isn't it another form of perpetuating the self? Yes, in the absolute sense. Even when you are aware that you are

aware of thoughts, images and sounds. And as long as there is brain activity, it may just have to go on. Then what the hell is all this writing about? Why am I doing it?

6) That's why UG kept saying that you have to clinically die! There is no final solution to problems except the "final solution!"

But then in UG's case at least, there may be thought functioning without there being a thinker and without its perpetuating the self.

But until then, at least relatively speaking, we could be disillusioned with our goals and attain some amount of peace. Or is that another one of our grand illusions?

12. Desire, Pleasure and Tension

I read in a "Network Chiropractic" brochure the statement that desire is a tension in the nervous system. I once mentioned this to UG without disclosing my source. He agreed and said, "Yes, it is."

This was borne out further in my own experience. When I let go of everything and am able to accept things as they happen, then my system relaxes totally. Then either I relax into the body and eventually fall asleep, or get into a state of awareness where there is no self, but just being, or I sometimes get into a state of ecstasy.

But you can't remain there forever. Something draws your attention and you are caught in this or that activity or thought process. Then again, you are aware of things as and when they are finished or you are finished with them, and you revert to the state of passivity.

There is a certain instability in the state of desirelessness or absence of thought. Our past simply impinges our memories on our consciousness, and there is a pull in the direction of seeking pleasure, of looking for things in the past which might give us pleasure now. And then you get lost in that memory, experience and pleasure-seeking, or whatever. Of course, if you are aware of it, you can return to Ground Zero.

The real test of freedom is the ability to stop anything you are doing at the moment, however important it is, to be totally detached from it and divert attention to whatever else is needed. That ability and flexibility are indeed what enable one to step out of any emotion, disappointment, depression etc., as well as any current activity.

13. The Self is a Set of Habits

A habit is no habit without continuity. You break up the continuity; then you break the habit. The self is a set of habits. Habits have a momentum. The momentum of a habit forces your consciousness to go back to a certain experience in the past and repeat it, or to seek a pleasurable experience, a novelty, an excitement, or something interesting relating to it. If you catch the urge as it arises, there is no need to "go" anywhere or "seek" anything. By interspersing the continuity with your consciousness, you break up the continuity of the habit into pieces. Then the habit loses its force.

You can say the force of habit is what in Indian philosophy are traditionally called *samskaras* (subconscious impressions of past experiences and deeds);. I think it is these that account for why there is such instability in consciousness when it doesn't have to think about anything. There is a constant urge to go out and seek something, as if without that something you are groundless and unfulfilled. This can especially be noticed when we sit doing nothing for a while and feel jittery.

What you seek, of course, is pleasure. You think, naturally, of what has given you pleasure in the past, with the assumption that it will give you pleasure again. The thinking of it itself gives you pleasure right now, and that pleasure creates the further urge to seek some more of the same or a similar pleasure in the future.

The same is true of our remembering of past painful events. The thought of the past painful event is itself painful. And that very thinking prompts the urge to avoid the recurrence of the same or similar painful event in the future. The self is nothing but such a habitual seeking for pleasure or avoidance of pain. These create the continuity of the self.

14. In and Out of Mental States

I wrote elsewhere about how the linking up of mental states not only creates mental problems, but also creates in us our sense of identity, a notion of self as a separate entity from others, the world and even from ourselves. It is indeed fascinating to see how this identity actually arises.

Without our interference, mental states have their own natural duration and then they fade out on their own. We pour life into them by either participating in them or resisting them by reacting to them through our memories and past knowledge, thus giving continuity and permanence to them.

Take grief, for example. Like anger, fear, depression, loneliness or boredom, it is a state of mind. Left to its own devices, it has a limited life and duration. Then it fizzles away, sometimes through distraction and sometimes naturally, without any effort on our part. But our past experience reacting to it through our thought process keeps it alive by interpreting it as something undesirable. In that very interpretation is the process of resistance. Since I, what I think about, and my thought about it, are not really separate entities, although I might presume they are, my very thought of the grief and my resistance to it pour emotional energy into the mental state, giving it continuity and life. In fact, we have no way of looking at a state of mind except through our thought of it. If we could, then we wouldn't even know we are in that state.

Thus, in my mind a duality is set up between me and my mental state (of course, through my thought process). I keep battling the state and can't understand why it continues in spite of my resistance to it or my trying to suppress it or get rid of it.

A mental state does not have any strength if I don't participate in it or resist it. Just suppose I come to terms with it by understanding that perhaps grieving is a natural process or that death is inevitable and so on. The state will have its natural life and die its natural death. The duration of the state would then depend mostly on the intensity of it.

Fear is another example of a mental state: Our initial attitude to fear is that it shouldn't be there, i.e., that we should not be afraid. And then whatever we do to address it will inevitably strengthen the fear, even if our attempt is merely to accept it. You cannot *will* to let it be. You just let it be. This is so because to "will" something presupposes a duality set between yourself and your fear, and as long as you operate within that duality, the fear not only persists, but is multiplied and strengthened. But suppose you surrender to it. Cease and desist from any effort to change it. On many such occasions, which generally happened when I was lying in my bed, in just a few moments, the fear not only fizzled away, but my organism relaxed and I fell asleep, waking up to notice I did not have the problem anymore.

The discussion about mental states gives us the hope that we can do something to change a given mental state. But unfortunately this essay can give no such direction or instruction. Even the instruction "Do nothing about mental states" can easily be taken as a direction. Then we tend to look upon a given state with a determination not to change it. That too has the motivation of wanting to bring about a result.

The reader can always ask: "Then what to do?" "Nothing," would be my answer.

2) But this talk may make it look all too easy. Actually, it's more difficult than it seems, because we are so used to living by the pleasure principle of pursuing and enhancing what is pleasant and avoiding what is painful. As long as we fall headlong into pleasurable experiences and want to repeat them, improve upon them and seek more of them, we guarantee some kind of continuity of ourselves. But this is the same mechanism of "self-preservation" that also automatically produces the negative reactions to some other experiences labeling them as painful. So, the learning about inaction regarding unpleasant mental states has eventually to be applied to the so-called pleasant or positive or pleasurable states of mind as well as to the negative painful states.

This is of course not to say that we shouldn't enjoy what happens in our life. But such enjoying is a far cry from preserving mental states as a way of perpetuating ourselves. The possibility of such inaction, however, may involve a fundamental overhaul of our systems.

What is the difference between letting a state be and being in a state? We are sometimes in a state, struggling in it (like in depression), and there may seem to be no end to it. This is an inevitable question. The answer lies within this dilemma that when you are struggling within a state, either you are aware of your struggling in it, or you are not. If you are aware, the fact that you are aware is itself in indication that you are other than that (although still involved with it). And that awareness of separation also implies that there is an attempt to become free from the struggle. Thus you are in that state and back to square one. If, on the other hand, you are not aware that you are struggling, then as such there is no problem. The state will wither away, unless, of course, it is generated by body chemistry or drug-induced. If it is, the solutions for such problems (which are observed by others) are not from within. You have to get help.

But if by some means you can get out of mental states, say by just letting them be and surrendering to them, there is a "neutral" zone, a zone of mere consciousness. Here you are merely aware of the innards of the body such as the throat, the stomach or the mouth, and you are not within the mental world. Thoughts may arise and pass, but you are not them or in them, and there is no reaction to them. Once you have a clear taste of this neutral zone, then you can move back into it whenever you find yourself caught in a mental state – you just have to let be whatever the state you find yourself – if it is fear, let it be; and if it is a hurt, let it also be. This is a skill of instantly freeing yourself from any mental state by thus letting it be and letting it last as long as it wants to. Please notice, once again, that I am not saying that this is a skill you can cultivate.

You can say this zone of consciousness is self-luminescent, to use a Vedanta phrase. You know it exists because there is a built-in self-awareness. UG himself talks about consciousness knowing itself (he says, for instance, in the *Mystique* that "Life knows itself"). You could call this a temporary state of enlightenment. On the other hand, you can say it is a shift in the brain. I am not so much interested in what you call it as the fact itself. When the "front" of your brain is active, you are in mental states and you struggle within them. When you shift to the "back" of your brain (or "head" if you prefer), then you are in the zone of the body and awareness of the innards. There are no values here, nothing bothers you, and you don't have to do or strive for anything. There are no relationships, including with yourself, no emotions, no love, and no fear of death. You can't say it is anything. But then it's not nothing either. It's just awareness.

15. Ending the Downward Spiral

The Build-Up Of Thought: We don't question our positive thoughts, because they give us pleasure. We tend to avoid the negative ones, because they are painful. Whether we have a positive or a negative thought or memory or impression or sensation, our mind builds on it, making the positive things seem more glorious and rosy, and negative things more gloomy and ominous. This build-up is forward-looking. In fact, because many memories we have carry an emotional charge, they prompt us to look toward future for further fulfillment and repetition, or avoidance and annulment, depending on the positive or negative character of the memory. In other words, as we move through time, it may seem like we are only repeating and reliving our past, but we are really trying to prolong or resolve the past mental build-ups for the future.

As we get older, we tend to emphasize worries and negative thoughts and dwell on them more and more, although we also reminisce the positive ones a lot. There are times when our minds seem to become stuck in downward spirals of negative thought. Whatever our actual problems are at the time, our minds seem to generate copious amounts of conjecture, dread, worry, etc., which are not only of no use, but also do not dissipate, but rather build up. Indeed, we build up on them so much that we panic and terrorize ourselves with them, turn them into nightmares and start trembling at the thought their possible occurrence. And it seems that there is a "tipping point;" in other words, if the ratio of negative to constructive "build-up is too skewed, we are in trouble. We sink into a paralysis of inaction and worry. We become mentally and therefore physically sicker and sicker.

My question is, if we come to find ourselves in such a situation, is there a way in which we can extricate ourselves from this burden of negative build-up, regardless of any actual problems being solved? First of all, one might suggest taking a hard look at their build-up, perhaps a look at things like one's attachment and conditioning, and we could, in facing those, make attempts to define them and let go of them. this may not work when we are under duress, as we may be adding to the build-up by attending to it in this fashion. Is it possible that, without confronting this build-up we can just "step aside"? This may entail our letting the

15. Ending the Downward Spiral

repetitive build-up "go", that is, complete itself by asking, what could be worse? or what is the worst thing that could happen?

There is no rut which we cannot extricate ourselves from. To be able do so it may not be enough to become aware of our conditioning or attachments and let them go, as they keep recurring. At times, we may have to consciously and deliberately say to ourselves, "I will accept whatever happens, and I am not going to obsess about this anymore." We have to make a conscious decision, like a young fellow saying to himself, "I am not going to be intimidated by this other kid anymore; what's the worst he can do to me?" or "I will work this out." It's not that you are using your will, which is generally based on identification with something. But rather it is that after seeing yourself get into the same rut repeatedly, you decide consciously not to slide into it. Buddhist Vipassana meditation recognized the role of such a decision. (Also, within the eightfold path, part of Buddhist meditation consists in encouraging our minds to think wholesome thoughts and discouraging them from thinking unwholesome thoughts. The Buddhists did realize that our minds do have a tendency to build up.)

When you once again find your thoughts beginning a familiar building up around something, you catch yourself before or right at the time you start to fall headlong into the thought habit pattern, and you stay out or step out of it. It doesn't matter if you have to do it repeatedly and it doesn't even matter if you have already been caught in the spiral. The moment you are aware of the rut, you step out. And you can.

The trouble with stepping out of things is that when you are involved in some thought process or state, you are within it and as such you don't even think that it's possible to get out of it, let alone for you to make any effort toward that end. But when the pain is great, and you see no way out, it might just occur to you to "surrender," and to drop the whole process. Or you might just say to yourself that you have had enough of the rigmarole and it's time to get out of it.

This stepping out of things brings one to a very unstable state. Consciousness, as Sartre would say, constantly seeks a grounding, a foundation. In other words, it seeks content. If there isn't any, it will try to find some. Being without any foundation is indeed a heroic task. But I suggest that if you could be there from moment to moment (unfortunately there is no continuity, because there is no mental state), then you stand alone outside the build-up of thought. You are truly being yourself. In some sense, you are always there catching the beginning of sliding into a mental state. I don't know if this is called freedom, but it can surely end the downward spiral and any descent into hell.

16. The Self, Meaning and Significance of Life

The Question of Meaning or Significance of Life: My former philosophy professor who later became my friend once bemoaned the fact that in spite of carrying the Bhagavad Gita under his arm for many years, he could never "believe" (in religious matters). He is a well-known scholar of Indian philosophy and culture as well as of Western philosophy and logic. I told him that he could never believe nor could he *make* himself believe because "he knew too much," meaning that his knowledge prevented him from naïvely believing in anything. The knowledge would prompt him to question and doubt any belief he might entertain. The same holds true with innocence in matters of living.

The question, "What is the meaning of life?" like questions such as "Who made God?" "What was there before everything?", is a metaphysical question. It does not lend itself to any satisfactory answer, because such questions are basically paradoxes created by our reason, which is a form of thought. For instance, suppose there is some meaning to life, say, for instance, serving God or His purposes (letting alone the question of whether there is a personal God or not), one could immediately ask the question of what God's purpose is, or why one should serve God. This questioning is endless. That's why the question has no general answer.

In order to satisfactorily answer this question, we must ask in what contexts the question of meaning of life arises. I used to point out to my students when discussing the question of meaning of life that a five year-old, for instance, just doesn't run to his or her daddy and ask him, "Daddy, daddy, what's the meaning of life?" We don't ask such questions when our lives are running smoothly. (I am not talking about asking such questions out of mere idle curiosity or academic interest.) Our lives must have run into some crisis and come to a screeching halt before we are prompted to ask such a question. As UG often said, a living man never asks the question of why he should live. You don't ask such questions until you have lost your innocence in living. You must have "known too much" to get to ask such questions.

Normally, when we do things, engage in various activities of life, we don't look for any external meaning to our actions except for keeping an eye on the goals we seek. It's natural that we confront various frustrations in life, particularly with regard to some significant goals, be it a girlfriend

15. Ending the Downward Spiral

or boyfriend we wanted, or a job we seek or the ill-health that we try to recover from. In striving for our goals, we make constant and repeated assessment of our status, where we are and how far we still have to go, what we have achieved, and what that "means" to us, and so forth, by reviewing not only our present situation, but also our life; and that reviewing becomes a habit. It is when we face some profound failures that we tend to review our life as a whole, assess its significance and ask if there is any meaning to life at all. We have to arrive at a general idea regarding the whole our life, which we didn't have earlier (even when as young people we constantly looked forward to our future), before we can ask such fundamental questions about life. This questioning can land us in various forms of malaise: one might lose one's taste for life, become bored with it, and worse, become an alcoholic or workaholic, or become addicted to achievement, or become chronically depressed or even go the limits of losing one's will to live and commit suicide.

The solution to the problem of meaning of life lies in the sources where it was generated, *viz.*, in the initial frustration in achieving one's basic desires or goals. In other words, the solution to this problem lies in its dissolution. If we could resolve, for instance, each specific frustration as it arises and move on with our life activities, we would be totally engaged in living and not be separated from life. Then the question of what is the meaning of life would not even arise.

Fulfillment and Frustration: Built into any activity geared toward goal-seeking are ideas of time and future. We labor under an implicit assumption that the satisfaction of each goal will somehow fulfill us. The feeling of fulfillment, the feeling that our life has been fruitful, could come not only from attainment of goals such as making money, having a good family, a house, a boat, power, or achievement, but also from religious sources: we ardently believe in God and His grace; we feel blessed; and through our devotion and piety we feel that someday our lives will be blessed, or we will reach the presence of God.

When goals are reached, when we get what we want, we do feel content and satisfied, and feel fulfilled for the moment. But the matter never ends there: the very awareness of what we have achieved spawns further goals, at least ones aimed at preserving the status quo or continuing it in time, for we once again feel we may be lacking or feel uncertain in some other fashion (we may not have what we want tomorrow or there is a risk that someone or something might take it away from us, and so on). When our striving process proceeds successfully without interruption, we normally do not tend to ask fundamental questions about living or its significance. If we happen to have religious beliefs, then as long as the beliefs are strong, they tend to give us support in tiding us over our frustrations: thus life with its travails, for example, might be viewed as a testing ground in which God or some other power morally and spiritually prepares us for a life of blessedness and guides us along the way.

But when we find that our goals are not achieved and frustration is the only outcome, and when we confront several such failures, we tend to believe that our lives have been a waste and we start wondering whether life itself has any meaning. We could even lose our faith in God, particularly if the shock of frustration is too great and none our prayers have been answered. It is not as much that we look toward a higher meaning as it is that we wonder whether there is any meaning at all: this is the crux of the issue.

The flow of life is interrupted when we ask such questions; our naiveté and unquestioning involvement in the life process are halted. When the frustrations are rather fundamental, no substitutions of goals or simple patching up will put us back on track. We have lost the taste for life. The lost belief or faith can never be restored. Is there any solution to such a problem short of being subject to boredom, depression, alcohol, or suicide?

Once the question of meaning arises, one then asks the further question of how to become free from this separation, this alienation between ourselves and our living.

As long as we are attached to setting goals and striving for something outside of us to fulfill us, frustrations are inevitable and the question of meaninglessness of life must arise, as we keep insisting that not only must our desires be satisfied, but that we must have no failures and we must be "permanently happy without a moment of unhappiness," to use UG's expression. The problem of meaningless of life is intimately bound with the problem of time and of our own future non-existence. For we try to fulfill ourselves because we feel we lack the time for all the things we desire, time for our very living.

If we can confront the idea of our own future non-existence (i.e. death), and our emptiness, then perhaps we could see the superfluous nature of the values and goals we have been seeking all our lives. That is, we can see that all the goals and values that have hitherto given meaning to our life are dispensable. This doesn't mean that we stop setting goals or stop having desires. Living simply requires us to. But we come to see the provisional nature of goals, and strive for them only when one needs to and not be daunted by failures. Each thing we undertake would have value only on its own merits, but not as part of an entire life-project, or to gain self-fulfillment or to find an ulterior meaning. When we don't succeed in our endeavor, we are flexible enough to try again or abandon the goal and move on to other things.

15. Ending the Downward Spiral

Notice that I am not advocating that we should not have goals, or not enjoy or suffer the results of our actions. Of course, we will do those things, as we currently do. Suppose we come to the realization that there is no external meaning to life, and thus whatever we do can only have meaning stemming from the goals of the specific actions we undertake. Further suppose that we realize that success and failure are equally possible outcomes of every action, and that when we are faced with failure, we accept it just as we would a success and move on to our next set of actions, perhaps even including reworking the entire project. If we could come to such a realization, it means that we have learned to become free from the residue of disappointment generated from previous failures.

Each failure is an invitation to revisit our goals and assess their feasibility as well as an opportunity to become aware of our attachments to things, people or situations and question them. As well, these processes allow us a glimpse of our own emptiness underneath all our goals and activities. Then we may come closer to living life on its own terms, and not by the dictates of some abstract values we have acquired here and there.

I am not saying that there is no significance to life or meaning in life; I am saying that if you don't need to ask fundamental questions about living, then each little thing we do will have its own temporary and provisional meaning. The metaphysical question of whether or not there is an ultimate, exterior meaning to life doesn't bother us anymore, because we realize that that need for meaning is bound up with all the goals and values that we have so far found desirable, and that in fact our "self" *is* that meaning. The loss of that self is what we have been afraid of. Once we are free from that fear, we don't have to look for any ulterior meaning. Life is its own meaning.

Meaning and the Self[45]: The world we build for ourselves, the world of our meaning, *is* our self. The self is meaning. The loss of meaning is the loss of self. Our thought process evaluates and categorizes various situations and events that occur in our life and assigns meaning and value to them. At various times we might feel elated or depressed, depending on the outcome of our evaluation. Thus meaning and value are assigned in terms of one's past experience; that's the measuring rod and the backdrop against which things and events acquire meaning. The meaning we assign to our world is *our* meaning and it defines us.

Our feeling secure is bound up with our being able to find positive meaning in our lives. The mind constantly tries to impose structure on any given situation. One has to find a place for oneself in this structure and evaluate as to how one measures up in relation to it. Not being able to do so makes one insecure, because life then is seen as fraught with uncertainty and one wouldn't know where one stands.

Boredom: One of the opposites of a meaningful life is a boring life. If things do not appear interesting or meaningful, then we feel bored. We constantly vacillate between the opposites of "boring" and "interesting" when we face various situations. What's interesting and what's not is determined, of course, on the basis of comparing the current situation, activity, idea, thought, conversation or whatever, with what we have experienced in our past as having been more or less interesting or meaningful than this. The ability of not looking for meaning in life is the ability to deal with situations not on the basis of such comparisons, but just as they are – i.e., neither interesting nor boring. You just do things because either you have to, or that's just what's in front of you. Everything you encounter, then, has its own interest.

Loneliness: One of the consequences of loss of meaning, particularly stemming from frustrations in love and relationships, is the problem of loneliness. Unless you are, once again, comparing and finding the present situation as lacking something you desire, there is no room for isolation or loneliness. The world is filled with things and people – they all keep us company. You don't get lost in them nor do you feel isolated.

Depression: Depression is another one of the consequences of the loss of meaning. Depression is considered a malaise. Unless it is generated from some physical condition (such as gloomy weather or chronic pain) or a chemical imbalance, it is always relative to something we have been missing or feel frustrated about. Depression is a withdrawal response. You don't reach out any more as you were frustrated earlier. Your energies, as it were, are turned inward as in withdrawal. And depression will be inevitable as long as you are still attached to the person or thing you have been frustrated by, and for some reason or other, continue to seek. If and when you could let the person or thing go, then depression will drop away from you like water off a duck's back.

Fear and Worrying about Future: We are not only proud of our past achievements, we also worry about our future – what will happen to our money, fortunes, job, health, family, house, and so on. We constantly live in hope, and yet when there is some doubt about future outcomes we worry. Our meaning structure, i.e., our self, is constantly in question. We feel threatened. As long as we think about our future, we must worry. The mind constantly calculates possibilities and measures one's progress in relation to them and we respond to these calculations through both worry and hope. Worry is a form of fear. We will never become free from one (fear) without becoming free from the other (hope). To become free from both requires an overhaul of our belief system, i.e., our cherished values and desires. We cannot be free from fear until we take it all the way to its limits and accept the worst possible outcome. If we could ever get to do that, that might engender the possible required disillusionment with our

15. Ending the Downward Spiral

desires and goals. Thus we become free from our attachments regarding future outcomes. Then we are not concerned with life's meaning. We just live.

In the final analysis, questioning of meaning in life in a blanket all-encompassing sense is tantamount to the readiness to let go of one's acquired values and meanings, that is, to let go and lose one's self. By facing one's possible annihilation, one might be able to break up the total meaning structure into pieces. Then perhaps one lives without having to have an overall meaning; each life situation or event has a meaning of its own. For instance, I am currently writing this essay because it falls within the scope of the issues discussed in this book, because there was some occasion in my previous writing where this sort of question arose, or because someone raised a question regarding this. Although I am drawing on many segments of my past experience, and I harbor some intention that in the future some person might find some interest or use for what I have written here, once I finish writing this piece, my purpose is served and I move on to other things. I don't have to have the writing of this essay to contribute to my sense of an overall meaning of life, nor do I have to feel disappointment if people criticize this, or do not understand it or agree with it. Those are their problems, not mine. As to the question of why I write at all, the answer is simply: for lack of anything better to do. It is, as a matter of fact, one among the many things I do in my day-to-day life, some necessary for living and survival, and some totally gratuitous. How else could it be? I cannot make myself believe in any artificial or religious structure and go about assigning meaning to my life on its basis. I have no disappointment in my life either. Life is what it is. I just live it as best as I can, and then I go!

I know all this sounds totally counter-commonsensical and absurd as we are all so used to living on the basis of a set of values to which we feel so committed and attached. We feel that there is no point of living without such a basis (I can hear a resounding response, "Then why live?" in my ears!) This is just one possible analysis and solution, and it may or may not appeal to you.

Part 4: Other Philosophical Essays

17. Whither Morality?

What is morality? It is not the following of enjoined rules of conduct. It is not a question of standing above temptations, or of conquering hate, anger, greed, lust and violence. Questioning your actions before and after creates the moral problem. What is responsible for this situation is the faculty of distinguishing between right and wrong and influencing your actions accordingly.

Life is action. Unquestioned action is morality. Questioning your actions is destroying the expression of life. A person who lets life act in its own way without the protective movement of thought has no self to defend. What need will he have to lie or cheat or pretend or to commit any other act which his society considers immoral?

--UG in *Mystique of Enlightenment.*

We do question our actions before and after, whether we like it or not. For one thing, we worry about the consequences of our actions, whether they will turn out just as we expected them, or will there be consequences to ourselves or others, or what will then happen to us if certain consequences follow our actions, and so on. We also feel guilty if a current action goes against our own previously accepted norms of right and wrong, or good and bad, and regret if our actions don't bring the desired outcome, and feel elated if they do.

I am not as much concerned here with which theory of morality and moral judgments is correct; for instance, whether utilitarianism is better than deontology or vice versa, or whether we should opt for egoism or altruism. My issue with morality is that even if we agree on which moral standards we should use in making our judgments, we are still left with a major problem.

The main problem with morality is not even that we worry about whether our actions may turn out to be wrong, but is that more often than not we do not act in accordance with what we ourselves have determined is the right thing to do. It was Aristotle who first grappled in his *Nichomachean Ethics* (Book VII) with the problem of moral incontinence. The problem appears in Christianity as the problem of the weakness of the will – "the spirit is willing but the flesh is weak." Socrates, followed by Plato, taught that if a person knows what is good, he then will automatically be good and therefore act accordingly. Thus the ultimate evil is ignorance. Plato's *Republic* is an attempt to connect knowledge of the good with a person's happiness (and by extension with the good of the state), thus ensuring the moral conduct of the individual (and of the society).

Whether we approach the problem as one of ignorance or of the weakness of the will, the problem of the gap between one's beliefs or intentions and one's actions remains. No matter what our ideas of right and wrong are, most of us say or believe in one thing and act in another way. Our desires and passions, or our "self-protectiveness", as UG said in the above passage, are the impediments to morality.

Once we act, publicly we tend to justify our actions or defend them, although, privately we may regret them or feel guilty. We learn to lead double lives – in public we try to appear to be virtuous, in line with our beliefs, while privately plotting against other people and scheming to get our way. No wonder morality becomes such a farce.

As I used to say sarcastically in the very first class of my Moral Issues class, "Morality is for other people only!" We are quick to judge other people's actions as good or bad, right or wrong, and we often use our judgments to bolster our egos, to help us feel superior to others, or to feel self-righteous, thinking that we operate on a higher moral ground than they do.

People always look for policies of living, for a policy which will make them permanently happy and bring them in harmony with the rest of the society. Unfortunately, even if they come up with one, I can hardly think of a single individual who doesn't, for whatever personal reason, violate his own policies (or moral standards) at the next turn, especially when no one is watching.

Then why this sham? Why morality at all? Why standards of right and wrong (and of good and bad which form their basis)?

I have thought for a long time that morality played out in these terms really has no place in our lives. Don't get me wrong: I am not advocating "immoral behavior" such as murder, rape, violence, lying or stealing, or acting on impulse or passion without regard to consequences.

UG talks about acting through the self-protectiveness of thought. Unfortunately, we do think, and by virtue of our thinking, more often than not, we *are* self-protective. To me, it's interesting to see how in fact we act in concrete situations: we have desires, some of which conflict with one another. And we have fears. In the face of any given situation, we consider the conflicts and act in a way consistent with the equilibrium of our mental economy. I think that's the most assurance we could have for moral behavior. Consider the following possibility:

A young woman comes to me for advice regarding an unwanted pregnancy. I could take a moralist pro-life position and tell her that she should carry the pregnancy to full-term, giving birth to the child, and if she has problems raising the child, give it up for adoption. Or, I could take the pro-choice position and tell her to go ahead and get an abortion.[46]

17. Whither Morality

But my advice ignores so many other factors the woman must consider in making her decisions. If she does have the baby, what economic hardship will she face? How about the social stigma, rejection or disapproval of others? But more importantly, my advice does not take into account how she will deal with her loneliness, feelings of guilt, remorse, and of being betrayed and so forth. Were I not to take these factors like these into consideration when I advise her, I might be missing the point and only imposing on her a "one-size-fits-all" advice from outside, as it were, thereby putting only more pressure on her instead of helping her solve her problem. Is my position here that of a moral judge or a friend and advisor or an interested party? (In fact, in giving advice, even use of terms such as "right" and "wrong" and "good" and "bad" would only exacerbate the confusion.) Where should I stand in this matter?

Leaving moral positions aside, if I were to advise her on this situation, my advice would be first, not to tell her what to do, and second, to tell her that the issue is not one of right or wrong, that she has to make up her own mind, listening to her feelings about the situation and considering how she would feel about the possible consequences. I would tell her that after considering all of these, she should come up with a decision which she could live with, and if she can't come up with a decision right away, she should keep working at it until she can come up with a solution, i.e., 'sit' on the problem. I also tell her that when she finds the right solution to her satisfaction, her mental turmoil will diminish and she can live peacefully.[47] She would then know that as far she is concerned she has the right answer. If she finds later that she was mistaken in her previous decision, then again she gives herself a chance to rethink the matter until she comes up with a more satisfactory solution. And unfortunately, there are no rules for this. And in this instance, there is a limited time frame to come to a decision. Of course, she knows that whichever way she decides, she has to face the moral judgments of other people, and that she has to live not only with herself, but with the society around her, and, more seriously, with the law.

I think this approach to the dilemmas we face bypasses the whole issue of rights and wrongs and goods and bads. (One might say, by taking consequences into consideration, she is adopting the utilitarian approach. But I think it's much more than that.) It's not that I provide any specific rules or guidelines for acting. But I think this approach more or less approximates actually the way we in fact act, and I also think that by broadening this approach (which aims at a state of equilibrium in our mental economy) we have a significantly better chance of bridging the gap between our professions and our actions. I know this is no easy solution to our problems, but I don't know of any easy ones.

By "to live with oneself" I mean that you work at a problem in a situation you confront until it is resolved in your mind and that it's no longer a problem to you; I mean to resolve a conflict until you can live in peace with yourself. And, of course, only you can be the judge of what you can live with.

One might ask the question, what if I lie or cheat or pull the ground out from under someone's feet, and I am still at peace with myself, either because I feel I am justified, or because I feel I did these things because others did similar provocative things. The answer to the question, of course, varies with the situation:

For one thing, I have to live with the fear of consequences: (of course, I could also just be paranoid and live in fear of unreal, non-existent possibilities). I remember that once, a long time ago, after smoking marijuana a couple of times, I refused to do it again, not just because I didn't like the taste of it, nor because of my respect for or fear of the law (I might easily break the law in other cases, if I thought it was worth it), but I didn't think the possible consequence of getting arrested and going to jail was worth it.

For another, if my lying or cheating does cause a problem to another person, and there indeed will be consequences as a result of that, then I still have a problem on my hand. I have to work to resolve that.

On the other hand, if what I do causes no problem to someone else or to myself, then why should I even bother to think about it?

One advantage of thinking in these terms is that such thinking provides a means to self-knowledge, and thus a way to free myself from all kinds of unnecessary goals, fears and worries, a self-knowledge which will hopefully ultimately lead to a life without self-protectiveness. Another advantage is that I am not quick to judge other people's behavior.

This type of thinking is not really Fletcher's situationism[48]. There is no talk here of God or love. It is subject, nevertheless, to charges of moral relativism which were leveled against situationism. But my thinking in a given situation is relative not just to the situation but also to myself, because my reaction or response to a situation is a complex result of what I see as the situation and of all the factors that go into making up myself including my background, conditioning, personality traits, psychological complexes and so forth. It is that entire complex which determines my response to the situation.

But my response is not a fixed response which can instantly be judged as right or wrong, although other people may in fact judge it as such. As far as I am concerned, at any given moment, my response to a situation is either satisfactory (to me, of course) or it is not. If it is satisfactory now, it may cease to be so when other factors come into the picture, and I may find another response more satisfactory and modify my previous one accordingly. If I don't intend to change my response, that means that I am willing to take the consequences.

To give an example: I once heard of a nun who made a decision to carry her unwanted pregnancy to full term and have the child. She was willing to face the consequences of her decision, including becoming a lay woman, finding a job to support herself and her child, facing social disapprobation. In other situations, the consequences I might be willing to face include physical punishment, prison or even death. But that would be my choice, that being the way I have decided to live. If I "chicken out" and change my mind, I have to face my fickleness too and that in turn becomes part of my situation I have to resolve.

Notice here, that there are no objective standards such as right and wrong, or good and bad that I use to judge my actions. (If others judge my actions with those standards, I, of course, have to face those judgments.) I can only talk about the responses I can live with and are satisfactory to me, and those I can't live with or have problems with.

An objection that can be raised against my approach is that it is purely psychological and has nothing to do with the moral issue of actions being right or wrong, and that it takes away the most powerful element affecting our communal living, moral decision-making and education.

I said above that we use morality as a means not merely to judge other people's actions, but to build our own sense of self-worth through those judgments, to feel righteous and morally or otherwise superior to other people. The one big problem I see in our society is that we are too quick to judge others (judging politicians about their sexual morals, for instance), knowing full well that we are not really much different from them and that under similar circumstances, we too would probably act in the same way or even worse. Then I ask, why play this game of morality?

Here I am distinguishing morality from obeying the law: if, for instance, someone burglarizes my home, I may report him to the police and get the culprit incarcerated. This is within the domain of law. I may feel justified in my action and may not feel any guilt for acting that way at all. On the other hand, I may feel that the criminal justice system does not care about the reasons why a person would commit a crime, that it only cares about punishing him, and thus I might not report the burglary to the police. Acting in that vein, I would bear the consequences of my action, including the one that I may be breaking the law in not reporting the crime.

What about situations like war? Haven't I removed the powerful tool of moral judgment, i.e., my ability to say that such and such a war, for instance, is morally wrong? My answer is the following: by criticizing either side in situations of war, we tend to polarize the situation further instead of resolving it. Instead of solving the problem of war, we perpetuate it by taking one side or the other. I remember the times when I was demonstrating against the War in Vietnam in the downtown mall in Riverside, California, as I also did earlier in Berkeley. While I was standing there in the mall holding hands with others in protest, I could see the animosity I was causing by my merely standing there -- people's hostile looks and angry debates and so forth. I asked myself, "What am I doing standing here? Instead of helping to solve the conflict in Vietnam, I am adding to it."

My reflections drove me to consider what the sources of war and violence in general are, and I discovered to my utter chagrin that I myself was not free from the qualities of intolerance, greed, aggression, violence, and quest for domination and glory, which I had identified as the qualities that perpetuate war. I similarly saw that the problems of hunger and poverty the world over are also perpetuated by the ways of my (and others') living: my self-protective self-interest, my urge to amass wealth beyond my need, and so on.

It's true that lack of sensitivity to other people and their needs causes untold harm in the world. How can I save myself and others from these horrendous consequences?

A person who is not sensitive to begin with is not affected by others' criticisms or moral judgments. His or her own needs have to shape such sensitivity.

Educating children when they are still young surely a holds a promise. If, for instance, we could show a child that hitting another child hurts the child (once I demonstrated this to my daughter who just hit another child in a park by actually snapping my fingers sharply on her forearm just once and telling her sharply, "this is how it feels to her, don't do it!"– and I never had do it again), then that's the best education I could give her. Of course, nothing I do might change her dislike for the other child, but at the least I provided an occasion for her to be aware of a problem (at least she had to deal with me!). To be sure, she might do it later stealthily, or she might like being violent for just the kicks of it -- but I don't need to dwell here on the endless consequences. Of course, the need to educate my child may be my own need (I wouldn't say moral need, but her behavior toward other kids did present a problem for me that I had to deal with).

Backing up, I also look for possibilities of change in my ways of living before I can even possibly contemplate changing others' ways of living or passing quick judgments on them. I think this sort of approach is more helpful than making moral judgments. This in fact not only helps me, but also the people I come into contact with to see things more clearly, and perhaps helps us all solve problems better in the long run.

The problem with the traditional moralistic approach is that it doesn't address the gap between what we profess and what we actually do: it ignores our desires, feelings and passions and our make-up in general. As long as we have our desires and goals centered around ourselves, there is bound to be a gap between what we think we ought to do and what we end up doing. The question I ask behind my approach is, how do we bridge that gap?

You might say that I am shifting morality from the objective to the subjective realm, thereby making it inaccessible to any public discussion. This is the same as saying that if we can't morally judge someone's actions as right or wrong, then we can't point a finger at the action of a person, however horrible it is, and indicate it is bad or wrong (or good); we can't publicly discuss such actions, and therefore, we can't praise or blame anyone. Thus one might draw the conclusion that we can't change people's anti-social behavior. While this all may be true, much of what we do in the public realm of morality can be transferred, practically intact, into the private realm of problem-solving. This move may help us make better progress.

You might also ask the question: suppose someone does make a moral judgment, would I say that making such a judgment is wrong? I say it's neither right nor wrong, as far as I am concerned. I might find a problem with it, and in fact might even feel guilty because they may point out a problem with my behavior (such as its having gone contrary to my own standards about myself).

What about feeling guilty then? Is that not a moral issue? (This is the crux of the objections to my approach.) "Guilt" and "guilty conscience" are expressions of conflict within a person between what he feels he ought to have done and what he in fact has done. The question of "ought" is not necessarily a moral "ought". It could just be a possible alternative action which the individual feels is more in accordance with his beliefs about how he should live or behave toward other people. That may or may not include adherence to moral standards.

One more remark about conscience: one might say my approach is akin to appealing to one's conscience in order to decide whether or not to act in a given fashion. This remark is only partially true, as "conscience" normally presupposes an inner moral voice with its dictates, whereas the problem-solving approach, in addition to including the moral considerations, also includes other considerations such as one's interests, passions, and so forth.

The fact of the matter is that we do have moral standards about ourselves, as we do about other people and other groups or nations. We have mostly acquired those standards from our society and use them to chastise ourselves or approve of ourselves and our actions. Of course, we believe in them. What my approach does is to bring them under the heading of "feelings" rather than "standards". We feel that such and such should be done or ought not to be done. Right and wrong are just expressions of those feelings. There is nothing very objectively correct about them, although we might believe that they are.

You might ask then whether those feelings ("oughts" and "ought-nots") are just viewpoints I might consider or not, or are they, according to me, what ought or ought not in fact to be the case? This is really the issue within the charge of subjectivism. My answer is that from my point of view there is no difference between "feelings" and "moral standards" and that I claim they are merely part of my mental economy.

It may be claimed that this approach is no different from that of any moral theory which attempts to reconcile one's interests and one's duties, taking into consideration how one's interests must pay attention to other people's interests in order to secure a moral society. To that degree, it might also be asserted, this theory is similar to the utilitarian or deontological ethics whose primary interest is to safeguard the welfare of the society as a whole.

My answer is that this claim is essentially true except for these basic differences: my approach doesn't lay an unnecessary burden of adherence to the so-called "rights" and "wrongs" principles on the individual; secondly, it allows a better integration of a person's interests and feelings with the unique aspects of each situation; and finally, this tends to diminish the gap, for the above reasons, between one's interests and one's duties.

One Final Remark: Again, one might claim that this is not very different from Hume's theory of morality, or a modern version of it such as "enlightened self-interest," which is a form of egoism. Here one might say that I am advocating individual happiness as the ultimate good, and all actions would be judged as good or bad, or right or wrong, according to this norm. My answer is, once again, that although it may very well sound like that, my approach tends to include moral psychology in the picture, which moral theories generally do not.

18. Is There Such a Thing as Selflessness?

UG used to proclaim that man is "selfish to the core." In fact, one of the articles written on him many years ago in a Kannada newspaper in Bangalore which he showed to me had the title of a quote from him, "Only selfishness is real, selflessness is an illusion." My comment on the title at that time to UG was, "Yes, it's a selfishness which does away with the very notion of self!"

The questions of egoism and altruism arise in the context of morality. Any moral theory must reconcile the conflict between self-interest and duty – at least that's how it is traditionally believed. Hobbes is a philosopher who claimed that man is like an animal, driven solely by self-interest and desire which "only ends in death." Some theories, like that of Hume, argue that there is basically no conflict between self-interest and duty, and that if one would only look deeply enough into self-interest, one would discover that one's duty is included in it. Similarly, Joseph Butler's moral theory claims:

> Every particular affection, even the love of our neighbor, is as really our own affection as self-love; and the pleasure arising from its gratification is as much my own pleasure as the pleasure self-love would have from knowing I myself should be happy some time hence would be my own pleasure.(*Quoted from Internet sources.*)

The extension of this notion is the modern theory of enlightened self-interest.

Various forms of utilitarianism attempt to reconcile the conflict between egoism and altruism in different ways with varying degrees of success. A more recent one, proposed by Rawls, includes self-interest in its notion of "acting under the veil of ignorance," according to which, people when they constitute themselves as a society should opt for such policies of the state that they would accept regardless of which position (high or low) they would occupy in the society. (Rawls, *Theory of Justice*) This notion seems like a version of the golden rule: "Do unto others as you would have them do unto you."

The political theory of Adam Smith, the theory of *laissez-faire*, believes in the Invisible Hand, which guarantees that if everyone in a society acts for his own self-interest, then the interests of the society as a whole will be automatically taken care of.

My interest here is actually not to address the issue of the conflict between interest and duty, but rather to inquire into the degree to which man is selfish: I particularly want to discuss the thesis that no matter what a man does, it always is done for his own self-interest. This is the thesis of psychological egoism. There are two problems with this thesis looked at from within the realm of morality. One problem is, how it is possible for a man sometimes to act in the interests of other people if by nature he is not endowed with the capacity to act in such a fashion, which is required by morality. The second problem, related to this, is that only one theory of morality becomes possible if the thesis of psychological egoism is true, and that is ethical egoism, which says that everyone ought to act according to his own self-interest. Ethical egoism leads to contradictions in contexts where two people's interests conflict, and, according to the theory, both of their actions must be right.

Now, rights and wrongs aside, the question must occur to anyone inquiring into human relations as to whether other people's interests have any role to play in our lives except as means for us to promote our own self-interest. Of course, we sometimes act contrary to our own self-interest, particularly when we don't know what it is – we think something is in our self-interest and it turns out that it is not truly so. And we do act for other people's interests – interests of our friends and relatives or strangers when we act charitably. When we do so, we tend to enjoy our actions. We find them in some way gratifying or fulfilling.

But can we act selflessly and contrary to our self-interest when the situation (and you might say, morality) demands it? The answer pretty much depends on what we mean by selfless action. Is selflessness action contrary to one's self-interest? If that's the meaning of "selflessness", the psychological egoist might claim that such actions are actually born out of our self-interest, because we only act altruistically (or contrary to our self-interest) when it suits us, i.e., when it gives us pleasure. When we no longer get the pleasure we seek in giving to others or in sacrificing our interests, as for example, when we don't get the thanks we expected or our actions are not appreciated or when the recipient turns hostile instead of being grateful, we revert to self-centered actions. The psychological egoist here will constantly look for a hidden motive of seeking pleasure (or other self-interest) even when it is not apparent on the surface. If we can't find any after a reasonable search, then he would say we haven't looked hard enough. When is the search enough? Could any interest count for him as altruistic? Doesn't that mean he is defining "interest" as self-interest? Isn't that begging the question?

I think this approach (of psychological egoism) misses some points. More specifically it ignores the mechanisms of our behavior, particularly our goal-seeking process. Our normal procedure is to direct our actions to achieve what we desire or to avoid what we don't want. Whatever we desire, we desire because we hope it will give us satisfaction or pleasure. If our action gives us the desired result, we feel satisfied. If we perform the action repeatedly and it no longer gives us the same satisfaction, the action tends to drop off, unless it is a long-standing habit and quitting it seems more painful than acting out of it. Masochism, although it seems painful on the surface, is pursued only because of the psychological pleasure one gets from physically inflicting pain on themselves: here strangely pain is pleasure.

Now, to repeat my question: when we think an action is right, yet it is not really to our self-interest or does not give us pleasure, would we still do it? If we still could, then altruism and morality are possible. If not, then only psychological egoism is true and morality is not possible. The discussion below explores the psychological process that precedes action, especially the goal-seeking of the self, in trying to arrive at an answer.

It is the mechanism of thought which has the built in process of seeking pleasure and avoiding pain. Anything it seeks, including doing good to others, has to fit into this scheme in order for it to be worthwhile to us. The values we hold and the things we desire are what give us satisfaction. They enhance our self. The thought process, in other words, is the process of the self. Through desire and fear, the thought process reinforces the self. All actions, even those we undertake intending to help others, must form a part of this "self (or mental) economy." Even when the actions we perform don't seem to give us satisfaction, or only give us pain, we would still do them if they conform to our values or concepts of what we want to achieve. The self, among other things, is a hierarchy of values we have built for ourselves consciously or have absorbed from the influences around us. We would do something painful because, as a value, it is bound up with the notion of ourselves. In other words, we sometimes do things for others even though they are painful, not because we might gain a hidden pleasure or item of self-interest, but because our very identity may be at stake; not to pursue that value would amount to losing one's self to that extent.

When our actions fail, and the goals or values are not achieved, we may quit the whole enterprise, or console ourselves saying that we have tried, or tell ourselves that that goal was not worth it, or that's not what we really wanted, or that we will try for it another time when conditions might be more favorable, or "who needs it anyway," and so forth. More often than not, we replace one goal with another. But we never quit striving for goals because we have an underlying belief that our happiness or fulfillment lies in achieving things which are out there, outside of ourselves, in becoming something other than ourselves. That is how we use our thought mechanism to perpetuate our "self".

At some point we become disillusioned with this striving; then perhaps not only the striving but also, our goals drop off, and, along with them, the thought process which is geared to achieving them. But that almost never happens.

Short of this total collapse of the self, which is perhaps possible in principle, at least temporarily, whatever we do is solely for the gratification, directly or indirectly, of the self. We are truly selfless only when such a collapse occurs. But then is there any purposeful action in such a circumstance? (I am speaking here of action other than automatically satisfying one's biological needs.) Or would a person's movements be merely random? If there was action, (I can't deny there would be), then it wouldn't be premeditated (to calculate a gain for oneself), or based on some moral or other rules or laws, but would depend on the situation (which may require thoughtfulness to achieve a certain result demanded by the situation). The action might even seem self-centered to others, and no rules could be made out of such actions as they would be so specific to any given situation.

You might ask, why would one even live in such a condition? There is no answer to that question, for any answer would presupposes a motive on behalf of the person, and that by definition is precluded for one in a selfless state. Any such action is gratuitous. To use a popular expression, it is a random act of kindness. It's just as if the person had no choice but to act that way. It is as if the action is extracted out of him, forced out of him by the situation. He acting is *wu-wei* (non-doing).

19. The Paradox of Being Yourself

UG often used to say that you don't have to be anything and that being yourself is the simplest thing there is. Unfortunately, being yourself may not be as simple as it sounds.

"Being yourself" is contrasted with trying to be (or become) someone other than yourself. If, for instance, you think you are inferior to someone else, or you feel inadequate or are afraid, in "being yourself" (trying to be yourself), you don't change what you are into something which you are not, namely superior, adequate or not fearful.

Part of not being someone or something other than what you are at the moment includes not being elsewhere at any time.

You accept your lot, whatever it is. Shall we say, you remain content?

Man's condition is such that more often than not he or she cannot just be (or be anything) without being aware of that condition. But the problem with simply "being yourself" is that the mere awareness of what you are also implies the formation of a judgment about yourself or your condition, and within that very act of judging is imbedded an attempt to transcend yourself, to be or become something other than what you are -- at any rate, there is an attempt to be rid of a problem and thereby change one's condition.

Unless you include these various attempts to be other than yourself (or be elsewhere) as part of being yourself, the notion of "being yourself" is a contradictory notion; or at least it seems so. For, as I said above, to the extent that it involves an awareness of yourself, being yourself is also an attempt to become someone or something other than yourself -- that is, not being yourself. So in this case, "to be yourself" paradoxically entails an attempt "not to be yourself". Or you could say, that "not being yourself" is a way of "being yourself."

When you are so aware, and at the same time also become aware of your attempts to transcend your condition, how *can* you be yourself? You can try to be what you are by telling yourself that there is no point in changing your condition, that there is nothing wrong with it, or that no solution to a problem has been shown to succeed, and so on. These instructions to yourself might help you succeed in returning to yourself momentarily. One could say then that one has learned to accept oneself or learned to be content with what one is.

Cutting the Gordian knot: This paradox, in my mind, can only be resolved by letting oneself be, even in the state of becoming. You are aware of the process of becoming, and you just do it without resistance to it. At some level or other you must come to terms with what you are – even if it be just to keep trying or keep becoming. When we are able "be" so even at the most superficial level, then sooner or later, the acceptance or letting go will penetrate through layer after layer of the self until you can accept your condition, fear, pain, guilt or whatever. Total acceptance has to involve surrendering, if you will, to pain, fear, guilt, or to whatever we recoil from. Then you are not your "self", because the self structure has been dissolved (at least relatively or momentarily), and you revert to mere consciousness or bodily awareness; you just *are*. So, in the final analysis, when we face the structures of the self, "to be yourself" means just "being", being without trying to become yourself or anything else.

20. Why I am a Vegetarian, On Taking Life, and On Abortion

Why I am a Vegetarian

People always ask me why I am a vegetarian, why I don't eat meat, fish or eggs, don't I kill the vegetables I eat, and so on. My answer is the following:

First, yes, I don't eat meat, fish or eggs. For one thing, I don't like them – I don't even like the flavor, smell or taste of any of them. I have tried them both in India and in the US many times. Furthermore, I don't like to eat meat or fish because I don't like to kill animals.

I have no quarrel with those who eat meat. Still, I believe that most of those who do eat meat (or even fish) don't quite realize what they are doing. Of course, a butcher kills animals or at least cuts them up into different parts as a routine to make his living. I don't really know how many butchers like their jobs or do it as a habit or do it because they have no choice. Most of the rest of us (except those who like to hunt) eat meat by killing animals by proxy.

My argument is not based on religion or morality. I think a person is justified in eating meat if he or she can kill an animal with their own bare hands, dress it, cook it, bring it to the table and eat it with relish. As for myself, I can't do any of these things.

I will recount a couple of experiences in this context: One, when I was living in Berkeley, I went on a camping trip with a Jewish girl from New York and her Norwegian boyfriend at that time. When the young man caught an oyster in the water and crushed it in his palm, the girl fainted at the sight of the blood in his hand. I have never forgotten that scene.

The other is from my own past. Once, in 1968, when I was in Waltair (Visakhapatnam), India, I lived in a cabin in the Shanti Ashram and this cabin had a patio, a bedroom and a kitchen, part of which was also used to take a bath. One night I woke up in the middle of the night to go pee in the bathroom, and I saw a rather long and very-slow-moving snake coming through the drainage hole in the wall. It must have been moving so slowly either because it had eaten a heavy meal or it was hurt or it was just too old -- I couldn't tell. I first used a broom and then an iron rod to move it forward with a view eventually to get it out of the cabin without hurting it. But somehow it managed to slither up onto the bedroom door and it was hanging right above the head of my bed. Tense and overcome by fear, I brought it down with the rod and, as it already seemed at least partly dead, beat it to death with the iron rod. Then ants collected around the snake and I called the caretaker of the ashram to come and take the dead snake away. An elderly man, the caretaker asked me in a voiced mixed with respect, disapproval and pity for the snake, "You killed it, sir?" The memory of that experience pricks my conscience (I must still have one!) to this day.

I can't make any general rules out of my experience (or anyone else's). I don't believe much in anything. Yet, I feel that a person is justified in eating meat if he or she realizes what they are doing. And of course, in some areas on the globe you have no choice.

Once, a colleague in my college who wanted me to give a talk on the subject of vegetarianism in her class heard my argument and countered it saying, "You can't always build a house from scratch with your own hands in order to be able to live in it." I replied that the cases are not analogous (a living thing is in question here). Of course, she promptly cancelled her invitation.

To be sure, I kill vegetables and fruit to eat them. Some ancient sages in India lived only on fallen grain and fruit just for that reason. But I can't. In addressing this question, J. Krishnamurti once said, "You have to draw a line somewhere." Some people don't draw a line at all, and I draw it at meat, fish and eggs. Why not eat eggs, you might ask. Actually, my family does. As for myself, I don't like the flavor, smell or after-taste of eggs. Also, I do consider the fact that it is potentially a living animal. Rarely, I might eat something which has eggs in it if I can't taste or smell them, and do not know they are there. If I eat eggs (or meat or fish) inadvertently, I wouldn't beat myself for it.

On Taking Life

Am I opposed to taking life? What would I do if I was attacked; or if someone in my family was attacked? Am I a pacifist? How about abortion? How about preventing babies with birth defects from being born through abortion?

First, my attitude to killing: I am not a pacifist. Yet, when I became a citizen of this country, I told the Immigration Department that I couldn't take an oath vowing that I would defend this country and its constitution by bearing arms if necessary. They asked me to write a statement of my religious faith explaining myself. I wrote in it that I consider all men as my brothers, and that I couldn't bear arms for any country including the United States. The Immigration judge ended up giving me a special oath which provided an alternative to bearing arms. Thus I became a citizen of the US by being eligible to be called a conscientious objector.

No one can make me take a gun and shoot another human being. I would rather go to prison. What would I do if someone attacked me and tried to kill me? I don't know. I will find out when I face such a situation. It's hard to answer hypothetical questions like that.

There was a time when a student actually did assault me in my office for calling him "stupid" (the word just slipped out of my mouth!) in an argument. I complained to the campus police and told them that I just wanted him "off my back" and that I didn't want to make any other trouble for him. His papers were later graded by my colleague. Each situation is resolved in its own fashion. I can't generalize and make up policies or rules of behavior for myself or for others on the basis of one or more experiences.

* * *

For similar reasons, I also will not serve on a jury. Of course, I am called once every couple of years (on the basis of my driver's license) for jury duty. So far, I have succeeded in avoiding it. A couple of times I was selected to be a potential juror. The first time, I was a bit disturbed and consulted a lawyer. He told me after consulting another lawyer, that by law I had to appear for the jury duty, and if I was called up to the jury box, I could explain to the judge why I couldn't serve on a jury. Something like that did happen: after I was called up and seated with the other potential jurors, the judge asked if anyone had objections to serving on the jury. I raised my hand. He asked, "What?" I told him, "My conscience does not permit me to sit in judgment of my fellow human beings." "You are excused!" was his quick reply. I left the courtroom in great relief.

The second time, when I was selected again and they asked me along with the others to fill out a questionnaire, I had an opportunity to express my objection. And that evening I was again excused.

The lawyer I had consulted the first time had asked me why I was opposed to being on the jury. I gave him my answer. He is a reputed lawyer who represented Cesar Chavez and others. I could see Mother Teresa's picture hanging in his office. He had countered my position a little, "There are a lot of evil guys out there." My reply was, "I can't deny that. But, as a philosopher, I can't be part of a system which only punishes people for their acts without considering their side of the picture and seeing what could be done to help them or prevent the crimes from happening." I think my comment is especially applicable to capital punishment.

On Abortion

This is one of the knotty issues that troubles people all over the world. Of course, an embryo is not a full-fledged but only a potential life. But the issue of abortion is not so simple. Read on:

First of all, this is a personal dilemma which by its nature is differentiated irrevocably by gender. Only women can actually undergo pregnancy or abortion. In most cases, but not all, a pregnancy carried to term would result in similar results for both sexes: an offspring to raise. It might be argued that it is easier for a man to step away from this result. As a matter of fact, either or both parties are capable of abandoning offspring, as they sometimes do, for various reasons. However, in the case of abortion only a woman can carry out both the decision and the result (at the very least of undergoing a medical procedure involving some discomfort) ultimately. Thus, the short-range issues of abortion are quite different for the man and the woman.

In my own experience, I did once first advice my girlfriend to abort her pregnancy; I did not think we could remain together and I did not think she could raise the child well on her own. For perhaps not the best reasons in my view, she insisted on having the child; so my position quickly changed: I would be with her and help her with the child until she could care for it on her own. We got married, our daughter was born, and of course that event changed my life.

Although my relation to my wife was tenuous, I saw that my connection to and responsibilities for this small child were profound and lifelong. And, as it turned out, after a few years of being together on and off, my wife did leave me with my daughter, and it was I who primarily and happily raised her. How could I have ever foreseen any of this when initially advising her on abortion? In fact, when my daughter was four or five, she asked me, "Daddy, did you want to get rid of me when I was Mommy's belly?" Somehow she had found out, on being told, about my initial advise. I had to collect my wits quickly and come up with a satisfactory answer, or I would have been her enemy for life. I said, "I'm sorry, but I didn't know it was you; if I did, why would I want to get rid of you?" Luckily for both of us, the answer pacified her and she never raised the question again.

Present in the above account are various positions regarding abortion. My initial decision about abortion was based on reasons of practicality. My ex-wife insisted that her body and that of the germinating baby, must be allowed their way. She was heedful of the process of life, but heedless of practicality. My subsequent surrender was to going along

20. Why I am a Vegetarian, On Taking Life, and On Abortion

with and giving myself up to the situation, one that I had not planned for or intended.

I have heard from several women their accounts of abortion, of the anxieties, depression and guilt they suffered, sometimes years after it had happened. They know that the potential baby that was aborted, even though it was a tiny bit of flesh, grew in their wombs, and they are deeply affected by the experience. For some women, abortion may be much less traumatic, and of course, they would have less of a tendency to dwell on it.

For men, it's more a matter of convenience, economics or parental responsibility for which they might not be prepared. I remember, in the case of both my children, it's the sight of them and my holding them physically that bonded them to me. But the issue is a lot deeper for women.

Now would I say that I am opposed to abortion? Of course not. Am I then in favor of it? I can only look at that question as applied to each individual situation, and advise one to consider carefully. How do *you* feel about it? Can you live with your decision? I can sermonize all I want, but if a woman feels so burdened by the baby and doesn't want the stigma or the travail of carrying the pregnancy to completion, and she feels her life would be thwarted or ruined by it, who can blame her for aborting? But, for either gender, do consider how you would feel if there was an abortion and consider if you could live with that decision. I would advise talking to the people who have had an abortion.

I see part of the problem that is generated in the controversy between the advocates of abortion (or the right to decide about your own body) and those who are pro-life has to do with receiving governmental permission and aid for abortion. There indeed are poor people who probably can't afford the money to go through with an abortion, let alone have money to raise the child. There are also related issues of birth control and care for unwanted or impoverished children. And the pro-life advocates, calling it murder of an unborn baby, don't want the tax-payer's money spent on it. The question then becomes political and I have no answer to that.

Also I have not addressed this question: What if the husband (or boy friend) or the families of either the husband or the wife may insist on the wife not going through an abortion, but giving birth to the child, since they feel that they have a need for an offspring and a right for it, and the woman has no business in taking that right away from them?

I have so far avoided the question of whether abortion constitutes the murder of an unborn child. True, we unscrupulously murder full-fledged human beings in situations such as war, executions, and so forth. When life begins, whether it begins at the time of conception or at the time of birth, or whether life is potential or actual before the child is born, are questions that cannot easily be decided by philosophical argument. (Much of the argument turns around how we define "life.") Nor can the question of whether a woman has a right to decide what happens to her body, as the unborn child is part of her body, or in some cases considered to be an unwanted guest in her body. Whichever way these questions are decided, the problem of how a woman feels when an abortion is carried out remains, nevertheless.

And to me, that's what should really decide whether she should go through with it. Surely, society does have a stake in the life of an unborn child. But ultimately, it's the mother (and not even the father) that bears the brunt of the emotional aftermath of an abortion. Giving the child for adoption does not take away some of the feelings that are generated when the unwanted child is allowed to be born. That is, of course, an option for the mother once she carries the pregnancy to full term, if she can come to terms with such an option.

21. Looking Within

Just the other day, I was watching how my mind was thinking of various possible solutions to the problem of the neck pain I sometimes have. Normally, every time I experience some discomfort or pain, there is an immediate looking for a solution, say a dietary supplement, a homeopathic remedy, a chiropractor, a surgeon or what not, even if I had already tried several of them before to no avail. If it is a new unfamiliar symptom I experience, it instantly triggers a panic response in me, and the effort to look for a solution immediately goes into operation. That particular day, I became aware of the process (not that it was the first time that it ever happened); then my mind stopped looking for a solution. My attention was turned inward to the discomfort itself, and soon there was no discomfort (not that this happens every time). One can say that I accepted the pain. (Please note that I am not suggesting here that merely "accepting" pain will always make it go away or that one should not get medical help when one is in pain or that medical help is useless.) It was in this context that the meaning of "looking within" became rather clear to me. When the problem disappeared on this occasion, I found that there was no "within" or "without," nor anything like "looking within."

What came through in this experiment was that my awareness of discomfort was enough to trigger the duality in the mind, in both defining my problem and immediately looking outside of myself for a solution (and, of course, making the effort of looking for it). A panic arose as all the various possibilities sprouted, along with an accompanying sense of time: a future to dread or hope for.

The experiment reminds me of one of the *angas* (components) of Patanjali's *ashtanga yoga*, i.e., *pratyahara*, which is normally translated as withdrawal of the senses. I used to explain this step to my students as withdrawal of one's attention from external objects. The next step is *dharana*, holding your attention on something, and then you have *dhyana*, meditation. Maybe my experiment condensed all these processes into one (which is traditionally called *samyama*) and removed the duality of the "inside" and "outside" as well as of myself and my pain. My experiment also presupposed that within the duality of the mind, there are no "external" or "internal' objects as such; yet the very idea of an object as other than myself *ipso facto* presupposes that it is external to me.

"Looking inward" and "looking within" are phrases used in the spiritual world. In psychology, the more common term is "introspection."

In either case, the most common things one does with oneself are being aware of one's memories (for instance, by recalling a past scene and reacting to it, often as if it were happening in the present), or being aware of parts of the body, or of thoughts, feelings, emotions, actions or intentions. What we are aware of and respond to is part of our mental world. All transactions take place within this field – the field of consciousness where objects are present in our mental world. And this response or reaction takes place from a certain point of view, which we had generally acquired in our past, and which we *are* at the moment. (We may say that the point of view is what constitutes the "I" or the ego.) Hence the duality. Time and time-consciousness are inherent in this process. That is, divisions of past, present and future are created through the process of self-consciousness.

We know that such introspective awareness is almost never neutral or impartial. We are partial to ourselves when we take a look at our own actions. More often than not, our point of view expresses itself through a thought which is more or less explicit, verbalized and conscious. In our attempt at introspection, we normally attempt to change what is given into what we think is more desirable or pleasurable (or less painful), so that eventually we arrive at a more acceptable state. When we do this consciously, we call the process self-consciousness. When we give directives to ourselves, we also do so with a view to better ourselves, be somewhere else or become someone better. Of course, the same processes might be done automatically; then we would not use the expressions "looking within," and "being self-conscious."

Often, the process of self-consciousness is a battleground. There is a constant striving that occurs and it is driven by goals or objects we are attached to. We use the process not just to solve problems, but to plan, scheme and plot our path to achieve our desires or avoid painful things (such as fear, inadequacy and guilt), to maintain, enhance or protect our status, and to defend, justify or glorify ourselves, often at the expense of other people. This striving process normally goes under the name of "thinking."

When we stop looking for external solutions to our problems, we are giving up trying to solve the problem. Then presumably we accept the problem. At least for that moment, we cease to strive. In others words, we "detach" ourselves from the problem. That's when we can say that our attention is turned "within." But there is really no "within" to look at. Just plain consciousness, if you will, or awareness of parts of the body, without any attempt to change anything or become something other than what we are. There is neither a "within" nor a "without." You just are.

Also, when we stop reacting to a problem, the personal point of view from which we look at the problem disappears. At least for the moment,

21. Looking Within

the point of view, or rather the ego, the reactive mechanism disappears; or at least it is held in suspension.

I know I am over-simplifying the introspective process, making it look too easy. My interest here is to point out the elements of the process, not to claim it's all that easy. I am not even claiming that the result is lasting.

Even when we become free from the thought process, i.e., when we give up a goal or an object we are attached to, this act is done consciously. That means, an internal dialogue goes on in which we either explicitly or implicitly tell ourselves to let go of something, just about the same way as we talk to ourselves when we plan, justify or defend ourselves, or try to calm ourselves when we are agitated. Directives are given through this talk, this verbalization, although, what unfolds may be nonverbal.

This leads us to the question of whether there is anything like consciousness without an accompanying thought process. You can't just say that thought goes on all the time. In fact, when, for instance, UG describes his state of mind when looking at a clock, for example, he reports that his whole being is like a question mark -- "What is that thing?" This just means that he is just conscious of the clock, (even to say that he is conscious of the clock or "that thing" is misleading; it's more appropriate to say that he is just conscious) without the knowledge that it is a clock nor the knowledge of what time it shows. Of course, when he is asked what he is looking at or what time it is, then, as he says, the answer "comes like an arrow." Only when the need arises does he know what he is looking at.

How long such a state of mere awareness or consciousness lasts is really not a relevant question. It is quite possible and indeed likely that when we get involved in a situation, or we are in the heat of the moment, we don't get the chance to look at an object dispassionately or ask ourselves questions regarding our relationship to an object or goal, thereby creating a "space" between ourselves (i.e. our reactive mechanism) and the object. Here I am more interested in analyzing the process itself and pointing out the elements involved in it.

22. Reflections on Meditation

Preface: I used to explain meditation to my students as having the main function of disrupting one's thought process. This explanation is consistent with the Yoga definition of meditation as the cessation of the activities of the mind. But unfortunately, like many other activities carried out by means of our mind, meditation is a mental activity, although its aim is to disrupt the thought process. In other words, its aim is psychological suicide!

Unless we have an intention to change ourselves to become someone different or better, or be in a more peaceful or "enlightened" state, we wouldn't take up meditation. Such an undertaking is the product of the mind, as it is our thought process which always attempts to change the given situation and help us to be somewhere else. Meditation presupposes an awareness of our condition and dissatisfaction with it, along with possible attempts to change our condition into something better. The following discussion demonstrates the paradoxical nature of meditation and how and why it is fundamentally frustrating. I will show some of its virtues as well as its limitations, and finally, I will discuss some other possibilities.

What is Meditation? In the West, meditation is used, more often than not, to relax, to gain a state of peace and freedom from anxiety. In the form of biofeedback it has been used to control blood pressure, promote alpha rhythm in the brain, or whatever. For purposes of relaxation, it is also coupled with deep breathing, differential relaxation, or visual imaging. Those who use meditation for such purposes don't have any pretense to enlightenment or liberation.

Traditionally, however, at least in the East, meditation has been viewed, not merely as a method of relaxation but either as a means of mind control or to attain Nirvana, or Release, or Enlightenment.

Forms and Methods of Meditation: There are many different forms of meditation: One of the most common forms is to focus totally on whatever one is doing, not minding anything else. The traditional story of a woman going around a *tulasi* plant three times with a pot of water on her head with nothing else in her mind, not even knowing that she was walking around, comes to mind. This is one of the means of transformation (*mukti*) traditionally recognized. It's what one might call the path of karma (action). You are focused so much on what you are doing that you are not even minding what it will get you or won't. Of course, normally, in any skilled action, you have to constantly adjust your means to the ends, or else your actions will misfire. That means that by meditating you don't care about the outcome; you do care, but not about what you will or won't get for yourself. This is implied in the path of karma.

Repetition of a *mantra* or a holy name is a more common method of meditation. Whether it is the syllable "*Om*" or the names of gods, or a prayer, it doesn't matter. The meditation could be helped further with the counting of beads and other repetitive acts. (Then one has to split one's attention between the recitation and the counting – which I think becomes a chore.)

Meditation can be engaging in contemplating God, or having a dialogue with Him. This could also take the form of singing the praise of God, as in *bhajans*. It is in this sense that meditation and prayer have been traditionally used by different religions to attain salvation.

One frequently adopted form of meditation is self-inquiry, looking into the true nature of the self. In a contemporary version, advocated by Sri Ramana Maharshi, it takes the form of the well-known "Who am I?" question one asks oneself constantly, peeling off layer after layer of the self. Assumed in this form of meditation is the idea that "I" am not either my body or my mind (and its thoughts). Its aim to disclose our true self which is pure awareness, peace and bliss.

Just sitting and being aware (passively) of one's mental contents is yet another form. Soto Zen is one form that advocates this practice. Non-interference with what is observed is essential. There is and should be no goal for this meditation. If there is a goal, then meditation becomes contrived: one begins to interfere with what is observed and a conflict is generated within oneself, since when goals are present, one constantly calculates, measures and compares.

Many times this method of passive meditation is aided by focusing visually on a dot on the wall, or the space between one's eyebrows or just one's breathing (watching the way the breath enters the nostrils and leaves them). In some forms of meditation, being aware of one's breath and counting the number of breaths constitutes meditation. It has been long known in yoga practice that making exhalations slower than inhalations can indeed help one to relax.

Some other methods of meditation employ the instrument of thought to create a space between oneself and one's problem, such as fear or depression, by thinking about the whole picture of a problem or situation, by contemplating the consequences of actions, or the opposite side of an issue, or by taking a third person's point of view. This method too can result in freeing oneself, relatively speaking, from the problem one is currently facing and perhaps even aid in development of detachment (Sankara's *Bhajagovindam* comes to mind, as well as the Buddhist descriptions of the various parts of the body, and its prospect of ending up in the cremation ground). Some types of meditation like Vipassana take an objective approach to one's actions and look at them as being an impersonal process than as something done through one's own agency. The aim here, once again, is to free one from an ego-centered point of view, thereby developing detachment. These types of meditation employ the instrument of thinking to solve, rather dissolve, the problems created by the thinking process.

Also in Vipassana meditation, like in some other forms, one is aware of one's parts of the body or emotions of the mind, without interfering with any activity. For example, while sweeping the floor, one is aware of how one's feet step on the ground or arms move. Or one is aware of how an emotion such as anger rises, has its life and passes away. This sort of awareness has not only the virtue of objectifying what one perceives, but also of breaking up one's identification with it.

One frequently used form of meditation in contemporary practice is differential relaxation – focusing on each part of the body and relaxing it. In contemporary practice, one finds similar techniques to reduce pain. Focusing on one's pain with awareness, and breathing and relaxing can deeply help one to be relieved of pain.

A meditative process of awareness in movement, such as in Feldenkrais method or the Alexander Technique, can be and has been used successfully in solving skeletal-muscular physical problems (and perhaps psychological problems as well). In some ways these forms are similar to practicing yoga *asanas* with breathing and awareness. Qui Gong is also similar: it combines breathing and awareness with movement to harness the *chi* in us.

Outcomes of Meditation: The outcomes of meditation vary with the belief system one participates in or the method of meditation one uses: you may gain a vision of Christ or Krishna, you may experience God. You may experience your true nature as pure awareness or you may feel oneness with the universe. You may have out-of-the-body experiences; you may lose all awareness of your body; or you may feel that your consciousness is expanding to encompass the whole universe. You may experience states of bliss or beatitude. Or the goal may be to attain peace and harmony, or become part of the universal energy. The list is endless. Some may claim supersensory powers, or the ability to peer into their past lives; others may claim to have precognition, psychic powers and power to heal, or the ability to know the internal structure of matter. Or one may more simply claim the ability to relax and move through day-to-day chores with increased ease and lightness of being.

Relaxation, Release and Self-Knowledge: We need to examine the mechanisms or operation of meditation to see how it works and how and if it can help. In meditation, you are either focusing or you are simply

22. Reflections on Meditation

relaxing. In either case, you don't interfere with the contents that show up in either the foreground or background of your consciousness. This is the primary reason why people who have been suppressing "negative" content in their minds, or who have difficulty facing their own "undesirable" thoughts, emotions or past experiences, have no business meditating unless they are able to face anything and everything that may show up in their minds when they meditate. But if one can let things go and not react as and when things show up, then there is a genuine possibility of being released from the mental content, particularly if one has gotten to the bottom rung of the ladder of the layers of a problem. One could term this process "self-knowing" or "self-knowledge".

Take, for example, fear. Normally we resist fear. But the fear there is stems from the threat we feel from an object of fear; we fear imagined consequences to us from the object. If we let the process of the fear unfold and figure out what might be the worst possible consequences from the threats that could happen, and let them all be, then the object of fear will no longer pose a threat.

This same process could be applied to objects of frustration or conflict or depression. Coming to terms with the incident which we dread or with the possibility of not obtaining what we so cherish and desire, we can achieve a release from either the fear or the frustration that is generated by our attachments, negative or positive, to the objects. We could apply this process to attitudes, beliefs and prejudices as well.

In adopting the process of meditation to enhance self-knowledge as described above, one might uncover our fundamental attachments to good health and to life itself, as well as our negative attachments to (or fears of) pain and death. We may find that through this discerning process of meditation enough space may be created between ourselves and these attachments and fears, such that we lose our connection with them and they drop away. We arrive at a state where nothing is important anymore, not even our living or dying, and there is just plain consciousness. In that moment of awareness thoughts might appear like sounds and experiences like images. One now has the ability to let them come and go. They have no longer the charge or hold on one they had before. The emotional charge is dissipated, as it were. (Of course, this can also happen in confession or confiding with a friend.)

Self-knowledge in the sense described above implies the awareness of the contents of the self, and since this awareness is of a non-interfering nature, it could be described as an automatic process of detachment. In other words, we are shedding the contents of the self.

Limitations of Meditation and of Its Effects: This freedom from may be just momentary. We may fall headlong into a thought or an experience or a habit pattern and react to objects of these as though they are currently happening. In other words, the attachments reassert themselves. We may have to go through the meditation again and again. So the relief and release we obtain in meditation may only be relative and temporary. We can't expect any permanent changes. The conditioning that generates our attachments may be too deep and perhaps even beyond the reach of our consciousness. And meditation may not be able to uproot these conditionings. We may have to accept meditation at that level; but that doesn't make it entirely useless.

Similar limitations apply to relaxation techniques. To the degree that we are able to let things happen or go, we are able to relax. Or we might say that the ability to relax physically in the face of the various attachments or hang-ups that show up in our consciousness is indeed what enables us to become released (detached) from them. This only shows that the body and the mind are not really two separate entities, but two aspects of the same entity.

We can re-invoke this relaxation process by consciously letting go of everything, even if it is for just a moment. Through repetition the process can become progressively shorter, telescoping a whole lot of previous self-knowledge into just a moment, as it were. But then we are back again in the thought-game.

The primary reason why release of this sort is only relative and temporary is that underneath all conscious activity is a holding on to existence, which is essential to the survival of the self, self in the psychological sense. The survival appears to be a physical survival – after all, the psychological is only a mental extension (or abstraction, if you will) of physical survival (at least, that's how it appears to the self). This holding on to existence manifests itself as fear of death, of old age, of disease, and most of all, of pain, as well as the attempts to strive for continuity through pleasure seeking. We can mislead ourselves into thinking that we are totally free from all this holding on, but when a situation presents itself, the fears might manifest themselves again, and thus we may have to work to loosen their grip yet again.

This is the reason why I say there is a radical difference between this relative freedom and total liberation, where one is free from the will to live, free from any attachment to living, as well as from any negative attachment to (or fear of) death, pain, disease and old age. This is witnessed rarely among human beings. I saw this in UG not only when he was face to face with death, but throughout the years I knew him. From my own perception, as well as from a detailed account I have read by Mahesh Bhatt who was with UG until the last moments of his life, I can say that after he had gone through his "calamity," UG never cared whether he lived or died, and almost *never* sought medical help[49] to become free from pain or sickness. And to me that's radical. I don't know if this is indeed desirable for any of us, but I do know that this is what constitutes true liberation, if there is such a thing.

Unfortunately, liberation is not subject to conscious choice, since, as far as the psychological self is concerned, such a choice would be tantamount to not just psychological, but actual suicide. No wonder UG kept saying that in order for such a thing to take place there must be a "clinical death."

Bonuses of Meditation -- Feelings of Ecstasy, Energy: Once one is momentarily free from the contents of consciousness (i.e., from the ego or self), at that moment, one might feel a surge of energy flowing through the body with or without an accompanying feeling of bliss. This can be (and is often) interpreted as an experience of enlightenment; but tradition warns us against such feelings: they are mere feelings and as such are fleeting. The consequence of such feeling may well be that the person feels unburdened, lighter and refreshed for the rest of the day, unless and until some concern, worry or obsession, stemming from the past, takes over.

But this is not what traditionally liberation is supposed to be. If one is liberated, it's final, once and for all. I can't see that happening through conscious meditation, and I give my reasons below for it. I don't mean that liberation can't happen at all; I just mean that it cannot happen through our conscious effort and will, or by any deliberate meditation.

Further Critique of Meditation: To repeat, meditation is an activity of the mind, although it is geared toward letting the mind cease its activity. It is, in fact, a "suicide mission," by definition: the hope is that through our meditation we will eventually reach our goal of becoming free from all mental activity, including that of striving for goals. But this is a contradictory process. We cannot succeed.

Practicing meditation is much like believing in God; we keep our faith and pray. We could say that one could eventually become free from the self by continuing the practice of meditation, just as we could say if one has enough faith they can move mountains. If one doesn't succeed, it's their own fault. It means they haven't done enough. This is a tautological requirement: you have meditated enough only when you have succeeded in becoming free from the self and you will succeed only if you have meditated enough.

So, we can go on without doing any ostensive meditation. But our awareness doesn't go away. We are stuck. We can't go forward and we can't go backward. Whatever is happening within us, we are still aware.

We keep going around in endless circles, getting more and more frustrated. We try in various ways not to meditate, to meditate, measure results, watch the activity of the self, and get frustrated again, let go of that activity, let go of everything, and so on and so on.

There are times when we don't care what happens and are merely aware, but only to again fall headlong into the habit of thinking and responding to the world through the self. This is an endless activity. And there is no end to it nor is there any hope. We are cornered.

But even this may not be a problem, given the nature of the mind – even this vicious cycle becomes comfortably familiar. We gain some facility of moving between "declutched" and "clutched" states.

Possible Conclusions: What possible conclusions can we arrive at so far? 1) It's a waste of time to meditate. 2) Meditation can at best help us arrive at "Ground Zero," a neutral state of awareness, but it cannot help us stay in it, for it is an unstable state, volatile; we are back in the automatic conditioned response cycle each time we have to deal with something in the world. Not only is the conditioned response mechanism brought into play, but also with it arises the duality between the self and the world. We cannot but respond to the world ultimately in terms of the self and its interests. Of course, through choosing to meditate, we may be able to work our way back to a state of pure awareness; but we have to do it over and over again. It's an endless cyclical process. Perhaps we could telescope the process somewhat and become skillful in moving between both worlds. That's about the best we might be able do.

Beyond Mediation -- A Possibility: If by some chance the mind does cease its activity, there is no meditation, and none is necessary. We are in the mode of being, rather than in the mode of becoming, of the mode of getting somewhere, where the future invites us, haunts us, where there is tension in our minds pulling us forward toward the future. This restlessness will not cease until we give up the goal of achieving anything, including any kind of liberation through any form of meditation; it will not cease until the very goal to meditate ceases to be. Then there is neither meditation nor any need to meditate.

When all activity of the mind stops, there is a respite. We are not meditating, nor are we not-meditating. I used to say in my Eastern Philosophy class that one truly meditates only when one is free from the very need to meditate. (As UG would say, "You are truly free when you are free from the very need to be free.")

I don't know if I would call this liberation. It's not liberation if liberation implies some kind of permanent state. There are no permanent states, at least in the conscious mental world. There is only a constant dynamic, a dynamic in which we typically respond to the world through the self, and yet at some point in time there may be no response at all -- one just is. As I discussed above, there, however, cannot be a radical change in oneself which may be called "total liberation."

23. The Bugbear of Spiritual Progress: So What?

Can One Be Unattached? Those who consider themselves as being in the spiritual path often try to measure their progress or achievement. Sometimes they feel elated when they see themselves freed from some hang-up or attachment and at other times they feel dejected at their failure to make any progress. They can even set themselves a high standard, say of total detachment, and yet find themselves still stuck with some basic attachments like money, sex, achievement, power or food. Their measurement lands them in these happy or frustrating crossroads.

But I think this problem caused by measuring one's progress is all bogus. As long as the measuring mechanism is operating, our mind is clearly active, looking forward to the future and measuring the past against the future. And this measurement just generates ideas. If a person is truly detached, he wouldn't care about enlightenment or liberation. He would be "stuck" with whatever or wherever he is in the present. In some sense, he is psychologically dead. There is no other life. If it is pain, he is the pain. (Of course, he may not be able to help himself taking a pain pill.) Whatever he is doing, he is involved in it. If he is not, he may just be merely aware of everything around him. But there is no other life and there is no enlightenment either. He has no choice but to let everything else be. Even when he is occasionally involved in what he is doing, he doesn't have judgmental feelings about it. That's what he is and there is no transcending it; because any attempt to transcend presupposes there is some other life. If he is attached, he is aware that he is attached. On the other hand, when he is deeply involved in what he is doing, he may not be even aware of any attachment. He may be stuck with it for the rest of his life. But that is his way of life. As UG says, it's the goal that's the problem, even the goal of letting go of attachment.

"Spiritual Hunger": The so-called "spiritual hunger" is part of the mind's deception. UG and others usually say that the person that is questioning them has no "hunger", meaning that the person has no real drive to break through. But having detachment as a goal and striving for it is just as much an involvement as any other. I realize that I don't have that kind of hunger. So I am stuck where I am. So what?

Is There a Thought that Results in No Thought? This question arises because when there is a moment of mere awareness, it is often preceded by a thought. (But then, for what state is this not true?) The thought may be one of understanding, or disillusionment or some such thing. If the thought results in such an awareness, the question is whether the thought itself is motivated (in other words fraught with duality). If you say it is motivated, the question arises as to how a dualistic thought can generate a non-dual state of mind? On the other hand, if you say, that it is not so motivated, that it is one of mere understanding and so forth, then the problem is how can there be a thought (or "understanding") without a motive? I think this paradox can only resolved by accepting the idea that the thought may very well be motivated, but then concluding "so what?" It doesn't matter if it is. If this awareness we are talking about is also dualistic, because it is generated by a dualistic thought, so be it. I don't care if one calls it pure awareness or dualistic awareness -- I just don't care about pure awareness or enlightenment. If it happens, that's fine, if it doesn't, that's fine, too. I think we generate unnecessary duality by worrying about the sources of thoughts.

The problem arises only if I want to be sure that what I have is pure awareness or if it just a thought-generated illusion. Why do I have to know?

Conclusion

My Relationship with UG: What was my relationship to UG? Was he my friend, or was he a master or teacher to me? I have been interested in the teachers I mentioned in my Introduction (Gora, Chalam, J. Krishnamurti and UG) primarily because they helped me in my own investigations. At different times, their teachings spurred me to make advances in my thinking and ways of living, and thus to various degrees they have become an integral part of my intellectual life as well as my living. Gora, Chalam and UG all became my friends as well. Yet, I never hesitated to criticize them, especially Gora and UG. This applies to J. Krishnamurti as well. In other words, I never submitted myself totally to any of them; I didn't implicitly obey them nor did I uncritically accept what they said.

With UG, "being in a relationship" is a paradoxical phrase, either as a "student" or as a friend. He always maintained that there was no teaching, nothing to be learned from him. By the time I met him (I was about 46), I had pretty much "burned my bridges;" my investigations had already brought me to a standstill in a spiritual sense. UG gave jolt to any complacency I may have had (and that was his effect on many others as well). His "negative" teaching of denying everything, combined with his elegant and persuasive speech, certainly lit a fire under me to continue to question my own world.

As a friend, again UG was an enigma. Because of our similar backgrounds and common mother tongue (Telugu), we sometimes shared a certain feeling of camaraderie. He was often quite attentive and hospitable to me and my family. Yet there was no lingering attachment or "relationship" on his part. I felt the extremes of both "oneness" and absolute "aloneness" with him that I have never felt with anyone else. Yet I have the greatest regard for UG as well as unbounded affection. So, in answer to my question, I have to look at these facets of "relating" with UG, and their effect on me, and just say that I had the good fortune to have both a most unique friend and teacher.

Main Conclusion of this Book: The main conclusion that might emerge from the different essays in this book is that release or liberation, while being total, sudden, final and acausal in someone like UG (and I can think of others), might also be piecemeal, relative and provisional in others.

UG on Freedom: Once, during a conversation, UG vehemently denied that there is any such thing as relative freedom. In fact, he at times even denied (although I doubt if he had meant it) that there is any such thing as enlightenment. UG also often said that you cannot strive for "enlightenment" or total freedom: "You do not choose it; it chooses you." Nevertheless, he laid down some necessary conditions: the mind must be stultified to the point that all desire must be burned away and all movement in any direction must stop. Yet, this, in his view, is not an effect you can aim at or try to achieve. This may be so. Yet the problem remains that the mind's nature is to seek, if not to seek goals, at least to seek to avoid pain. The question is whether one can give up seeking ultimate goals such as what UG might call "permanent happiness," "*nirvana*" and what not. As UG always said you don't really give up anything.

My Approach to Freedom: I might want to opt for shutting life down, renouncing everything that I am and all that I have, say my house, relationships, property, food (when I am hungry I will figure out where to get food), and so on. I could just walk away from everything. But would I be free from the goal of shutting life down? As UG says, it's the goal you have to be free from. But could I? Giving up the goal still presupposes a reason for the giving up, which is in itself a goal. Thus it becomes a game we play with ourselves. (As UG said, "the negative approach is still positive.")

My discussions in the book should have shown that while we have persistent goals (or attachments), there are also moments when we can just simply surrender to the inability to let those goals go. That effortlessness, to my mind, lets one become detached from the goal itself. So, the distinction I am trying to make here is not just to try to let things go, but to discover in oneself a place where there are no goals and surrender oneself to the prospect of living without any goal. Once we see the state of mind where there are no goals of any kind, including being free or enlightened, then I think stepping out of the process of striving for goals is not such a hard thing to do.

While a total and final change to our thought process may be the "real" thing, I can't just sit on my hands and wait for it. For whatever it is worth, I have to live my life now, facing my problems and working things out, nevertheless not losing sight of what is fundamental in life. Regarding myself, I see a gradual evolution (or development, if you will) in this process and it may or may not culminate in a total transformation. For example, it's a lot easier for me now than before to let go of things and people.

I know such a release is at best relative and provisional and there is no finality about it. Total and final release can only come about when the will in some fashion or other withers away and that unfortunately is not in my hands.

Can I say that I have attained some kind of a fundamental breakthrough, or release? I can make no claims to this. At times I feel that with the limitations of my present makeup, physical and psychical, it may not possible for me to be anything other than what I am. That doesn't render what I have been discussing in this book useless.

One of the facts of my life is that I too am conditioned like everyone else. UG used to say, "You can never be free from conditioning; conditioning is intelligence." I don't know if these statements are indeed true. But I know that I do react and it may take me some time to let those disturbances to run their course. I can see that as long as conditioning operates, one must live in the world of duality. In that sense, UG himself, as far as I know, to the extent he was operating under his own conditioning, was also subject to moments of duality (as he would say, "'UG' comes into the picture").

Method: The whole book may seem to advocate adopting a method, practicing it and thereby trying to make progress toward a goal. It may seem as if I haven't become free from goals myself. (You might ask, "Or why write this book?") Also, what I have written cannot but be taken as a "directive," to use UG's term.

The Other Side Of The Picture: If having goals is a problem, and yet UG says that you cannot give up anything (including goals) except in order to gain something in return, then my question is, why did he talk about anything at all? Why didn't he just say what he had to say once and walk away? If UG kept hammering away at these issues, dinning the same thing over and over again into people's ears, it may be that he was doing it so that it might have the effect eventually of people quitting their goal-seeking and their quests.

UG's common response to this dilemma was to say that when people asked him questions, the answers would come out of him as if from a machine, automatically. When involved in some discussion or debate, UG often ended the debate by asserting, "This is just a dog barking," implying that there was no real debate going on, but rather that his words were merely coming in response to the other person's comment or question. He claimed that we "interpret" whatever he says or does according to our background, prejudices or predilections. There may be no problem with the words, his or others', they simply being noises, and everything being mainly our interpretation. This response of UG may have been a consequence of his non-dual state, but it also had the effect of his being wrapped up in a bubble of immunity to criticism, challenge or personal involvement. You could either admire him or throw up your hands in despair.

People who heard or read UG often couldn't help but take what he said as being directives, either. He knew that. But he kept talking, knowing full well that people would interpret him in the ways they in fact do. His answer to the problem is to say, "Being exposed to what I say will unburden you." For instance, UG told someone who was bothered by a neurotic fear of silence that he should change nothing but should merely accept his fear. And that person eventually did find relief by letting his fear be. To my mind, such changes are possible only because people have learned to let things go, especially their goals. That is indeed how their lives become unburdened.

My wife used to remark that while people would come to see UG hoping to unburden themselves from some kind of inner malaise, they often ended up "leaving behind more than they had bargained for." That is, they would come hoping to divest themselves of a bothersome aspect of a problem, but did not expect to have their underlying attachments and conditioning, even their sense of self, exposed.

One of the common answers UG gave to people raising their problems in front of him was to say, "There are no problems. You have no problem." If a person was saying he gets depressed, UG would say, "Be depressed!" or he would say, "Unless you are contrasting it with another state, where is the problem?" Or he would say "You have problems only because you want two things at the same time. If you want just one thing (and are willing to do everything to get it), there is not a thing you cannot get." When he himself was in a rage, he never looked at it as a problem. He just freely rode it out. In that sense he never wanted to change the given. He never moved out of his nonduality (except, in my opinion, when "UG" came into the picture).

Goals and Lettings Things Go: To come back to my own writing: what I have been trying to do is primarily to agree with what UG says about the illusoriness of goals (my writing should confirm this), yet, at the same time, I am trying to work out the nitty-gritties of it (i.e., how goals exert power over us). My talk of "letting things go" may sound like I am advocating a method. It's rather a "non-doing" without any specific goal in mind, done only because one is confronted with a problem or set of problems. You might say that this, i.e., becoming free from a problem, is indeed a goal and is bound to set up a duality in one's mind between oneself and the problem one is trying to deal with. I agree, and that's where I point to the idea of "surrendering to a problem" (including to the inability to give up a goal). In other words, although your intention (or goal) is to solve a problem to begin with, you realize at some point that as long as you are attached to the goal, you cannot truly solve the problem.

Notice that in view of my analysis of mental states, it should be clear that I am not advocating any advancement toward or achievement of some goal. Rather, I am talking about repeatedly letting things go. In that sense there is a progress or evolution, but not in any sense of gaining something. In fact, the "letting go" will surely backfire if one does it with a view to achieve some result or gain something or attain a state (even if it is just to become free from a problem). If one has in view any solution outside of the problem, that surely would set up a duality and throw one headlong back into the problem.

I am writing more in the spirit of explaining the structure of problems and gaining an insight into how we relate ourselves to them rather than trying to provide a solution or method which can be mechanically applied to rid ourselves of them. Of course, just as with UG, this too can easily be misconstrued as advocating and teaching a certain method, a path, a practice and so on.

To me, what words one uses doesn't really matter. What matters are the facts: One can be relieved from the burden of one's past by becoming free from specific problems as well as problems in general, and land in a field of awareness (energy if you will). This "landing" is a function of our ability to relax totally to the point where nothing matters, including living, dying or enlightenment. For me, when I stop caring for any problems or solutions by letting things go (and letting the problems be), I not only relax totally, but the problems disappear; I am then in the field of mere awareness or awareness of the body. The body is itself a surface phenomenon. When the relaxation is deep enough, even my awareness of the body as such merges into a general awareness. I can feel the tension in my head when I am in the middle of a problem and when I let things go, my attention goes back into the spine area in the back of my head, instead of being caught in the top of my head. Thus my system relaxes and that helps the energies in my body flow freely.

I am hoping this possibility of stepping out of things can be used by others as well. In that sense, the book is hopefully within the realm of understanding and communication.

I believe what I have written here is sufficiently highlights the meaning and importance of effortlessness. UG often said that any movement of the mind, in any direction, will make you stray from your natural state: I have explored the problems encountered in trying to achieve the natural state while trying to keep that goal in mind and making use of various methods. It seems any effort in this area is ultimately futile. Of course, even this can be construed as some kind of positive teaching or offering of a method, but unfortunately, nothing that is written or communicated can escape that fate. The human "hearing" mechanism is such that the very language creates a goal and looks for a directive.

Thought and Knowledge: The final problem I have to deal with is thought -- namely, that any of one's relaxing is an activity of thought, driven by the motivations of the self. For instance, how do I really know whether I am totally relaxing or giving up everything? How do I know whether I am in a state of being merely aware of the body? Isn't this whole enterprise driven by thought? If it is, one cannot be said to be really free of the self as long as there is the self in the background, calculating and contriving. Indeed, I have myself raised such a question to UG: how does he know whether he is free from thought? What told him? Couldn't one say that the self, and hence knowledge, has always been there in the background? UG's answer always was that he didn't know, that Life knows itself.

Sometimes he said he knew it (that he was free from thought) now (when he was talking), but didn't know it then (when it was happening). My answer is somewhat similar to this last answer of UG: although one starts with the motivation of the self, one realizes that as long as there is any motivation to be free one cannot be free. But when one is free, there is an awareness of freedom; and when thought and knowledge operate, then one knows that he or she has been free. Of course, such knowledge can trigger further motivation and duality, but that's in the nature of things.

Differences: Therein lies the essential difference between UG and me. With UG, the freedom was permanent and final. (You could say there was a change in his "hardware".) The getting rid of motive had become automatic. (In this context he would say, "thought cannot enter; it will get burnt up every time it enters.") In UG there was a perpetual state of unknowing in which knowledge occasionally entered and created a temporary duality of UG and the other. In me, it's freedom that is occasional.

There is something else that is totally different about UG: I felt at times that UG was a mere appearance and that some force or power from another dimension was operating through UG. Thus to my mind UG represents the unknown. We get hints of this when we know that UG's words and deeds are not what they seem to be, and have effects which are unfathomable to our ordinary knowledge and experience. I have no problems with that unknown. To that I totally surrender myself and pay homage. And I have no way to speak of or account for it. I just simply am awed when I sense its presence.

In spite of these differences, I feel that the attempt here is not futile. Although the release that I experience may be only provisional and may lack the finality of the liberation of UG, it shows possibilities of freedom in everyday life.

Despite any differences, I have always felt there is a fundamental unity between UG and me. Underlying us is the unity of life, of existence or whatever you may call it, as was attested to so many times by my sense of being in the same "field of awareness" when I was around him, where there was (and is) neither UG nor me. I know that some others had similar experiences.

The End

NOTES

1. "Fragmentation, Meditation, and Transformation: The Teachings of J. Krishnamurti," published in *Journal of Indian Council of Philosophical Research*, Vol. 5 No. 2, 1988.

2. Till his final days, on special occasions, especially on full moon days, UG would show the swollen glands to those around him.

3. I know that treatment: there were times when I slept in UG's living rooms. He would come early in the morning at 6 or 7 am, stand by my side and say in a soft and gentle voice: "It's 7 O'clock, you want to get up now?"

4. Chandrasekhar was a frequent visitor to Chalam's house and regarded Chalam as his "father" besides being devoted to Sowris.

5. Having been a widow and having no place to go, she took shelter in Chalam's place and became part of the family.

6. Probably sometime in October, 1981.

7. She had been staying with us for about a month. She was recently separated from her husband and apparently they had both met UG once before in India.

8. He did make a few fruitless attempts later [sometimes with me helping him] to break up the relationship. They ended up having a child and then separating.

9. Sometime later, I asked him at my home why he kept visiting me. His reply was: "because you fit in!"

10. My article on UG, "Pulling Yourself Up by Your Bootstraps" was added at the end of the book later in its second edition.

11. Julie sent me the following remark upon reading what I wrote: "I wouldn't call those 'fights' with UG. He was always blasting me and I was stupid and stubborn and couldn't listen. But I have yet to see anyone really listen to him; it was impossible on some level. We were all just listening to ourselves. Nobody really knew the nature of the relationship I had with UG and that is okay with me, even I am only beginning to understand it now, a little too late."

12. Of course, Paul Arms was always in the background, to be of service whenever it was needed.

13. Of course, Mahesh was chastised for not helping Usha, Chandrasekhar and Suguna with their visas. But Mahesh protested saying that he wasn't asked to.

14. Julie writes to me saying: "UG told Guha he could come back just before he (UG) died. He definitely did not come against his wishes; he would never have done that. And Mahesh told Guha that he could stay on nearby until the end, just as it was Mahesh who asked Mario and Sarito to stay on, not UG." I stand corrected.

15. I learned later from Mahesh's his then-unpublished journal *A Taste of Life* that on his request UG's ashes were scattered soon after in the Mediterranean

Sea by Lucia, UG's hostess, as Mahesh had to return to India right away on some urgent business.

16. Sarito has written an e-mail saying, "UG never asked me to do that!" So, it must have been someone else.

17. I know of several people who did want to come, and even made arrangements, but couldn't, for various reasons.

18. UG fell in the bathroom and hurt himself once before, about four years ago, and was nursed back to normalcy by Louis, Sidd, Paul Arms and other friends. Apparently, it took him five weeks then to recover.

19. "...a super-information field of the whole universe, a super-implicate order which organizes the first level into various structures and is capable of tremendous development of structure." (Bohm in Weber, p.33).

20. "The theory of morphogenetic fields proposes that there's a field, or a spatial structure, which is responsible for the development of the form (in living organisms)." (Weber, p. 75).

21. We have learned this quite clearly in Kant, as when he shows how reason generates paradoxes when it is applied to the universe or the soul beyond the limits of any possible experience -- paradoxes such as that the universe has an unconditioned condition or first cause and yet there must be a cause for that cause, and another cause for that, and so on.

22. Even to use the term "knowledge" is misleading in this context. Knowledge presupposes in our ordinary life continuity in the self such that we can say, "I did not know then, but now I know it." Such continuity is nonexistent in the case of UG. Yet in some sense UG's past knowledge or experience is coming into operation here. But the knowledge is operating for the moment only, only as much as it is relevant to the present context, without, however, being related to a "reference point" or a project of the self, which might prompt us to formulate our desires and plans on the basis of such knowledge, or seek a repetition of the current experience.

23. Some mystics did realize the problems in expressing themselves. In my opinion, Sankara, Nagarjuna and Chuang Tzu all had an inkling of these problems and resorted to dialectical reason to "point the way" to an "experience of reality" without giving a positive verbal expression in statements which can be understood as representations of an experience of reality.

24. *UG Krishnamurti – A Life*, Penguin Books India (Private) Ltd., 1992.

25. In the following, by "goals" I do not mean the goals necessary for day-to-day living, but goals for self-improvement and self-fulfillment – goals which involve the "self" in some fashion or other. While the former set of goals will have no relevance and cease to be once they are achieved, the latter persist in our consciousness and create endless striving. Indeed, the continuity of the "self" is perpetuated by the contemplation and striving for these goals.

26. I discussed this question in Chapter 5 above.

27. Disillusionment can not only be unsettling but also traumatic and can happen in stages.

28. Although the following is based mostly on specific instances, I have not, except occasionally, made references to specific names lest anyone might take it personally.

29. When Mahesh was writing his biography, UG himself had said, "After the Calamity, there is no biography to write." There are only isolated instances with no connecting link between them.

30. A few times when I was alone with UG, he would describe something to me, whether it be his current state of the body or the senses or some way of looking at things such as the tree in front of you being only two-dimensional. I couldn't always make sense of what he said. Sometimes I would give my interpretation and he would either agree or keep silent.

31. Once he remarked to a couple who are friends of mine: "I am trying to sever all your connections so that you can be related to everything around you."

32. That man was critical of UG for allowing all "these Rajneeshis to gather around him and sit in meditation with closed eyes." He was obviously missing UG's discussions from earlier times, because now UG was going along with the Rajneeshis by sitting in silence. UG yelled at him in reply: "They too are people like you. You have your background and they have theirs." Then the man timidly said, "I see your point, UG."

33. The gathering, recorded on video tape, was organized by Professor John Wren-Lewis.

34. He bought into a time-share in Lake Havasu once and soon realized it was a mistake – it didn't deliver the convenience he thought it might provide for his periodic stay. He exposed the misleading nature of the sale to the seller and forced her to take it back.

35. UG's pat answer on such occasions was, "You can pack up and leave!"

36. Louis even wrote a humorous song about UG's driving instructions and sang it with the young girls, Shilpa, Sumedha and Claire: "Don't go left, don't go right, go straight!"

37. See my account in Chapter 3 (pp. 43-44 above) about how UG's planned to decide where he was going to go next after leaving Chennai.

38. I know of many occasions when his decisions, particularly about travel, were based on the outcome of tossing a coin.

39. Most of his life, UG ate very small meals, often a piece of *idli* with some spice powder and chutney or *upma* or rice flakes, when in India; or about half a cup of oatmeal with heavy cream and frozen pineapple juice, or a piece of bread with butter and some soup, or angel hair with tomato sauce with grated Gruyere cheese on top, or couscous with frozen broccoli or spinach added to it (with a little curry powder for taste), or bread and some European cheese like Cambozola, and other such small meals, while he was in the West. Of late, friends always brought packages of Leonidas chocolate; those, as well as Swiss Lindt milk chocolates, were freely passed around in gatherings. He himself used to make extremely simple but quick and delicious meals and feed people at times. He always asked a few friends to come early in the morning for breakfast and coffee.

40. That was in 1986 when I first visited UG in Bangalore.

41. At other times, UG would ask Nataraj to sing Beethoven, read astrological signs, cook or go on car rides.

42. "Thought, the Natural State and the Body"- see above, Ch. 6.

43. Division in consciousness, which constitutes UG and what he experiences.

44. Of course, there may be other physiological cues, instead of images, that may achieve the same end. What could be said about images, then, perhaps could be said about those cues as well.

45. I wrote about this in a previous article, but it can bear some repetition in the present context.

46. I actually did advice someone to do this once, but I had a vested interest in giving that advice, leaving aside the main consideration of whether it was good for the mother or the unborn child.

47. I am assuming, of course, that the woman is sane and in a stable mind, capable of making decisions, carrying them out and standing by them.

48. Situationism advocates taking into consideration the context or circumstances surrounding an action as the basis for moral judgments. In Joseph Fletcher's Christian form of situationism, moral laws and rules are only valid if they happen to serve love in a particular situation. They may be violated or ignored if another course of action would achieve a more loving outcome. (J. Fletcher, *Situation Ethics: The New Morality*, Philadelphia: Westminster, 1966.)

49. Except on rare occasions as when he consulted a doctor about his "plumbing problem" (hiatal hernia) or when he wanted his teeth extracted by a dentist.

Please e-mail your comments, if any, to: *moorty@pacbell.net*

Printed in Great Britain
by Amazon